8/15

2

W9-BUZ-355

WITHDRAWN

America the Possible

James Gustave Speth

America

Yale UNIVERSITY PRESS

the Possible

Manifesto for a New Economy

NEW HAVEN AND LONDON

Published with assistance from
the foundation established in memory of
James Wesley Cooper of the Class of 1865,
Yale College.

Yale University Press books may be purchased in quantity for educational, business, or
promotional use. For information, please e-mail sales.press@yale.edu (U.S. office) or
sales@yaleup.co.uk (U.K. office).

"Look Out" by Wendell Berry. Copyright © 2005 by Wendell Berry from *Given*. Reprinted
by permission of Counterpoint. Excerpt from "The Cure at Troy: A Version of Sophocles's
Philocretes" by Seamus Heaney. Copyright © 1990 by Seamus Heaney. Reprinted by
permission of Farrar, Straus and Giroux, LLC, and Faber and Faber Limited. "Whitman and
the Moth" by Clive James, *The New Yorker*, November 22, 2010. Copyright © Clive James
2010. Reproduced by permission of United Agents (www.unitedagents.co.uk) on behalf of
Dr. Dannie Abse. "The Gardener" by Linda Pastan. Reprinted by permission of the author.

Set in Fournier type by Newgen North America, Inc.
Printed in the United States of America.

Library of Congress Cataloging-in-Publication Data

Speth, James Gustave.
America the possible : manifesto for a new economy / James Gustave Speth.
p.   cm.
Includes bibliographical references and index.
ISBN 978-0-300-18076-3 (hardback)
1. United States—Economic policy.   2. Environmental policy—
United States.   3. Social justice—United States.   4. Progressivism
(United States politics).   I. Title.
HC106.84. S66 2012
338.973—dc23   2012012170

A catalogue record for this book is available from the British Library.

This book was printed with low VOC, vegetable-based inks on FSC-certified acid-,
lignin-, and carbon-free recycled paper that contains 30% postconsumer waste. The case
materials are FSC-certified: binders boards of 100% postconsumer waste and cover paper
that contains postconsumer pulp and is acid-, lignin-, and carbon-free.

This paper meets the requirements of ANSI/NISO z39.48-1992 (Permanence of Paper).

10 9 8 7 6 5 4 3 2 1

For
Cameron, Rodgers, Lilla, Charlotte, Grace
and all the grandchildren,

and

For all those with whom I've had the privilege of working over
these past four decades. If I could gather you in my arms,
it would be a bouquet to save the world.

Good reason to despair, yet grief was purged
By tracing how creation reigned supreme.
A pupa cracked, a butterfly emerged:
America, still unfolding from its dream.

——CLIVE JAMES

She starts old, old, wrinkled and writhing in an old skin.
And there is a gradual sloughing off of the old skin,
towards a new youth. It is the myth of America.

——D. H. LAWRENCE

Contents

Preface

Like most Americans, I love this country. I love its boundless energy and spirited people, its natural beauty, its creativity in so many fields, its many gifts to the world, and the freedom and opportunity it has given me and others to write books like this one—which is why on August 20, 2011, I became a jailbird.

Along with sixty-five others, I was arrested in front of the White House protesting the proposed Keystone XL pipeline, all 1,700 miles of it intended to carry oil from the tar sands of Alberta, Canada, to the Gulf Coast to satisfy our country's insatiable thirst for oil. Our modest act of nonviolent civil disobedience landed us in the central cellblock of the District of Columbia jail for two nights.

Some protesters were acting to stop the desecration of the North American land. My motivation was climate change: after more than thirty years of unsuccessfully advocating for government action to protect our planet's climate, I found myself at the end of my proverbial rope. Civil disobedience was my way of saying that America's economic and political system had failed us all. Having served as President Jimmy Carter's White House environmental adviser, helping to found two of our country's major environmental groups, leading the United Nations' largest program for international development, and serving as dean of Yale's environment school, I was once dubbed the "ultimate insider" by *Time* magazine. But my conclusion in August was and still is that working inside the system is insufficient. We have to step outside America's broken system of political economy and begin the difficult job of transforming it. As the slogan goes, "system change, not climate change."

This book tells the story of how system change can come to America. At its heart is a vision of an attractive, pleasant, and successful America that is still within our power to realize by mid-century. In this America the Possible, our country will have rejoined the leading nations in realizing social justice and well-being, in building peace and real global security, and in sustaining our planet's environmental assets both domestically and globally. We will have reclaimed our democracy from what were once quite properly called the "moneyed interests." And we will have seen a deep transformation in our country's dominant values and culture.

Now that is all very nice, you might be thinking, but how do we get there? I will endeavor in this book to chart a course to an America the Possible—a course from today's decline to tomorrow's rebirth.

The journey to America the Possible begins when enough Americans have come to some important conclusions. The first is that something is profoundly wrong with our overall political economy—the operating system on which our country now runs. That system is now routinely generating terrible results, and is failing us socially, economically, environmentally, and politically. The second conclusion follows from the first. It is the imperative of system change, of building a new political economy that routinely delivers good results for people and planet.

The third conclusion is that, contrary to what one frequently hears, a better alternative does indeed exist. We certainly do not yet understand all the details of how this alternative will look, and much hard analysis and creative experimentation lie ahead. But we do know enough to have confidence that something much better can be built, and we know enough to start building it.

These conclusions are not today's conventional wisdom, but more and more people are embracing them. They are the foundation from which the work of system change can move forward. From the vantage point they provide, we can see how the dynamics of fundamental change might emerge. As conditions in our country continue to decline across a wide front, or at best fester as they are, ever-larger numbers of Americans lose faith in the current system and its ability to deliver on the values it proclaims. The system steadily loses support, leading to a crisis of legitimacy. Meanwhile, traditional crises, both in the economy and in the environment, grow more numerous and fearsome. In response, progressives of all stripes coalesce, find their voice and their strength, and pioneer the development of a powerful set of new ideas and policy proposals confirming that the path to a better world does indeed exist. Demonstrations and protests multiply, and a popular movement for prodemocracy reform and transformative change is born. At the local level, people and groups plant the seeds of change through a host of innovative initiatives that provide inspirational models of how things might work in a new political economy devoted to sustaining human and natural communities. Sensing the direction in which things are moving, our wiser and more responsible leaders, political and otherwise, rise to the occasion, support the growing movement for change, and frame a compelling story or narrative that makes sense of it all and provides a positive vision of a better America. The movement broadens to become a major national force.

The Tea Party, whatever its fate, shows that it is possible to move from protest to movement to political power with amazing speed. The progressives I know are hoping that the Occupy, labor, climate, and other protests will help spark the beginnings of a new movement in America.[1]

We do not know exactly how these and other forces will emerge and interact. But we know this: pleas for immediate amelioration—for jobs, for tax justice, for climate action—will at best be met with proposals for modest accommodations and half measures, and the struggle for deep, systemic change will be met with fierce opposition and determined resistance. So an all-important conclusion emerges—namely, that the prospects for systemic change will depend mightily on the health of our democracy and the power of the social and political movement that is built. Transformative change, and even most of the proposals for reform offered by progressives in Washington today, will not be possible without a new politics in America. So prodemocracy political reform and building a new progressive movement in America must be priority number one. Popular movements can have near-term political objectives, like amending the Constitution to protect the public's right to regulate campaign finance, or they can seek transformative change in values and the way the world is perceived, as many of the Occupy movement now seek. And the diverse aims can be complementary.

As I developed these themes, I returned often to the question: Is the assessment I offer in this book too optimistic or too pessimistic? To those who believe a bleak future for our country cannot be avoided, this book will seem too optimistic. I have encountered many such people, in person and in print. To those who believe the problems our country faces will soon yield to the reforms currently offered to address them, or who do not acknowledge the seriousness of those challenges in the first place, it will seem excessively pessimistic. There are doubtless many of this view. I find myself in neither camp.

A well-placed optimism is healthy, and as Dee Hock has said, "Things are much too bad for pessimism."[2] Rather than optimism versus pessimism, however, I prefer to think in terms of realism and hopefulness. I have tried to be realistic about where America is today and where we are headed. I'm saddened that we find ourselves adrift in a sea of troubles, but I find it impossible to reach any other conclusion. At the same time, I believe the central message of the book is one of good hope. Throughout the book, I try to show that hope for a better America is not hollow but reasonable and well grounded. Amid all the difficulties we face, current and foreseeable, there are grounds for plausible hope that a bright future is still within our reach. As David Suzuki says in his powerful essay "The Legacy," "It is not too late to take another path."[3]

In preparing this book, I have been encouraged by the emergence of the "new economy movement" and supported by constant interactions with its members.[4] In the words of the New Economy Network, the new economy is one where "the priority is to sustain people and planet, social justice and cohesion are prized, and peace, communities, democracy, and nature all flourish."[5] Many initiatives are now engaged in developing new economy themes. Those in the United States with which I've had the pleasure to work in recent years include the New Economics Institute, the New Economy Network, the New Economy Working Group, the Institute for Policy Studies, Demos, the Democracy Collaborative at the University of Maryland, *Yes! Magazine*, the Center for a New American Dream, the Capital Institute, *Solutions* journal, the Tellus Institute, the Business Alliance for Local Living Economies, the American Sustainable Business Council, and the Fourth Sector Network—an extraordinary collection indeed.[6]

Readers will undoubtedly remember the old Yogi Berra–ish quip that "predictions are hazardous, especially about the future." But this book is not full of predictions in the normal sense, though there are some. The possible future for our country sketched here is not a "base-case scenario" where policies, institutions, and behaviors stay as they are today. Just the opposite. The future described herein rests on massive change that will be realized only if the American people insist on it. So the book is more about what can be than what will be. In any case, I hope my mistakes of judgment and fact are small and easily forgiven.

In late October 2011, my wife, Cameron, and I drove across Vermont to a wildlife management area near Lake Champlain, hoping to find the migrating snow geese heading south. We heard them first, and then there they were, thousands of them feeding and resting in a cornfield on the banks of Dead Creek. Stretching across almost the entire horizon to the southwest, these magnificent creatures from the tundra were a joy to behold. We climbed up onto the car for a better view and watched for about an hour. Then, just when we'd decided to go check out the ducks and mergansers, the geese suddenly levitated en masse. In only a few seconds they were high in the sky, honking and whirling in ever-widening circles. We thought at first that they were heading off again on their journey, but slowly they descended on another rich area of corn and water. It was one of the finest sights I'll ever see, and I was reminded of John James Audubon's description of flocks of passenger pigeons darkening the sky.

It was a moment of hope as well as pleasure, seeing nature still strong despite all the wounds we have inflicted. But, as we stood there, it grew on me that this grand display was made possible not only by Mother Nature but also by people and their government, state and federal, acting together decades ago to create Vermont's Dead Creek Wildlife Management Area. They cared enough to create something wonderful for future generations. When Cameron said, "We will bring them here one day," I did not have to ask to whom she was referring.

A great many people helped me with this book, and I wish to recognize and thank them profusely. At the top of the list is my dean at the Vermont Law School, Jeff Shields, who not only ensured that I had the time to work on it but provided steady encouragement. My wife, Cameron, provided wise counsel throughout, a service matched only by her skillful help in manuscript preparation. Megan Hustad was invaluable as editorial counselor, sharpening and enlivening the presentation. Executive Editor William Frucht at Yale University Press provided many helpful suggestions and skillful guidance. Many colleagues read some or all of the manuscript and provided excellent comments, advice, information, and, where needed, corrections. Included here are Peter Barnes, Kelly Levin, Betsy Taylor, Noel Ortega, John Cavanagh, Robin Broad, David Korten, Edward Strohbehn, Heather Ross, Marianne Tyrrell, Chris Brooks, John Fullerton, Richard Rosen, Gar Alperovitz, Neva Goodwin, Herman Daly, Fritz Schwarz, Paul Raskin, Bill Butler, Helga Butler, Mary Evelyn Tucker, John Grim, Robert Repetto, Bill Rees, Dahvi Wilson, David Grant, Ned Coffin, Peter Victor, Juliet Schor, Steve Dubb, Tom Powell, Chris Ryan, Kirsten Moran, Peter Brown, Mike MacCracken, John de Graaf, Will Raap, Roger Masters, Lew Daly, Steven Dycus, Susan Witt, Emerson Blake, Andrew Blechman,

Sarah Stranahan, Bob Costanza, Allen White, Robert Lane, Servaas Storm, and Bob Edgar. In addition, a group of very sharp students at the Vermont Law School helped with research, including Paige Davis, Brian Martin, Lisa Stevens, Emily Slagle, Veronique Jarrell-King, Ashley Campbell, Stephen Campbell, Allie Silverman, Ben Jones, and Josh Donabedian. My great thanks to all.

James Gustave Speth
Strafford, Vermont

America the Possible

I Manifesto

This is a book about the American future.

The plainest truth is that, as a country, we have let conditions of life in America deteriorate across a broad front and are headed straight to a place we would not want for our children and grandchildren. There is another future, an enormously attractive one, that is still within our power to build, but only if we mobilize and fight for it. It's time, indeed past time, for our country to chart a course to this better place.

That task begins with knowing where we are today. So let's look at the present, and at a group of advanced democracies, specifically the major countries of the Organization for Economic Cooperation and Development (OECD)—twenty in all, including the United Kingdom, France, Germany, the Nordics, Japan, Canada, and others. They can be thought of as our peer countries. What we see when we look at these countries is that compared with them, the United States now ranks at or very near the bottom in a host of important areas. America now has:[1]

- the highest poverty rate, both generally and for children;
- the greatest inequality of incomes;
- the lowest government spending as a percentage of gross domestic product (GDP) on social programs for the disadvantaged;

- the lowest score on the United Nations' index of "material well-being of children";
- the worst score on the UN's gender inequality index;
- the lowest social mobility;
- the highest public and private expenditure on health care as a percentage of GDP, and yet the highest infant mortality rate, prevalence of mental health problems, obesity rate, percentage of people going without health care due to cost concerns, and consumption of antidepressants per capita, along with the shortest life expectancy at birth;
- the third lowest scores for student performance in math and middling scores in science and reading;
- the second highest high school dropout rate;
- the highest homicide rate;
- the largest prison population, both absolutely and per capita;
- the highest water consumption per capita and the second-highest carbon dioxide emissions per capita;
- the lowest score on the Yale–World Economic Forum's Environmental Performance Index, and the second largest Ecological Footprint per capita;
- the highest rate of failing to ratify international agreements;
- the third-lowest spending on international development and humanitarian assistance as a percentage of GDP;
- the highest military spending in total and as a percentage of GDP; and
- the largest international arms sales.

International comparisons are only one way to examine what's gone wrong. As I will discuss in Part I, these comparisons miss many of our most worrying challenges.

It is not for lack of knowledge, technology, or thoughtful policy proposals that we face this overwhelming, colliding collection of problems. One can easily identify a set of intelligent policy responses to almost all of these challenges. Groups advocating them pound constantly on Washington's doors. Extraordinary technological opportunities remain untapped. Nor did these deplorable consequences simply happen as the result of larger economic and geopolitical forces over which we have no control.

When big problems emerge across the entire spectrum of national life, it cannot be for small reasons. We have encompassing problems because of fundamental flaws in our economic and political system. The many problems listed here and others discussed in Part I are the product of that system, compounded by conscious political decisions made over several decades by both Democrats and Republicans who have had priorities other than strengthening the well-being of American society and our environment. Many countries, obviously, took a different path, one that was open to us as well.

I think America got off course principally for two reasons. First, in recent decades we failed to build consistently on the foundations laid by the New Deal, by Franklin Roosevelt's Four Freedoms and his Second Bill of Rights, and by the United Nations' Universal Declaration of Human Rights, to which Eleanor Roosevelt contributed so much. Instead, we unleashed a virulent, fast-growing strain of corporate-consumerist capitalism.[2] Here, I am referring not to an idealized capitalism but to the one we actually have. This system of political economy—the basic operating system of our society—rewards the pursuit of profit, growth, and power and does little to encourage a concern for people, place, and planet. "Ours is the Ruthless Economy," say Paul Samuelson and William Nordhaus in their text *Macroeconomics*.[3] Indeed it is. And in its ruthlessness at home and abroad, it creates a world of wounds. As it strengthens and grows, those wounds deepen and multiply.

Such an economy begs for restraint and guidance in the public interest—control that must be provided mainly by government. Yet the captains of our economic life, and those who have benefited disproportionately from it, have largely taken over our political life. Corporations have long been identified as our principal economic actors; they are now also our principal political actors. The result is a combined economic and political system of great power and voraciousness pursuing its own economic interests without serious concern for the values of fairness or justice or sustainability that democratic government might have provided.

The other big and relevant development in recent American history is that our political economy evolved and gathered force in parallel with the U.S. role in the Cold War. After World War II we "lost the peace," as Robert Dallek puts it, and took up in earnest the demands of the Cold War.[4] The Cold War and the rise of the American security state powerfully affected the political-economic system—strengthening the priority given to economic growth, giving rise to the military-industrial complex, and draining time, attention, and money away from domestic needs and many international challenges. This deflection of attention and resources continued with the rise of peacekeeping operations in the wake of the Cold War's end and, more recently, with the response to international terrorism and other perceived threats.

As a result, America now confronts a daunting array of challenges in the well-being of our people, in the conduct of our international affairs, and in the management of our planet's natural assets, at precisely the moment that it has become unimaginable that American politics as we know it will deliver the needed responses. Washington isn't even seriously trying to address most of our challenges. Neglect, stalemate, and denial rule the day.

So what are the critical features of today's failing operating system that have been given such free rein?[5] First, and most obviously, our system gives priority to economic growth to the neglect and often the detriment of social and environmental needs. The reigning policy orientation holds that the path to greater well-being is to grow and expand the economy. Output, productivity, profits, the stock market, and consumption must all go up. This growth imperative trumps all else. Growth is measured by tallying GDP at the national level and sales and profits at the company level, and pursuit of GDP and profit can be said to be the overwhelming priorities of national economic and political life.

We tend to see growth as an unalloyed good, but an expanding body of evidence is now telling us to think again.[6] Economic growth may be the world's secular religion, but for much of the world it is a god that is failing—underperforming for most of the world's people and, for those in affluent societies, now creating more problems than it is solving. We've had tons of growth in recent decades while wages stagnated, jobs fled our borders, life satisfaction flatlined, social capital eroded, poverty and inequality mounted, and the environment declined. The never-ending drive to grow the overall U.S. economy has led to a ruthless international search for energy and other resources, has failed at generating needed jobs, and rests on a manufactured consumerism that does not meet the deepest human needs. Americans are substituting growth and ever-more consumption for doing the things that would truly make us and our country better off. Psychologists have pointed out, for example, that while economic output per person in the United States rose sharply in recent decades, there has been no increase in life satisfaction. Meanwhile, levels of distrust and depression have increased substantially.

Politically, the growth imperative is a big part of how we the people are controlled: the necessity for growth puts American politics in a straitjacket—a golden straitjacket, as Tom Friedman would say[7]—and it gives the real power to those who have the finance and technology to deliver that growth.

Second, the profit motive powerfully affects corporate behavior. Profits can be increased by keeping wages low and real social, environmental, and economic costs externalized, borne by society at large and not by the firm. Today's corporations have been called "externalizing machines" because they are so committed to keeping much of the real costs of their activities off their books. One can get some measure of these external costs from a recent analysis of three thousand of the world's biggest companies; it concluded that paying for just their external environmental costs would erase a third of their profits at least.[8] Profits can also be increased through subsidies, tax breaks, regulatory loopholes, and other gifts from government. Together, these external costs and subsidies lead to dishonest prices, which in turn lead consumers to spur on the businesses that do damage to people and planet.

Third, as Karl Polanyi described in 1944 in *The Great Transformation*, the constant spread of the market into new areas can be very costly both environmentally and socially. American capitalism has carried this forward with a vengeance with its emphasis on privatization, commercialization, and commodification.

Polanyi wrote that "to allow the market mechanism to be sole director of the fate of human beings and their natural environment . . . would result in the demolition of society. . . . Nature would be reduced to its elements, neighborhoods and landscapes defiled, rivers polluted, military safety jeopardized, the power to produce food and raw materials destroyed."[9] Of course, the ever-expanding, self-adjusting market that Polanyi feared did not collapse as he predicted in 1944. It took off again after World War II, and in America it steadily became more fearsome and expansive, and the consequences that Polanyi warned against came to pass.

But the system that drives the capitalism we have today includes other, more contemporary elements. The modern corporation, the most important institution and agent of modern capitalism, has become both huge and hugely powerful. Of the one hundred largest economic entities in the world, fifty-three are corporations, not countries, and of the three hundred largest corporations, a third are U.S. companies. American business wields great political and economic power and has routinely used that power to restrain ameliorative governmental action. And U.S. corporations have led the process of economic globalization with all the challenges that introduces.[10]

Then, there is what our society has become. Dominant American values today are strongly materialistic, anthropocentric, and contempocentric. Consumerism and materialism place high priority on meeting human needs through ever-increasing purchase of goods and services. We say "the best things in life are free," but not many of us act that way. Instead we have what Juliet Schor terms "the insidious cycle of work and spend."[11] The anthropocentric view that nature belongs to us rather than we to nature eases the exploitation of the natural world. The habit of focusing on the present and discounting the future leads away from a thoughtful appraisal of long-term consequences and the world we are making.

Next, there is what our government and politics have become. Growth serves the interests of government by boosting politicians' approval ratings, keeping knotty social justice issues on the back burner, and generating larger revenues without raising tax rates. Government in America doesn't own much of the economy, so it must feed its growth habit by providing what corporations need to keep growing. Meanwhile, Washington is hobbled, corrupted by money, focused on the short time horizons of election cycles, and guided by a pathetic level of public discourse on important issues. Finally, our government seeks to enhance and project national power, both hard and soft, in part through economic strength and growth and in part through sustaining a vast and costly military deployment.[12] One upshot is that American citizens feel increasingly unable to shape the contours of their own lives.

Lastly, there is what our system of money and finance has become. We think of money as the cash in our pockets, but in truth, virtually all the money in circulation today is created by the banking system when loans are made. If everyone paid off all of their debts, there would be hardly any money. As David Korten has stressed, money is a system of power, and Wall Street wields that power. "The institutions that control the creation and allocation of money shape the fate of nations, businesses large and small, and the boom and bust cycles of economic life," Korten writes. "Where money flows, there will be jobs; where it doesn't flow, jobs will be in short supply."[13]

Today, the big banks are financing, among much else, the destruction of the planet's climate. In 2010 Citi raised more than $34 billion for the coal and oil industries. Within Citi's portfolio is $1 billion raised for the proposed pipeline intended to carry tar sands oil from Alberta, Canada, to Gulf Coast refineries. Since January 2010 ten big banks have supported mountaintop-removal coal mining with more than $2.5 billion.[14]

These features aptly characterize key dimensions of today's operating system—the actual political economy that we have, the political economy of today's American capitalism. It's important to see these elements as part of a system, linked and mutually reinforcing. Together they have given rise to an economic reality that is both enormously large and largely out of control and therefore very destructive. An unquestioning society-wide commitment to economic growth at any cost; powerful corporate and banking interests whose overriding objective is to grow by generating profit, including profit from avoiding social and environmental costs unless corrected by government, but government that is itself beholden to corporate interests and thus not strongly inclined to curb corporate abuses; and rampant consumerism spurred endlessly on by sophisticated advertising—all combine to deliver an ever-growing economy insensitive to the needs of people, place, and planet.

Progressive causes in America today all confront the challenge of trying to make progress within this system. It is up to us as citizens to inject values of justice, fairness, and sustainability into the system, and we look to government to that end. We develop new policy options and hustle to get the best result we can. We work the media and other channels to raise public awareness of our issue and try to shift public understanding and discourse in our favor. We lobby Congress, the administration, and the federal agencies with well-crafted and sensible proposals. When necessary, we go to court. With modest resources, we devote what we can to the electoral process and to candidates for public office. And we hope somehow that lightning will strike and events will move in our favor.

But it is now abundantly clear that these approaches are not succeeding. The titanic forces unleashed by American capitalism and the Cold War lie behind most of the big challenges America now faces and strongly influence the others. These forces perpetuate existing problems and give rise to new ones. The ceaseless drive for profits, growth, and power and other system imperatives keep the problem spigot fully open. By not dealing with the root causes— the underlying drivers—the well-trod path of incremental reform cannot deliver the responses needed. Our enfeebled politics are no match for these forces.

Progressives endeavor to make the system work for their causes, but many long-term Washington observers, like former *Washington Post* reporter William Greider, are now skeptical. "The regulatory state has become a deeply flawed governing mess," he writes in *The Soul of Capitalism*. "Many of the enforcement agencies are securely captured by the industries they regulate, others are blocked from effective action by industry's endless litigation and political counterattacks. Stronger laws are tortuously difficult to enact and invariably studded with purposeful loopholes designed to delay effective enforcement for years, even decades."[15]

Some of our best analysts and modelers have reached a similar conclusion by different routes. For example, the Tellus Institute, after examining quantitatively a comprehensive range of future scenarios, concluded that "within a conventional economic development paradigm, implementing remedial technologies and policies at the required pace and magnitude would be daunting, indeed, like trying to go up a down escalator. A twenty-first century world of rising population, consumerism, and universal convergence toward affluent lifestyles would create incessant pressure for ever more energy and materials, land and food." The only future they find truly attractive is a Great Transition involving deep, systemic change— "a values-led shift in which citizens of the world drive fundamental change towards a just, sustainable, and livable future."[16]

We thus have encompassing problems that place in grave peril much that we hold dear and that defy the reformist approaches that have been attempted so far. To deal successfully with all the challenges America now faces, we must complement reform, incrementalism, and working within the system with at least equal efforts aimed at transformative change leading to a new political economy—a new operating system that routinely delivers good results for people and planet at home and around the world.

At the core of this new operating system must be a *sustaining* economy based on new economic thinking and driven forward by a new politics. Sustaining people, communities, and nature must henceforth be seen as the central goals of economic activity. The purpose of a sustaining economy is to provide broadly shared prosperity that meets human needs while preserving the Earth's ecological integrity and resilience—in short, a flourishing people and a flourishing nature. That is the paradigm shift we must now seek.[17] But how?

I believe this paradigm shift in the nature and operation of America's political economy can best be approached through a series of interacting, mutually reinforcing transformations—transformations that attack and undermine the key motivational structures of the current system and replace these old structures with new arrangements needed for a sustaining economy and a successful democracy.

Elaborated in the chapters that follow, these transformations hold the key to moving to a new political economy. Consider each as a transition from today to tomorrow.

Economic growth: from growth fetish to post-growth society, from mere GDP growth to growth in human welfare and democratically determined priorities;

The market: from near laissez-faire to powerful market governance in the public interest; from dishonest prices to honest ones;

The corporation: from shareholder primacy to stakeholder primacy, from one ownership and motivation model to new business models and the democratization of capital;

Money and finance: from Wall Street to Main Street, from money created through bank debt to money created by government;

Social conditions: from economic insecurity to security, from vast inequities to fundamental fairness;

Indicators: from GDP (grossly distorted picture) to accurate measures of social and environmental health and quality of life;

Consumerism: from consumerism and "affluenza" to sufficiency and mindful consumption, from more to enough;

Communities: from runaway enterprise and throwaway communities to vital local economies, from social rootlessness to rootedness and solidarity;

Dominant cultural values: from having to being, from getting to giving, from richer to better, from separate to connected, from apart from nature to part of nature, from transcendent to interdependent, from near term to long term;

Politics: from weak democracy to strong, from creeping corpo- ratocracy and plutocracy to true popular sovereignty;

Foreign policy and the military: from American exceptionalism to America as a normal nation, from hard power to soft, from military prowess to real security.

We know that systemic, transformative change along these di- mensions will require a great struggle, and it will not come quickly. The new values, priorities, policies, and institutions that would con- stitute a new political economy are not at hand and won't be for many years. The truth is we are still mostly in the design stage of a new operating system. That system won't be yesterday's socialism, by the way, and it won't be today's American capitalism either.

It follows that effectively addressing the many serious challenges America faces will take more time than we would like, and mean- while, America's decline will persist. By decline I am referring here not to losing world power relative to China and other countries but to decline in human and natural conditions—the actual conditions of life and living in America.

That is a depressing conclusion, but we must face it. More im- portantly, we must use it as a framework for understanding what we must now do. Indeed, there can be a very bright light at the end of this gloomy tunnel. Consider the diagram on page 12. We are in a pe- riod of decline and we haven't hit bottom yet, though we may now be close to the point of bifurcation or crisis.[18] The imperatives we face as citizens are therefore threefold: (1) to slow and then halt the descent, minimizing human suffering and planetary damage along the way and preventing a collapse, the emergence of fortress world, or any of the dark scenarios that have been plotted for us in science fiction and increasingly in serious analysis;[19] (2) to minimize the time in the bot- tom and start the climb upward, moving forward the transitions just

American Passage: Decline and Rebirth

described and building a new operating system; and (3) to complete, inhabit, and flourish in the diversity of alternative social arrangements, each far superior to ones we will have left behind.

Here is a fair question: If we are failing at modest, incremental reform, how can we hope to achieve deeper, transformative change? I believe there is hope, especially in three things. The persistence of our many problems will progressively delegitimize the current order. Who wants an operating system that is capable of generating such suffering and destruction? One good thing about the decline of today's political economy is that it opens the door to something much better. Second, people will eventually rise up, raise a loud shout, and demand major changes. That is already happening with some people in some places, including the Occupy Wall Street movement and other protests in the United States and abroad. Protests can quickly grow to become a national and global movement for transformation, demanding a better world.

Beyond these things that are likely to happen, there is also great hope in something already happening. Evidence of the birth of something new and better is all around us, and it goes far beyond the green products and corporate social responsibility about which we've heard much more.

We are seeing the proliferation of innovative models of "local living economies," sustainable communities, transition towns, as well as innovative business models, including social enterprises and for-benefit and worker-owned businesses that prioritize community and environment over profit and growth. Initiatives that may seem small or local can be entering wedges that lead to larger changes later. These initiatives provide inspirational models of how things might work in a new political economy devoted to sustaining human and natural communities. One recalls here Rebecca Solnit's words: "The grounds for hope are in the shadows, in the people who are inventing the world while no one looks."[20]

Simultaneously, while the struggle to build a new system goes forward, we must do everything we can to make the old system perform. If, for example, we do not act now on climate change, both nationally and internationally, the consequences will become so severe that the dark visions of those predicting calamity will become all too real. Climate disruption is already well under way. Should we fail to act now on the climate front, the world will likely become so nasty and brutish that the possibility of rebirth, of achieving something new and beautiful, will simply vanish, and we will be left with nothing but the burden of climate chaos and societies' endless responses to it. Coping with the wreckage of a planetary civilization run amok would be a full-time job. On this issue and others, then, reform and transform are not alternatives but complementary and mutually reinforcing strategies, especially if we pursue non-reformist reforms that lay the groundwork for deeper changes.

I believe the case is strong that something new will be born. To elaborate, the case for transformation of today's American capitalism into something truly sustaining of people and planet rests on these propositions:

System failure. Today's system of political economy and its principal product, economic growth, are destructive of the environment, and not in a minor way but in a way that profoundly threatens the planet. Equally, they are not delivering economic and social well-being. People will therefore increasingly demand solutions, but the current system will not be able to deliver credible answers and so will lose legitimacy.[21] Dissatisfaction will multiply. Meanwhile, America's political economy will be severely stressed by multiple pressures, general overload, and buffeting events at home and abroad, including scarcities and rising prices. Having lost resiliency and coping capacity, it will be highly vulnerable to crises that will open the door to major change[22]—and

A better world. The affluent societies have reached the point where, as John Maynard Keynes forecast, the "economic problem" has been solved;[23] the long era of ceaseless striving to overcome hardship and deprivation should be over; there is enough to go around if it were shared. But this prospect and other attractive possibilities contrast sharply with everyday reality, so people are increasingly fed up and are looking for and building something more meaningful. A positive alternative to the current order is coming into view, taking shape on the horizon. People and groups are busily planting the seeds of change through a host of alternative arrangements scattered across the landscape, principally at the local level, and still other attractive directions for upgrading to a new operating system have been identified.

These developments will raise consciousness, inspire hope, open the door to deep change, and help launch a powerful movement that can transform the current system.

Implicit here is a "theory of change." It begins with the view that people act out of both fear and love—to avoid disaster and to realize a dream or positive vision. Plausibility is key. The risks of great loss must be realistic and credible, and the vision of a better world must be grounded in honest possibility. The theory affirms the centrality of hope and hope's victory over despair. It locates the plausibility of hope in knowledge—that people will eventually rise up and fight for the things that they love; that history's sole constant is change; that deep, systemic change is part of our human legacy and human potential; and that we understand enough to strike out in the right directions, even if the journey's end is a place we have never been. It embraces the seminal role of crises in waking us from the slumber of routine and shining the spotlight on the failings of the current order. It puts great stock in transformative leadership that can point beyond crisis to something better. The theory adopts the view that systemic change must be driven both bottom-up and top-down, that it requires communities, businesses, and citizens deciding on their own to build locally as well as to develop the political muscle to adopt system-changing policies at the national and international levels. And it sees the growth of a powerful citizens movement as necessary to spur action at all levels.

So imagine: a major national crisis (or, ideally, the widespread anticipation of one brought on by many warnings and much evidence) occurs in a time of wise leadership. The crisis both reflects and exacerbates severe, existing shortcomings in our country, and American leadership rises to articulate a new narrative that makes sense of it all and to provide a positive vision of a better America. Meanwhile, an ongoing and contagious proliferation of real-world examples points the way to the future, and a powerful set of new ideas and policy proposals confirms that the path to a better country and world does indeed exist. Such circumstances can open the door to transformative change. It is a moment of democratic possibility.

In the end it all comes down to the American people and the strong possibility that we still have it in us to use our freedom and our democracy in powerful ways to create something fine, a reborn America, for our children and grandchildren. At the deepest level we must build the moral force that can encourage and sustain the human energy for change. This mobilization of the spirit begins in our hopes and dreams and is nurtured by our religions, the arts, music, and the poetry we can find in books and in everyday life.

We can realize a new American Dream, America the Possible, if enough of us join together in the fight for it. This new dream envisions an America where the pursuit of happiness is sought not in more getting and spending but in the growth of human solidarity, real democracy, and devotion to the public good; where the average American is empowered to achieve his or her human potential; where the benefits of economic activity are widely and equitably shared; where the environment is sustained for current and future generations; and where the virtues of simple living, community self-reliance, good fellowship, and respect for nature predominate. These American traditions may not prevail today, but they are not dead. They await us, and indeed they are today being awakened across this great land. New ways of living and working, sharing and caring are emerging across America. They beckon us with a new American Dream, one rebuilt from the best of the old, drawing on the best of who we were, are, and can be.

In Part I of this book, I focus on the challenges America faces, because any hope of changing the system to better serve people and the planet rests on an accurate assessment of the full scope of our problems. My chaplain at Yale in the 1960s, William Sloan Coffin, was fond of quoting St. Paul: "The truth will make you free." But, he quickly added, "First it makes you miserable." In that misery is our salvation. We will do what is needed only when we fully appreciate the situation we face. The drive to change the system is born in appreciation of the many ways it is failing us, in the great suffering and loss those failings bring forth, and in the prospects for declining conditions of life and living in the absence of such change.

When systemic change does come, it does so because the people agitating for change have painted a compelling vision of what a better future might look like. This is the subject of Part II. How do we envision an America the Possible that we want to see for future generations—a very different and attractive America that could be built, say, by 2050? What new sets of values and cultural preferences will have arisen that allow—even encourage—us to live well and prosper despite the serious constraints and limits that may confront us?

Of course, the feasibility of system change is acknowledged by a critical mass of people only when they see what the changes are and that a path forward exists. That is the subject of Part III. It describes the areas where transformative change is necessary to realize America the Possible, and it identifies policy and other measures needed for each transition. It deflates the myth that there is no alternative to our failing system of political economy.

Finally, Part IV describes how political force for system change can be built. Part IV is therefore about building a new political reality in America. It is unimaginable that American politics as we know it today will deliver the transformative changes needed, but the prospect of these changes comes alive with the presence of a powerful social and political movement focusing first and foremost on pro-democracy political reform.

Part One A Nation in Trouble

If we could first know where we are, and whither we are tending, we could better judge what to do, and how to do it. —ABRAHAM LINCOLN

To set in motion the conditions of a better America and a better world for our children and grandchildren, we must first carry out a reconnaissance, as Lincoln said, of "where we are, and whither we are tending." Such an assessment must be both honest and comprehensive. If we don't view the complete picture, we are unlikely to do the right things.

Readers of congenitally sunny dispositions may wish for relief from cataloging the many serious challenges America has to address in the years ahead. But even they, as well as those who advise us always to be positive, will appreciate the importance of pausing, standing back from our daily rounds, and taking in the full situation, regardless of how uncomfortable it makes us.

When we see our predicament whole, we can glimpse the parallels between our mistakes at home and those made abroad, the common origins of the social and environmental challenges we now face, and the ways in which our broken political system has served as both midwife and guarantor of the destructive trends from which we must now escape. We can also see the many ways that continued neglect of urgent issues at home and abroad can lead to crises that interact with and build upon each other.

2 Society at the Breaking Point

The U.S. has not just misplaced its priorities. When the most powerful country ever to inhabit the earth finds it so easy to plunge into the horror of warfare but almost impossible to find adequate work for its people or to properly educate its young, it has lost its way entirely. —BOB HERBERT

Plutocracy is not an American word and wasn't meant to become an American phenomenon. —BILL MOYERS

The United States, as we all know, is a fabulously wealthy country, with the world's biggest economy and a GDP per capita near the top. Unfortunately, these numbers, like the plantation mansions of the antebellum South, can disguise grave social injustice. If it is true that a society should be judged by how it treats its less fortunate members, then the judgment on today's America should be harsh indeed.

Poverty Amid Plenty

Poverty is the destroyer of lives, a condition where dreams are still-born and hope imprisoned. In our abundant land, an abundance of citizens are poor. The number of Americans living in poverty declined sharply in the 1960s, leveled off in the 1970s, and then began growing, so that by 2008 forty million Americans, almost one in every seven of us, lived in poverty, an all-time high in the data going back to 1960.[1] By 2010, with the burden of the recession fully on us, Americans in poverty grew to number about forty-six million.[2] If one uses the new and greatly improved measure of poverty developed by the Census Bureau, the 2010 number swells to forty-nine million, close to one person in six.[3]

There is nothing generous about our national definition of poverty. In 2010 the official poverty line was family income below $22,491 for a family of four, or $5,622 per person per year ($469 per month), or about $100 per week. And $100 is the ceiling, not the average. It would be a mistake to imagine that families in poverty cluster just below the poverty threshold. More than 40 percent of poor U.S. families have incomes of less than half the poverty line. They are the "severely poor," and their ranks are growing. During the pre-recession 2000–2005 period, the number of the severely poor grew by 26 percent, more than 50 percent faster than the overall population in poverty.[4]

Poverty hits American children hard. A fifth of American children live in poverty and two-fifths in low-income households, with family incomes below twice the poverty line. The number of poor children grew by 33 percent since 2000, ten times faster than the number of children generally. Poverty is most prevalent among minorities, with the poverty rate among blacks almost three times that of whites and the rate among Hispanics more than twice that of whites. But the poverty rate among whites stood at 10 percent in 2011, and white children are the largest group afflicted.[5]

Being poor creates a host of deprivations. A recent UN report, for example, noted that a boy born to the top 5 percent of income earners in the United States would live, on average, 25 percent longer than a boy born to the bottom 5 percent.[6] In 2005, thirty-five million Americans, a third of them children, lived in households that could not consistently afford enough to eat.[7] In late 2009, the U.S.

Department of Agriculture reported that forty-nine million Americans are "food insecure," meaning they lack consistent access to adequate food.[8] And, of course, if you're poor, and especially if you're poor and dark skinned, you're much more likely to run afoul of the law. Barbara Ehrenreich calls it "the criminalization of poverty."[9]

Contrary to popular myth, the high rates of poverty in the United States are not mainly because the poor here are less likely to be working. They arise from the fact that the United States does less than other countries to reduce poverty. In a survey of twelve nations, the U.S. poverty rate was better than average if market income alone was counted. But after taxes and transfers were counted, the United States had the highest poverty rate among the twelve.[10] In the well-to-do countries of the OECD, public cash transfers and taxes have the effect of reducing poverty by 60 percent on average. In Sweden the reduction is 80 percent. But in the United States, public policy reduces poverty by only about 35 percent.[11]

Vast Economic Insecurity

But the problem is larger. Poverty is the desperate side of the more pervasive American problem of economic insecurity. Long before the 2008–2009 recession, the economic security of American families was being assaulted by plant closings and layoffs, declining worker benefits, and stagnant and even declining wages. In his 2006 book *The Great Risk Shift*, Jacob Hacker called attention to a set of appalling trends, the cumulative effect of which has been that "more and more economic risk has been offloaded by government and corporations onto the increasingly fragile balance sheets of workers and their families."[12] Hacker points out that personal bankruptcies rose from fewer than 300,000 in 1980 to more than two million in 2005, home mortgage foreclosures rose fivefold between the early 1970s and 2005, traditional "defined-benefit" pensions offered by corporations to their employees dropped over a twenty-five-year period from 83 percent of larger firms to less than 33 percent, the portion of companies offering retirees health benefits fell from 66 percent in 1988 to half that in 2005, and the odds of working Americans experiencing at least a 50 percent drop in income for one to two years climbed sharply between the early 1970s and the early 2000s. All this happened before the recent recession.[13]

In a sophisticated analysis of middle-class vulnerability, the policy center Demos and others developed a Middle Class Security Index to gauge how secure middle-class families were in that status. They found that only 31 percent of American middle-class families met their criteria for being securely in the middle class. More than two-thirds of American middle-class families lacked the basics to ensure financial security.[14]

The American Human Development Report for 2008–2009 estimated that eighty million Americans are unable to generate enough income to meet basic expenses.[15] In 2011 the *Wall Street Journal* reported that nearly half of Americans are "financially fragile"— definitely or probably unable to come up with $2,000 in thirty days— and the *New York Times* reported that well over half of American families were earning less than needed to cover core living expenses and save for retirement and emergencies.[16] Americans have seen the value of their homes decline by more than $7 trillion since the economic crisis began. More than a third of home mortgages were underwater in 2011, and seven million families had already lost their homes by early 2011, with another three million foreclosures expected through 2012.[17]

Many factors have contributed to this pervasive economic insecurity:

- Between 2001 and 2010, about forty-two thousand U.S. manufacturing plants closed. About six million factory jobs have disappeared over the past dozen years.[18] In 2011, the U.S. Department of Commerce reported that during the 2000s, U.S.-based multinational corporations added two million employees abroad while cutting payrolls at home by 860,000.[19]
- While the U.S. economy has grown well since 1980, 90 percent of Americans saw average income rise from $30,941 in

1980 to $31,244 in 2008. That's a gain of $303 in twenty-eight years.[20]

- A 2011 U.S. Census analysis found that a startling 17 percent of the population, or fifty-one million people, were near-poor with incomes less than 50 percent above the poverty line.[21]
- Private-sector union membership has declined from 39 percent in 1955 to a mere 7 percent today.
- The federal minimum wage, adjusted for inflation, has fallen 42 percent since its 1968 peak.
- The official unemployment rate, though improving, was reported in mid-2011 at 9 percent, and if one takes into consideration involuntary part-time workers and discouraged workers who have dropped out of the labor force, the rate would be at least 15 percent.[22] Unemployment insurance covers less than 30 percent of the unemployed. About a quarter of the jobs lost in the Great Recession were low-wage, but about half of the jobs added back by 2011 were in low-wage sectors.[23]

The pain, suffering, and deprivation are not the result of something inevitable about today's world but the foreseeable result of policy choices (see Box 1). Given that, one might expect to find considerable international variation in poverty and economic insecurity. Indeed we do. As Steven Hill points out in his book *Europe's Promise,* "What stands out is that in nearly every index [of social well-being] the United States is rated at the bottom among developed countries. . . . European countries always occupy the top ratings." Hill explains that Europeans took the American "idea" of the middle class and improved upon it, putting "some meat on the bones of their family values." Systems can be constructed, in short, to minimize the exposure to risk that individuals and families face in an age of globalized capitalism.[24]

You get what you pay for. Or should, at least. In Europe, public spending on social programs tends to be about a quarter to a third of net national income; in the United States it is 18 percent.[25] "Active labor market programs" (unemployment, retraining, and so on) are five or more times more generous in much of Europe than in

"How We Got into This Mess"
Damon Silvers from *The American Prospect*, May 2008

For 30 years, America's economic elites and their political allies have pursued policies designed to produce this low-wage economy. But at the same time, policy-makers of both parties have sought, with some success, to maintain high levels of consumer spending. . . . The ultimate unsustainability of this strategy has brought us to our current economic crisis.

In the 1980s, the United States began to set the course that led to the present economic crisis. This was the period when both the Reagan administration and the business community began to seriously attack the institutions that drove the high-wage postwar economy. This was the period when the progressive income tax was substantially eliminated for high-income Americans and when the federal government ceased in a meaningful way to protect workers' right to organize and collectively bargain, fueling a dramatic decline in union strength.

In the 1990's, these trends were accelerated by a series of trade agreements and technological developments that fully exposed the U.S. economy to goods and services produced by low-wage labor around the world. . . . U.S.-based global corporations began to see their non-U.S. operations not just as sources of raw materials but also as cheap production sites.

The resulting downward pressure on wages meant that although the productivity of U.S. workers improved dramatically since 1980, their real wages remained flat, with the exception of a brief period in the late 1990s.

But the story of the decoupling of wages and productivity doesn't do justice to the full destructiveness of our low-wage strategy, since it also destroyed our savings and our ability to invest. Employers not only reduced wages but also dismantled our pension system.

In the public sector, starting in the 1980s, tax cuts that overwhelmingly benefited the rich robbed government of revenues necessary to fund public investment, both at the state and federal level. The nation is now left with schools that do less and less just when we need them to do more and more, with no money for infrastructure just when the roads and bridges we built during the great postwar infrastructure boom are wearing out, and, perhaps worst, no public resources to take on the great challenge of global warming and sustainable energy.

Ultimately, even the retreat from public and private saving was not enough to maintain a healthy consumer-driven economy in an environment of falling wages. So as a nation we went from eating our own seed corn to borrowing money in order to buy more seed corn to eat. . . . As our trade deficit skyrocketed, our trading partners in Asia accumulated trillions of dollars. China, Japan, and, more recently, the oil-producing countries lent their dollars back to us.

The consequences of these policies are very clear. We have just gone through the first postwar economic expansion in which real wages did not rise. Pension and health-care coverage for Americans has shrunk dramatically. . . . Our negative balance of payments keeps growing, and the dollar keeps falling against the euro. We are losing the very high-tech jobs that we were supposed to keep in an era of globalization—jobs in aerospace and information technology. The price of oil is over $100 a barrel, and oil production on a daily basis is not increasing, while demand from other countries is growing apace. And hanging over our future is the threat of a radically destabilized climate because of our refusal to address the damage done by our carbon emissions.

Source: Damon Silvers, "How We Got into This Mess," *The American Prospect*, May 2008, 23. See also Harold Meyerson, Testimony Before House Appropriations Committee, http://prospect.org/article/middle-falling-out-economy, February 13, 2008.

the United States.[26] U.S. unemployment insurance pays on average 14 percent of lost wages; the portion is twice that in Germany and four times higher in the Netherlands.[27] Of course, taxes are higher in Europe. In major European countries, taxes range from 36 to 44 percent of GDP; in the United States they are 28 percent.[28]

In short, it is a matter of where the political process puts its priorities. Journals and books are full of well-conceived policy measures that could reverse America's appalling and growing economic insecurity and deprivation, and there are proven models abroad to consult. But these tools work only if we use them. We haven't. America has instead chosen to do something else.

Income Inequality Matching 1928

What America has done in the past few decades, instead of addressing the needs of the desperately poor and its shrinking middle class, is to take the lion's share of its impressive GDP and productivity gains and engage in a far-reaching project of income redistribution upward, to the rich.

From 1973 to 2005 overall labor productivity per hour in the United States increased by about 80 percent,[29] and GDP per capita almost doubled in constant dollars. So where did the money go? If we take all of the income growth from 1979 to 2007, we find that 64 percent of it went to the top 10 percent of households and a startling 39 percent went to the top 1 percent. A mere 11 percent went to the bottom 60 percent of families.[30] Here's another distressing comparison, this one from a Congressional Budget Office report released in October 2011: between 1979 and 2007 the poorest fifth of American households saw their real after-tax income increase by 18 percent, but for the richest fifth it went up 65 percent, and for the top 1 percent it went up 275 percent.[31]

Back in 1928, right before the Great Depression, the richest 1 percent of Americans received 24 percent of the country's total income. Starting with the New Deal, public policy favored greater equality and a strong middle class, so that by 1976, the share of the richest 1 percent of households had dropped to 9 percent. But then the great re-redistribution began, so that by 2007, right before the Great Recession, the richest 1 percent again had regained its 1928 position—24 percent of income.[32]

Much more can be said about inequality in today's America. The skew in wealth is worse than the skew in income: Those very rich 1 percent of Americans hold assets that exceed by $2 trillion the collected assets of the bottom 90 percent.[33] The richest 10 percent of Americans own 80 to 90 percent of all U.S. financial wealth—the assets that produce income, including stocks and bonds, business equity, commercial real estate, and trusts.[34] The levels of executive compensation are also scandalous; the CEOs of our largest companies take home more than five hundred times what the average worker earns, up from only forty-two times in 1980.[35] Our tax code also exacerbates the inequality divide. The change in the "effective federal tax rate," which combines income and employee tax rates for a family of four, was 42 percent in 1961 for the top four hundred U.S. taxpayers. By 2007 that rate had dropped to 17 percent. Meanwhile, the effective rate for the median taxpayer climbed from 10 percent in 1961 to 14 percent in 2007. Here's another comparison: Between 1960 and 2004, for the wealthiest 0.1 percent of taxpayers, the portion of their income paid in all federal taxes declined from 60 to 34 percent, while for the middle fifth of all taxpayers the percentage stayed constant at 16 percent.[36] In other words, Congress has been cutting taxes sharply for the rich, but not for the middle class.

As noted in Chapter 1, the United States is the most unequal society among the affluent countries of the world. Some might say, so what? There has in fact been a running debate in the United States about whether we should worry about inequality per se. A major new analysis entered this debate in 2010, *The Spirit Level: Why Greater Equality Makes Societies Stronger* by Richard Wilkinson and Kate Pickett. A number of critiques have been written about their work, but their analysis has held up well. What Wilkinson and Pickett show is that the more unequal societies are, the more health and social problems they have.[37] They find that high levels of income inequality correlate with low levels of social trust and mental health, high levels of drug use and obesity, a high teenage birthrate, high incarceration, low child well-being, and more. Most compelling, they find an extremely high correlation across rich countries between income inequality and their index of health and social problems. When it comes to infant mortality rates, obesity, mental illness, teenage births, homicide rates, incarceration rates, and low social mobility, statistically three-fourths of the intercountry differences in this index can be explained by inequality. In their analysis, the United States is not only the most unequal country, it is the most dysfunctional.[38]

Finally, Wilkinson and Pickett find one of the tightest relationships between high inequality and low social mobility. Their analysis is now one of many that deflate the myth that America is a land of equal opportunity. Examining the relationship between fathers' incomes when their sons were born and their sons' incomes at age thirty, they found that the United States had the lowest social mobility.[39]

Many globalization advocates see America's growing inequality as the inevitable outgrowth of market and technological forces. But Jacob Hacker and Paul Pierson, in their 2010 book *Winner-Take-All Politics: How Washington Made the Rich Richer—and Turned Its Back on the Middle Class*, roundly disagree. They argue cogently that it is the result of public policies that have cut taxes on high incomes and investment earnings, undermined unionization, facilitated lavish executive compensation, and deregulated banking and finance.[40]

It is hard to improve on Robert Reich's analysis of how the great divergence of rich and poor in America happened: "Starting in the late 1970s, and with increasing fervor over the next three decades, government . . . deregulated and privatized. It increased the cost of public higher education and cut public transportation. It shredded safety nets. It halved the top income tax rate from the range of 70–90 percent that prevailed during the 1950s and '60s to 28–40 percent; it allowed many of the nation's rich to treat their income as capital gains subject to no more than 15 percent tax and escape inheritance taxes altogether. At the same time, America boosted sales and payroll taxes, both of which have taken a bigger chunk out of the pay of the middle class and the poor than of the well-off. Companies were allowed to slash jobs and wages, cut benefits and shift risks to employees. . . . They busted unions and threatened employees who tried to organize. The biggest companies went global with no more loyalty or connection to the United States than a GPS device. Washington deregulated Wall Street while insuring it against major losses, turning finance—which until recently had been the servant of American industry—into its master, demanding short-term profits over long-term growth and raking in an ever larger portion of the nation's profits."[41]

Wounded People

America is now a land of economic insecurity for most and unprecedented wealth for a small minority. Whether it is accurate to attribute as much of America's social deterioration to income inequality as Wilkinson and Pickett do, I will leave to others. But it's worth reviewing some of the key features of that deterioration, each a problem that took a long time, typically decades, to mature and will likely take decades of determined effort to correct.

Decline of Social Capital

American society is increasingly fragmented, and intimate social ties are shrinking. In his pathbreaking 2000 book *Bowling Alone*, Robert Putnam described "several decades of decline in sociability and civic participation across the United States" whereby, beginning in the late 1960s, "Americans in massive numbers began to join less, trust less, give less, vote less, and schmooze less." Putnam showed that from 1970 onward we have become less likely to join a civic association, church, social club, or union; spend time with neighbors; give to philanthropy; even join a bowling league—all by factors of 25 to

50 percent.[42] Other studies have confirmed this growing social isolation: a fourth of Americans now say they have no one with whom to discuss their personal troubles, more than double the number isolated in 1985.[43]

Our increasing isolation from one another has had consequences of its own. The portion of Americans who believe people are as "good and honest as they used to be" declined from 50 percent to 27 percent between 1950 and 1998.[44] Trust in our political and business institutions also declined. Between 1973 and 2006, the public's trust in medicine, religion, the press, and Congress all fell by ten percentage points or more. By 2006, trust in Congress was at 12 percent, the media at 10 percent. Meanwhile, trust in the military climbed from 32 to 47 percent, the highest of all.[45]

Trust is essential to social cohesion, commercial dealings, and political stability. In *The Moral Foundations of Trust*, Eric Uslaner concludes that inequality places too great a strain on mutual trust. In an unequal society, "those at the top can enforce their will against people who have less. . . . And those at the bottom have little reason to believe they will get a fair shake." Wariness of motives becomes the order of the day. Uslaner also notes that higher rates of upward social mobility aid trust. "If you believe that things are going to get better—and that you have the capacity to control your life—trusting others isn't so risky."[46] It's not surprising, then, that, as Bruce Judson observed in *It Could Happen Here*, "We now live in a society permeated by distrust."[47] There is a connection, perhaps, between this pervasive distrust and our gun culture. The United States has about ninety guns for every one hundred Americans, the most in the world.[48] More than 150,000 Americans have been murdered in the past decade, mostly with guns.[49]

Social isolation can be seen also in the sharp decline of empathy among America's students. College students today score about 40 percent lower in measures of empathy than their counterparts of twenty or thirty years ago, according to the University of Michigan Institute for Social Research.[50] Students are now much less likely to try to understand others by imagining how things look from their perspectives and much less likely to report concern for people less fortunate than they are. The Michigan researchers suggest that behind this decline is the explosion in exposure to information, the prevalence of violence in the media, the rise of social media and fake friends, today's hypercompetitive atmosphere and inflated expectations of success, and the frenetic pace of life.

Failing Health Care

As reported in Chapter 1, one of the great tragedies of health care in America is that we spend the highest percentage of GDP on our health system but get some of the poorest outcomes. Health-care costs already exceed 17 percent of GDP and are slated to rise to almost 20 percent by 2019.[51] Doctor and hospital costs are soaring, and U.S. citizens experience more cost barriers to health care than citizens of other advanced economies. In 2011, fifty million Americans lacked health insurance.[52] In 2006 *Business Week* reported that the health-care industry had added 1.7 million jobs since 2001, while the rest of the private sector added none.[53]

Failing Educational System

In late 2010, the OECD released the results of its student assessment tests, covering fifteen-year-olds in sixty-five countries. As before, U.S. students performed poorly: twenty-ninth in the international rankings in math, sixteenth in reading, and twenty-first in science.[54] Even privileged U.S. students don't score competitively with average students in other well-off countries.[55]

The United States is now ranked twelfth internationally in the percentage of young people with college degrees, an area where we once led the world.[56] An admirable 70 percent of high school grads go to college, but fewer than 60 percent finish with degrees. The national high school graduation rate is only about 75 percent.[57] Major efforts are being made nationally to keep kids in school at all levels and to improve teaching and learning, but it will take a much larger sustained effort to get American schooling where it should be. Poor student performance at advanced levels is a regular feature of our own U.S. testing as well.[58] In February 2011, New York State reported that fewer than half of its high school graduates were prepared for college.[59]

Jobs Deficit

Being thrown out of work is devastating psychologically and economically. The scars persist even for those lucky enough to find new jobs. Though the situation is slowly improving, the Great Recession cost nine million Americans their jobs, and, given labor force growth, the economy in 2011 was still missing ten million jobs. The ranks of the long-term unemployed—jobless for six months or longer— have surged 400 percent since the end of 2007 and reached over six million in early 2011.[60] Sixty percent of the unemployed received no notice that their jobs were being terminated; 84 percent received no severance pay. Half of the currently unemployed have cut back on medical treatment and borrowed money from friends and relatives. Half also report suffering from depression or anxiety, and report that they feel embarrassed or ashamed most of the time. They also feel angry and hopeless. About a quarter report that they have either lost or risk losing their homes; a quarter are also on food stamps.[61] The chance of reentering the employed ranks dims for the long-term unemployed, especially those aged fifty and over; many may never find a job.[62]

We would have problems even if the labor pool stayed the same size it was in 2007, but of course it isn't and won't. New entrants into the labor force create additional pressure, but those new entrants— the young and new immigrants—will not be able to anticipate high wages given the slack job market overall. Many economists predict that job growth will be sluggish, and it could take the better part of a decade for the unemployment rate to return to pre-recession levels. Meanwhile, American companies have been taking advantage of the recession to lay off more workers than required. They have been pushing up productivity with fewer workers, pocketing the profits, and sitting on them; substituting temporary jobs for permanent ones; and foreclosing on mortgages with scant regard for legal and ethical standards.[63]

With Congress in gridlock on jobs action, Paul Krugman is right to worry that "a once unthinkable level of economic distress is in the process of becoming the new normal."[64] Meanwhile, by mid-2011 GDP had bounced back to its pre-recession level with eight straight quarters of growth, and the stock market had recovered. So much for either as a barometer of national well-being.

The Welfare of American Children

In late 2010 UNICEF released an international assessment of children's well-being. Among the twenty-four OECD countries surveyed, the United States ranked twenty-second in children's health, nineteenth in educational well-being, and twenty-third in material well-being.[65] The rate of reported child abuse in the United States increased fivefold between 1976 and 2005.[66] The average child between eight and eighteen spends 6.5 hours a day using electronic media.[67] Richard Louv has written movingly about the increasing isolation of American children from the natural world, leading to what he calls "nature deficit disorder."[68] America's "shrinking vacation syndrome" can't be good for children, either. Gallup reported in 2006 that 43 percent of American families had no plans to take a summer vacation, and another national survey found that 40 percent of families had no plans to vacation in the coming six months, the lowest number recorded in three decades of polling.[69]

Minorities

For the most part, I have reported average national conditions. But the welfare of minorities in the United States is generally much worse than the average. The proportion of blacks, Hispanics, and Native Americans in low-income households is twice that of whites and Asians.[70] If current incarceration rates continue, nearly a third of African American males will spend some portion of their lives in state or federal prison.[71] The jobs dearth has been particularly severe for minorities. While black men constitute about 5 percent of the labor force, they are almost 13 percent of the long-term unemployed.[72] In 2011, when the national unemployment rate was 9 percent, it was 16 percent among blacks and 11 percent among Hispanics.[73] The list of indicators where minority groups fare worse than average goes on and on.

Incarceration

America has in jail 24 percent of the world's prisoners. The United States locks up more people, both in total and as a percentage of the population, than any other country in the world.[74]

Denial

Badly stressed and perplexed, many Americans are simply rejecting or ignoring information they find threatening. When there is often not much else to cling to, rejecting the experts ("my-views-are-as-good-as-anyone's") is a form of self-protection and taking back control.[75] Troubling news is frequently brought forward by scientists and other pointy-headed intellectuals, never a popular group, and sometimes it runs counter to a major source of comfort and consolation in America, religion. A majority of Americans see science and religion as often in conflict, and 64 percent report that if science were to disprove a particular religious belief, they would reject the scientific facts in favor of their faith.[76] A National Science Foundation survey recently found that only 45 percent of Americans support evolution.[77]

Add to this the fact that Americans are not well informed scientifically in the first place (only half of us know that the earth journeys around the sun once a year and that electrons are smaller than atoms),[78] and the playing field is wide open for unscrupulous manipulation of public views on policy issues with high scientific content. That includes an increasing number of public issues such as climate change, sexual orientation, stem cells, abortion, health effects of chemicals, genetically modified organisms, and much more.

In their excellent book *Merchants of Doubt,* Naomi Oreskes and Erik Conway have documented how some scientists backed by private corporations and think tanks applied a strategy of sowing the seeds of doubt to "challenge scientific evidence on a host of contemporary issues. In the early years, much of the money for this effort came from the tobacco industry; in later years, it came from foundations, think tanks, and the fossil fuel industry. They claimed the link between smoking and cancer remained unproven. They insisted that scientists were mistaken about the risks and limitations of SDI [the Strategic Defense Initiative, popularly known as 'Star Wars']. They argued that acid rain was caused by volcanoes, and so was the ozone hole. They charged that the Environmental Protection Agency had rigged the science surrounding secondhand smoke. Most recently— over the course of nearly two decades and against the face of mounting evidence—they dismissed the reality of global warming. . . . The failure of the United States to act on global warming and the long delays between when the science was settled and when we acted on tobacco, acid rain, and the ozone hole are prima facie empirical evidence that doubt-mongering worked."[79]

On matters complex and intangible like climate change, the public needs help, but it gets hustle.

The Unnamed Problem

What happens in a society when community bonds break down, when the message becomes "you're on your own; you'd better look out for number one," when average salaries languish while incomes for some soar? It would seem that the incentives to practice self-control and internal restraint have proved harder to find.[80] Barbara Ehrenreich observes, "Somewhere along the line, the ethos changed from *we're all in this together* to *get what you can while the getting is good.*"[81] One upshot has been a long string of corporate scandals and excesses: Enron, Arthur Andersen, WorldCom, Global Crossing, Tyco, Bernie Madoff, Wall Street and Lehman Brothers, Nortel, AIG, Goldman Sachs, Citibank, Halliburton, Countrywide. Conscientiousness and a sense of fair play seem to be in steep decline.[82] Demos's David Callahan has looked at the polling results on American values and concludes that the "rising tide of bad behavior suggests that the great moral struggle of today . . . is between the relentless, amoral logic of self-interest, profit, and the bottom line . . . and, against that, the fuzzier bonds of human connectivity—our integrity, our empathy, and our obligations to others. This divide, pitting market values against human values, is the real culture war of our time."[83]

The Debt Bind

Over the decade from 2000 to 2010, total federal debt climbed from $5.7 trillion to $13.6 trillion, an increase of about 140 percent. That seemed plenty large, but by late 2011 it had climbed to $15 trillion. You can watch it grow at www.usdebtclock.org. According to the debt clock, our total national debt is now 100 percent of current GDP. The International Monetary Fund believes that America's structural deficit and the growth of its debt "are among the worst in the rich world."[84]

This enormous federal indebtedness is, of course, driven ever upward by annual budget deficits. In 2010 the federal deficit was $1.7 trillion, or 9 percent of GDP, much higher than the 3 percent considered safe. The years 2009 and 2010 saw the highest deficits since World War II. Meanwhile, according to the debt clock, total personal debt is now $16 trillion, or about $50,000 for each American. Given that both government and individual households are in debt and spending beyond their means, the United States has been buying and borrowing abundantly from abroad. Much of this borrowing and buying has to do with China, which by 2009 had invested over

$1 trillion in U.S. bonds and government-backed mortgage debt.[85] In 2005, foreigners held about $2 trillion in long-term federal treasury debt, and by 2010 these holdings had roughly doubled, with China as the largest holder.

Meeting America's many social challenges, as well as the environmental and international ones addressed in the chapters that follow, will require large and sustained commitments of funds in federal budgets for decades ahead, as will the need to expand entitlement programs for retirement and health care for the aging boomer generation. Meanwhile, taxes in the United States are the lowest in a group of twenty well-to-do OECD countries, and our military spending is almost as high as the rest of the world's combined. It is not hard to spot from where the needed funds should come.

3 The Weight of the World

Who can doubt that there is an American empire?—an "infor-
mal" empire, not colonial in polity, but still richly equipped with
imperial paraphernalia: troops, ships, planes, bases, proconsuls,
local collaborators, all spread around the luckless planet.
—ARTHUR M. SCHLESINGER, JR.

The world is home to a bewildering array of threats and problems
that require serious international attention and action. The United
States finds itself potentially affected by almost all of them. In its
assumed role as the "indispensable state," the United States has undoubtedly benefited both us and other countries in many ways over
the decades since World War II. But our actions have also cost us
and others dearly. I will argue here that the U.S. posture in the world
reflects a radical imbalance: a hugely disproportionate focus on the
military and on economic issues and a tragic neglect of some of the
most serious challenges we and the world now face. On both sides of
the balance, very large costs have been borne, and they will continue
to mount until a new balance is struck.

Consider this list of twenty major international human well-
being and security concerns:

1. terrorism
2. interstate rivalry, conflict, and war

3. intrastate conflicts and insurgencies
4. failed and fragile states
5. weapons of mass destruction and nuclear proliferation
6. genocide and mass rape
7. resource disputes involving energy, water, minerals, and land
8. arms sales, legal and illegal
9. global warming and climate disruption
10. global-scale impoverishment of biological systems
11. food supply and famines
12. natural disasters, floods, and droughts
13. refugees and displaced people
14. migration
15. poverty, underdevelopment, and joblessness
16. drug trafficking and other transnational organized crime and corruption
17. diseases and pandemics
18. human rights and antidemocratic, autocratic regimes
19. women's rights and gender equality
20. population pressures

Add to these issues a host of international economic ones—globalization, trade, financial flows, foreign direct investment, multinational corporations, intellectual property, access to oil and other fuel and nonfuel minerals, corruption, rule of law, and others—and one gets a sense of the extraordinary weight of comprehensive international engagement. Dealing successfully with these challenges, even with improved approaches very different from today's, will inevitably require huge, continuing commitments of time, energy, and money. Success will be made dramatically more difficult by the impacts of climate change and resource scarcities discussed in the following chapter. And all of this is coming at us, along with our compelling domestic needs, at a time of incessant drumbeating to reduce the federal deficit by cutting spending. This is not a pretty picture.

A prominent feature of the U.S. response to these challenges has been the projection of military and economic power around the world. Many of America's engagements and roles abroad are well conceived and beneficial; many others are blunders with disastrous results for us and others. Our foreign policy leaders often contend there is no real choice regarding U.S. involvement, at least some of it. Leslie Gelb, former president of the Council on Foreign Relations, recently noted, "For over half a century, U.S. foreign policy had to give priority to stemming real and serious threats. No other nation could or would shoulder the responsibilities. Even now, no other nation or group of nations can lead coalitions against terrorists and nuclear proliferation threats. . . . Today, the United States continues to be the world's power balancer of choice."[1]

Still, we have let our international priorities get off track, just as we have done domestically. Much as we have favored the rich in domestic policy, we have favored the military in our foreign policy. And much as we have badly neglected many real needs at home, we have badly neglected many real needs abroad. The upshot is severe imbalance in our approach to the many international challenges we face.

American Empire

Let's look first at what has been referred to by many as the American empire. Its existence is welcomed by some and decried by others.[2] It has undoubtedly benefited both us and many other countries over the decades in various ways, but its accomplishments have come at a very high price in terms of our security, our economy, our democracy, and our society.

Consider first the sheer size and reach of the American security state. Late in 2010, Congress authorized $725 billion for the Defense Department budget for fiscal year (FY) 2011. That's the most the United States has spent on defense since World War II. In other words, our defense spending today is higher than at any point in the Cold War. According to the Stockholm International Peace Research Institute, the United States spends nearly as much on military power as the rest of the world combined—43 percent of the world total.[3] But this official Defense budget is just the beginning. If one adds spending generated by U.S. national security efforts—such as "homeland security," the nuclear weapons work in the Department of Energy, military retirement pay, counterterrorism activities, and Central Intelligence Agency (CIA) and other intelligence operations—the total easily climbs to over $1 trillion annually.[4] One trillion dollars is a bit more than a fourth of total federal spending in fiscal year 2011. In the budget proposal for fiscal year 2012 submitted by the Obama administration, two-thirds of all discretionary spending is officially allocated to "national security."[5] To get another view of how expensive our military engagements and homeland security efforts can be, consider that, when it is all said and done, the full costs of the wars in Iraq and Afghanistan and homeland security spending through 2011 have been estimated to be about $4.1 trillion.[6]

The Pentagon's 2010 Base Structure Report reveals that the United States maintains 662 military sites in thirty-eight countries around the world. Some of these should be deleted to get a better sense of actual bases, but many more need to be added because bases in Afghanistan, Iraq, Saudi Arabia, and elsewhere aren't listed in the report. It's estimated that the United States actually has more than a thousand military bases around the world.[7] In other words, the United States garrisons the world in a way that no empire has ever done.

There's more. The United States also leads in the international arms trade, accounting in 2008 for about 70 percent of the global arms business.[8] As part of the U.S. antiterrorism effort, by 2010 we had an estimated thirteen thousand Special Operations troops deployed in seventy-five countries. In other words, we're on the ground with covert and clandestine forces in about 40 percent of the 192 nations in the United Nations.[9]

Despite President Dwight D. Eisenhower's warning in his Farewell Address, the military-industrial complex has developed into an iron triangle—Pentagon, industry, Congress—of unprecedented power in our politics. The poster child for this system is Lockheed Martin, the premier defense contractor that received $36 billion in government contracts in 2008. William Hartung reports that Lockheed Martin spent $12 million on lobbying Congress and making campaign contributions in 2009. With facilities in forty-six states, the company (as with other defense contractors) typically relies heavily on the jobs issue to support their legislative needs.[10] Andrew Bacevich has described other dimensions of how the system works: "The revolving door connecting the world of soldiering to the world of arms purveyors continues to turn. . . . Throw in the former members of Congress who lobby their successors on behalf of defense contractors, and the serving members who vote in favor of any defense appropriations that send money to their districts, and one begins to get a sense of the true topography."[11]

In July 2010, the *Washington Post* began running its alarming series on the size of America's antiterrorism programs. It reported: "The top-secret world the government created in response to the terrorist attacks of Sept. 11, 2001, has become so large, so unwieldy and so secretive that no one knows how much money it costs, how many people it employs, how many programs exist within it or exactly how many agencies do the same work. . . . Some 1,271 government organizations and 1,931 private companies work on programs related to counterterrorism, homeland security and intelligence in some 10,000 locations across the United States."[12]

Later, in December 2010, the *Washington Post* released another disturbing analysis: "The system, by far the largest and most technologically sophisticated in the nation's history, collects, stores and analyzes information about thousands of U.S. citizens and residents, many of whom have not been accused of any wrongdoing. The government's goal is to have every state and local law enforcement agency in the country feed information to Washington to buttress the work of the FBI, which is in charge of terrorism investigations in the United States."[13]

Whatever it has gained us, this National Security State has also created a world of trouble for us and others. I have already mentioned some of the costs it has brought: a phenomenal drain on the federal budget (as President Eisenhower said, "Every gun that is made, every warship launched, every rocket fired signifies, in the final sense, a theft from those who hunger and are not fed, those who are cold and are not clothed"), a major assault on privacy and civil liberties, and a serious distortion of our national politics by the military-industrial complex. But the unfortunate consequences don't end there.

William Pfaff has noted, "The global base system, it seems, tends to produce and intensify the very insecurity that is cited to justify it."[14] Chalmers Johnson analyzed this pattern in three books, his well-known "blowback trilogy."[15] He noted linkages large and seemingly small between our empire of bases and blowback—retaliations for things we have done around the world.[16] "Imperialism means one nation imposing its will on others through the threat or actual use of force. Imperialism is a root cause of blowback. Our global garrisons provide that threat and are a cause of blowback."[17]

Another "sorrow of empire" stressed by Johnson, Bacevich, and others is the rise of militarism in the United States and its often ill-fated consequences. Johnson associates militarism with the rise of a professional military class, the adoption of policies in which military preparedness becomes the highest priority of the state, and the tendency to see and to seek military action as the solution to problems that might be addressed otherwise.[18] Nicholas Kristof put it well: "If you're carrying an armload of hammers, every problem looks like a nail. The truth is that military power often isn't very effective at solving modern problems, like a nuclear North Korea or an Iran that is on the nuclear path. Indeed, in an age of nationalism, our military force is often counterproductive."[19]

A consequence of militarism, of course, is that one does end up in wars. Here is Pfaff's summation: "Between the beginning of the Cold War in Europe and the present war in Afghanistan, a period has passed that included the Korean War; the Vietnam War and the Cambodian invasion; U.S. interventions in Lebanon, Grenada, Panama, the Dominican Republic, El Salvador (indirectly), and Somalia (in connection with a UN operation, followed by sponsorship of an invasion of Somalia by Ethiopia); and two invasions of Iraq and one of Afghanistan. None except the Gulf War deserves to be called a victory. The United States' millenarian notions of a national destiny and the militarism that has infected American society have been responsible for a series of wars from which Washington has gained little or nothing, and suffered a great deal, while contributing enormously to the misfortune of others."[20] Today, Iran and others are tempting us again. But, as the future unfolds, a more likely prospect may be for the United States to be drawn into wars linked to energy, natural resources, and environmental calamity. Recent books bear the titles *Resource Wars, Water Wars,* and *Climate Wars.*[21]

Another consequence of empire stressed by Johnson, Garry Wills, and others is the threat to our democracy.[22] As Johnson puts it: "The combination of huge standing armies, almost continuous wars, an ever growing economic dependence on the military-industrial complex and the making of weaponry, and ruinous military expenses as well as a vast bloated 'defense' budget, not to speak of the creation of a whole second Defense Department (known as the Department of Homeland Security) has been destroying our republican structure of governing in favor of an imperial presidency. We are on the brink of losing our democracy for the sake of keeping our empire."[23] On another front, David Shipler in his *Rights of the People* reviews the extensive erosion of privacy and other Fourth Amendment protections since 9/11.[24]

A final sorrow of empire is the huge, draining psychological burden that U.S. actions have on its citizens. As events unfold, we experience by turns sadness and depression, denial, or worse, a hardening of the spirit. We see our own military, the CIA, and U.S. contractors engaged in torture, large killings of innocent civilians, murders and the taking of body parts as souvenirs, renditions, drone assassinations, military detention without trial, collaboration with unsavory regimes, and more. As Chris Hedges has put it: the endless warring is "a parasite that devours the heart and soul of a nation."[25]

Needless to say, many of our actions since 9/11 have also deeply distressed our allies and damaged U.S. standing around the world.

Johnson looked hard at all these issues for over a decade and ended up not very hopeful: "If, however, we were to dismantle our empire of military bases and redirect our economy toward productive, instead of destructive, industries; if we maintained our volunteer armed forces primarily to defend our own shores (and perhaps to be used at the behest of the United Nations); if we began to invest in our infrastructure, education, health care, and savings, then we might have a chance to reinvent ourselves as a productive, normal nation. Unfortunately, I don't see that happening. Peering into that foggy future, I simply can't imagine the U.S. dismantling its empire voluntarily, which doesn't mean that, like all sets of imperial garrisons, our bases won't go someday."[26]

Pfaff also notes the difficulty of real change: "U.S. security is far more likely to be found in a noninterventionist foreign policy. . . . So drastic a reversal of U.S. policy will not be possible without heavy political costs, both domestic and foreign. Nevertheless, the time has come for U.S. policymakers to begin considering reversing course."[27]

Many American foreign policy experts resist the idea of a smaller projection of American power around the world, and they look to economic growth to keep us strong internationally.[28] Leslie Gelb, for example, called for American leaders to take difficult steps to "rejuvenate the U.S. economy," to "elevate economic priorities as never before," and to "recognize that economics is now at the center of geopolitics." In sum, "to an unprecedented degree, the major powers now need one another to grow their economies."[29] Michael Mandelbaum says that "foreign policy is the province of the expert."[30] That disqualifies me, but one must doubt whether our foreign policy leaders give sufficient weight to the points made by Johnson, Pfaff, Bacevich, and others, and they clearly do not take into account the shortsightedness of relying on economic growth, a matter discussed in several chapters that follow.

Malign Neglect

Meanwhile, outside the Pentagon of plenitude, a world of wounds has festered without much help, and quite often with harm, from the United Sates.

Is the United States a good global citizen? Certainly one test would be the United States joining with other nations in addressing the big challenges that require international attention. Here, the story is sad indeed. The following are among the long list of treaties ratified by all nations except for a few rogue states, but not by the United States: the Convention of the Rights of the Child, the Convention Against All Forms of Discrimination Against Women, the Land Mine Convention, the Criminal Court Convention, the Biodiversity Convention, the Law of the Sea, the Kyoto Protocol of the Climate Convention, and the Convention on Persistent Organic Pollutants, to mention some prominent ones.[31]

America's international generosity is largely a myth. For many years, the United States was last among twenty-two OECD countries in the percentage of national income allocated to official development assistance generally and last also in the percentage allocated to the least-developed countries, where aid is needed most. In 2010 the United States pulled a bit ahead of Japan and Italy. Quite apart from the humanitarian and ethical issues involved in shortchanging the almost half of humanity who live on less than $2.25 a day, including the 1.75 billion people the UN estimates live in severe deprivation and the one billion who are chronically hungry and undernourished, development cooperation is one of the principal tools we have to address the capacity-building needs of fractured and failing states, which former Defense Secretary Robert Gates said is "the main security challenge of our time."[32]

While the United States has not ignored global population issues, it has not done nearly enough given the stakes involved and has often withheld support of major international population programs to further anti-abortion objectives. The United Nations projects that global population will grow by more than two billion by mid-century, reaching nine billion by then. Population pressures will exacerbate already difficult challenges in meeting demands for food and water, in protecting biodiversity and other resources, and in coping with climate change.[33]

The United States' failure to have done anything significant to address its huge releases of climate-changing greenhouse gases is, at this point, an international scandal. This is part of a more encompassing U.S. neglect of global-scale environmental and resource threats, issues taken up in the following chapter.

In terms of helping to build the needed international institutions and arrangements, the United States has concentrated heavily on institutions and issues involving security, trade, globalization, and other economic concerns while neglecting other areas (although, to be fair, the United States has often led on human rights issues). For decades, the United States has been at best neglectful of the United Nations and its many agencies and programs, including failing to pay its UN bills for a number of years. The United States is one of the principal reasons the world does not now have a World Environment Organization. Making the United Nations work successfully for all has just not been a U.S. priority, and too often the world body has been the target of U.S. hostility.

Another neglected area for the international community is the increasing size and strength of transnational criminal activity. In 2000, the U.S. National Intelligence Council, a group allied with the CIA, prepared a report looking ahead to 2015. Here's what it said: "Criminal organizations and networks . . . will expand the scale and scope of their activities. They will form loose alliances with one another, with smaller criminal entrepreneurs, and with insurgent movements for specific operations. They will corrupt leaders of unstable, economically fragile or failing states, insinuate themselves into troubled banks and businesses, and cooperate with insurgent political movements to control substantial geographic areas. Their income will come from narcotics trafficking; alien smuggling; trafficking in women and children; smuggling toxic materials, hazardous wastes, illicit arms, military technologies, and other contraband; financial fraud; and racketeering. The risk will increase that organized criminal groups will traffic in nuclear, biological, or chemical weapons. . . . Available data suggest that current annual revenues from illicit criminal activities include: $100–300 billion from narcotics trafficking; $10–12 billion from toxic and other hazardous waste dumping; $9 billion from automobile theft in the United States and Europe; $7 billion from alien smuggling; and as much as $1 billion from theft of intellectual property through pirating of videos, software, and other commodities."[34] Illegal wildlife trade is now estimated at between $10 and $20 billion annually. The black market in bluefin tuna alone is now put at $4 billion annually.[35] The estimated annual cost of Somali piracy in the Indian Ocean is between $5 and $7 billion.[36] The United States has focused on these issues to some degree, but not enough and too often neglecting to address root causes. And we seem unable to do the big things needed in the Mexican drug wars and the international drug situation generally. In Mexico, the United States is both a main source of the illegal guns being used and the main market for the sale of the illegal drugs.[37]

U.S. oil imports remain astronomically high, about nine million barrels a day, subtracting about $1 billion a day from the U.S. balance of trade, contributing greatly to one of the worst balance of payments deficits in the OECD and ensnaring us in a host of international troubles. In his book *The Frugal Superpower,* Michael Mandelbaum observes that "a different way to lower the costs of carrying out its responsibilities in the Middle East is available to the United States: a substantial reduction in the American consumption of oil through a major increase, via taxation, in the price Americans pay for gasoline. No single measure, in fact, would do as much to secure American interests worldwide in the face of the new economic limits on American foreign policy than a large reduction in American oil consumption. Mustering the political will to achieve this goal looms as the single most important foreign policy test the United States will face in the coming age of scarcity."[38]

American economic and political life is infected with a bad case of militarization that, in turn, has led to a severe imbalance in our allocation of public and private resources among the many international challenges America faces. We have overinvested in an approach to national security dominated by a vast military deployment, expensive and increasingly exotic weapons systems, and burgeoning intelligence operations at home and abroad, and in the process, we created the imperial presidency, sacrificed American rights and liberties, misspent a goodly share of the federal budget, and found ourselves moving from one costly and largely unsuccessful military conflict to another. Meanwhile, many international threats to our security and well-being have been badly neglected. It's time to strike a very different balance.

4 Running Out of Planet

The fact is that no compound growth is sustainable. If we maintain our desperate focus on growth, we will run out of everything and crash. We must substitute qualitative growth for quantitative growth. . . . From now on, price pressure and shortages of resources will be a permanent feature of our lives. This will increasingly slow down the growth rate of the developed and developing world. —JEREMY GRANTHAM

However demanding the challenges described so far, they may be overshadowed by developments on the environment, energy, and resources fronts. The rapaciousness with which we have run down the natural assets on which future well-being depends is staggering, and the U.S. record on these issues is deplorable. Since our early leadership in addressing ozone depletion, we have not accorded global-scale environmental challenges the priority needed to elicit determined, effective responses.

We live now in a world dramatically unlike the world of 1900, or even that of 1950. One does not have to look far ahead to see tighter supplies of energy, water, food, and various minerals. Prices will rise. We will see far fewer species in the planet's ecosystems, both terrestrial and aquatic. Most important will be the impacts from global warming and the resulting climate disruption. All can combine in predictable and unpredictable ways around the globe, undermining development prospects, giving rise to humanitarian emergencies, and bringing forth major threats to peace and security. And atop the list of threats, because it is the lynchpin that holds together our system of political economy, is the threat to economic growth. Historian J. R. McNeill has observed that in the twentieth century, "economic growth became the indispensible ideology of the state nearly everywhere. . . . The overarching priority of economic growth was easily the most important idea of the twentieth century."[1] But this commitment to growth at all costs has now given rise to a world economy that is so large and voracious that the "indispensible ideology" is itself headed toward the dustbin of history.

Environmental Decline

How serious are global environmental threats? Here is one measure of the problem: all that we have to do to destroy the planet's climate and biota and leave a ruined world to future generations is to keep doing what is being done today. Continue to release greenhouse gases at current rates, continue to impoverish ecosystems and to release toxic chemicals at current rates, and the world in the latter part of this century won't be fit to live in. But, of course, human activities are not holding steady at current levels—they are dramatically accelerating. It took all of history to build the $7 trillion world economy of 1950; more recently, economic activity has grown by $7 trillion every decade. At typical rates of growth, the world economy will now double in size in twenty years, perhaps fewer. We are thus facing the possibility of an enormous increase in environmental deterioration, just when the world needs to move strongly in the opposite direction.[2]

Half of the world's tropical and temperate forests have disappeared,[3] and a high rate of deforestation in the tropics continues.[4] About half the wetlands and a third of the mangroves are gone.[5] An estimated 90 percent of the large predator fish are gone, and 75 to 80 percent of marine fisheries are now overfished or fished to capacity.[6] Twenty percent of the corals are gone, and another 20 percent damaged and threatened.[7] Species are disappearing about a thousand times faster than normal.[8] The planet has not seen such a spasm of extinction in sixty-five million years—not since the dinosaurs disappeared.[9] Over half the agricultural land in drier regions suffers from some degree of deterioration and desertification.[10] Persistent toxic chemicals can be found by the dozens in essentially each and every one of us.[11]

Human impacts are now large relative to natural systems. We have pushed atmospheric carbon dioxide up by more than a third. The earth's ice fields are melting almost everywhere.[12] Industrial processes are fixing nitrogen, making it biologically active, at a rate equal to nature's; one result is the development of more than two hundred dead zones in the oceans due to overfertilization.[13] Human actions already consume or destroy each year about 40 percent of nature's photosynthetic output, leaving too little for other species.[14] Freshwater withdrawals doubled globally between 1960 and 2000, and are now over half of accessible runoff.[15] The following rivers no longer regularly reach the oceans in the dry season: the Colorado, Yellow, and Nile, among others.[16]

Though decried for decades, the decimation of the planet's rich endowment of species and ecosystems continues. One major 2010 assessment reported in *Science* concluded that despite efforts to stem this dramatic erosion of life, "Biodiversity loss is not slowing down. Recent assessment shows a continued, steady overall decline in wild species' population sizes and in the extent, condition, and connectivity of many habitats with accelerating levels of extinction risk and accelerating or steady declines in the benefits people derive from biodiversity."[17]

The proportion of mammals threatened with extinction today is estimated to be about 20 percent. The list of threatened species grows annually.[18] If seeing Africa's big game is on your bucket list, leave for Africa tomorrow. The index that measures animal population abundance in seventy-eight protected areas in Africa shows an average decline of almost 60 percent in the populations of sixty-nine key species, including lion, giraffe, buffalo, and zebra, between 1970 and 2005.[19]

In just the first five years of this century, the extent of world forests declined by 3 percent.[20] Mangrove forests are now being destroyed at four times the rate of other forests.[21] A recent assessment by the United Nations Environment Programme (UNEP) concluded that if overfishing trends continue, we will have largely exhausted commercial ocean fisheries in forty years.[22]

Unfortunately, losses to date are modest when compared with how they will be dramatically worsened by climate change. Emissions of greenhouse gases have already committed the planet to a global average warming of 1.4°C over the preindustrial (1880) level. Even if all the emission cuts pledged by governments in Copenhagen in 2009 are met, it is estimated that global average temperatures will rise between 2.5°C and 5°C over the preindustrial level by 2100.[23] Estimates vary, but additional global warming of 1.5°C to 2.5°C over today's level will likely put 20 to 30 percent of species at increased risk of extinction.[24] One huge impact of climate change already under way is the loss of a Washington state–size amount of forests in the United States and Canada due to die-off caused by tree-killing insects that global warming has allowed to proliferate through mild winters.[25]

But the adverse consequences of climate change do not end there. Staying on the course we are on today will likely lead us to:[26]

Extensive drought. A 2010 report by the National Center for Atmospheric Research forecasts increasingly severe drought conditions by 2030 over much of the world due to climate change, including the western two-thirds of the United States, much of Latin America, southeastern Asia including China, and most of Australia and Africa.[27] In fact, anyone following the news closely will know that the drying has begun. Major portions of the U.S. Southwest have experienced prolonged drought since 2001.[28] A 2011 report from the World Resources Institute notes that Brazil has experienced "two '100 year' droughts within five years in the western Amazon basin, suggesting that this destructive weather pattern may soon become the country's 'new normal.' China is facing its longest drought in over 60 years, endangering its wheat crop. Climate change promises to alter both the structure and function of ecosystems, thereby transforming the lives of hundreds of millions of people who depend on these critical life-support systems over large parts of the globe."[29]

Sea level rise of 2–3 feet in this century, and possibly up to five feet. Sea levels are already up eight inches since 1900, and from 2003 to 2010 NASA satellites measured the earth's melting land ice and found that it added about 4.3 trillion tons of water to the oceans, enough itself to raise sea levels a half an inch.[30] So the process is well under way. A two-foot rise would put 190 million people a year at risk from floods.[31] Greenland's ice sheet holds enough water to raise sea levels by seven yards. It is melting and its glaciers are moving much faster than predicted.[32]

Extensive loss of forests. In a +4°C world—a possibility for this century—over 80 percent of the Amazon forests could be destroyed by 2100.[33] The National Academy of Sciences has estimated that each 1°C of global warming will increase the area burned by wildfires in the western United States by 200 to 400 percent.[34]

Killer heat waves. The year 2010 was the hottest year yet (tied for first with 2005). Seventeen nations set temperature records. In the United States, a Stanford study predicts that long and extreme heat waves could be commonplace in thirty years.[35] The European heat wave of 2003 killed more than thirty thousand people, and summers like that will likely happen every other year by 2040 if current emission trends continue.[36]

Millions of climate refugees. Lack of water, crop failure, and sea level rise could force two hundred million people from their homes by 2050.[37] A 2010 report on changing conditions in Africa's Sahel noted, "Millions of people are on the move. The question now is whether to encourage them to migrate—or to salvage their ravaged land with long-term investment, instead of simply handing out emergency aid. . . . Evidence like this is convincing some experts that the Sahel is becoming uninhabitable. Across most of Africa, average temperatures have been steadily rising for decades, while rainfall has been declining. The Sahel is one of the worst-hit regions. Climate change and human exploitation have left it vulnerable to extreme weather and a destructive cycle of drought and floods."[38]

More-intense hurricanes and floods. Category 4 and 5 storms, which can do the most damage, are projected to double in frequency in the Atlantic in this century.[39] One study has linked the recent increase in heavy rainfall and resulting floods to climate change.[40]

While many people assume that the impacts of climate change will unfold gradually as the earth's temperature slowly rises, the buildup of greenhouse gases may in fact lead to abrupt changes.[41] The possibility of abrupt climate change is linked to what may be the most problematic possibility of all—"positive" feedback effects wherein the initial warming generates more warming. First, the land's ability to store carbon could weaken. Soils and forests can dry out or burn, thereby releasing carbon. Less plant growth reduces nature's ability to remove carbon from the air. Ocean warming could also lead to a reduction of carbon sinks in the oceans. As the planet warms and becomes drier in various regions, the potent greenhouse gas methane could be released from peat bogs, wetlands, and thawing permafrost, and even from the methane hydrates in the oceans.[42] Finally, the earth's albedo, the reflectivity of the earth's surface, will be compromised. Large areas now covered by ice and snow will be covered by meltwater, and so the sun's rays—heretofore reflected off the earth and back into space—will not be reflected, and the water will warm even more. All these effects would tend to make warming self-reinforcing, greatly amplifying the greenhouse effect.

The extra carbon dioxide being released has a further consequence: ocean acidification. Here's a recent report from *Science:* "Now ocean pH is lower than it's been for 20 million years, and it's going to get lower."[43] Organisms that build shells or skeletons of calcium carbonate will suffer as a result. "When the hydrogen ion concentration of seawater gets high enough," the *Science* article notes, "the calcium carbonate in these organisms begins to dissolve."[44] Loss of corals due to ocean warming and acidification has huge implications for the five hundred million people worldwide who depend on corals to support fisheries and tourism. Pavan Sukhdev, a successful banker now leading major analyses for UNEP, noted recently that if coral reefs—now valued by economists at between $30 billion and $172 billion per year—collapse, huge numbers of people in Southeast Asia and Africa regions will migrate from the coastal areas where they've lived for generations, causing political instability and strife.[45]

The Food-Water-Climate-Energy Complex

Meeting the world's growing demand for food, water, and energy in the context of ongoing climate change is one of the greatest policy and technological challenges human societies have ever faced. On the subject of food: World food output will have to approach a doubling by 2050 in order to feed a world population of nine billion, and this will have to happen despite the impacts of climate change, the need to reduce agriculture's contribution to climate change (currently greater than that of transportation), competition for freshwater supplies, higher energy prices, and widespread losses of soil and biological resources.[46]

A series of articles on food in *Science* stresses the problems posed by climate change. One notes, "The average temperature in Europe's hot summer of 2003 was only about 3.5°C above the average for the last century. The 20 to 35 percent decrease in the yields of grains and fruits that summer drew little attention. But if the climate scientists are right, summers will be that hot on average by mid-century, and by 2090 much of the world will be experiencing summers hotter than the hottest summer now on record. . . . It will be increasingly difficult to maintain, much less increase, yields of our current major crops as temperatures rise and drylands expand. Climate change will further affect agriculture as the sea level rises, submerging low-lying cropland, and as glaciers melt, causing river systems to experience shorter and more intense seasonal flows, as well as more flooding."[47]

Meanwhile, freshwater shortages have also become more severe. A comprehensive overview in *Nature* in 2010 reported that roughly

80 percent of the world's population is vulnerable to freshwater deficits.[48] The American Geophysical Union reported in 2010 that the groundwater depletion rate is accelerating worldwide. "In recent decades, the rate at which humans worldwide are pumping dry the vast underground stores of water that billions depend on has more than doubled. . . . Soaring global groundwater depletion bodes a potential disaster for an increasingly globalized agricultural system."[49] Water scarcity is a particular threat in some of the world's most volatile areas: Pakistan, India, Iraq, Egypt, Sudan, Uzbekistan, and elsewhere.

The Pacific Institute, which keeps the record book on water conflicts, recently noted, "Global climate change will increase the risk of conflict over shared international freshwater resources." Its Water and Conflict Chronology shows "a growing incidence of disputes over water allocations leading to conflict across local borders, ethnic boundaries, or between economic groups, as well as in international conflicts. Climate change will only make these problems worse."[50]

Regarding food, Lester Brown has noted that food shortages and rising food prices have the potential to destabilize and collapse failing and fragile states. "Unable to buy grain or grow their own, hungry people take to the streets. Indeed, even before the steep climb in grain prices in 2008, the number of failing states was expanding. Many of their problems stem from a failure to slow the growth of their populations. But if the food situation continues to deteriorate, entire nations will break down at an ever-increasing rate."[51] The United Nations found that at least 40 percent of recent civil wars had access to natural resources as a primary or contributing cause.[52]

While concerted international efforts must be going forward to deal with the linked challenges of food, water, and climate change, the world's nations will also be in the midst of a confusing mix of trends and pressures on the energy front. Oil prices will likely continue to rise and do so in a highly volatile way. Energy prices will be driven upward by surging demand, more costly supply, and the push to put a price on carbon emissions. Huge efforts will be under way to shift to efficiency and renewables, and huge efforts will also be under way to find new fossil fuel resources, including in the Arctic. An international scramble for energy resources has already begun, including exploitation of supplies that are more difficult and expensive to access and more environmentally risky. Controversies will undoubtedly swirl around nuclear power and its attendant proliferation and safety risks.

Energy expert Michael Klare has described the rise of the permanent energy crisis: "The primary vectors of the permanent energy crisis can be identified and charted. Three such vectors, in particular, demand attention: a slowing in the growth of energy supplies at a time of accelerating worldwide demand; rising political instability provoked by geopolitical competition for those supplies; and mounting environmental woes produced by our continuing addiction to oil, natural gas, and coal."[53]

The Pentagon has concluded that climate change poses a broad strategic challenge to the United States. As the *New York Times* noted in August 2009: "The changing global climate will pose profound strategic challenges to the United States in coming decades, raising the prospect of military intervention to deal with the effects of violent storms, drought, mass migration and pandemics, military and intelligence analysts say.

"Such climate-induced crises could topple governments, feed terrorist movements or destabilize entire regions, say the analysts, experts at the Pentagon and intelligence agencies who for the first time are taking a serious look at the national security implications of climate change."[54]

In his remarkable book *Why the West Rules—for Now,* Ian Morris reflects on how all the issues discussed here might interact in the future: "As when the horsemen rode in the past, climate change, famine, migration, and disease will probably feed back on one another, unleashing the fifth horseman, state failure. . . . Every year we avoid Armageddon the threats from the horsemen of the apocalypse keep building. Pressure on resources will mount, new diseases will evolve, nuclear weapons will proliferate, and—most insidious of all—global weirding will shift the calculus in unpredictable ways. It seems crazily optimistic to think we can juggle all these dangers indefinitely." His conclusion: "The odds look bad."[55]

Facing Up to Climate Change

We can be confident, or at least hopeful, that an international political tipping point will eventually be reached and major programs to reduce global warming emissions will be launched, even by the U.S. Congress. But every year of delay is costly.

The international community has set a target of keeping global average warming from rising an additional 2°C above the preindustrial level, even though many climate scientists and others believe that that goal is too lax and would much prefer limiting warming to +1.5°C. Huge efforts involving many hundreds of computer runs have been expended over the past couple of years to advise governments on what they must do to have any hope of staying below the +2°C ceiling. Others believe that even with the most strenuous international efforts, we're already fated to a +3°C or +4°C world by 2100, far beyond the +2°C goal and deep into dangerous territory.[56]

The UNEP has recently reviewed this burgeoning literature to explore what will be needed to stay below +2°C. It concludes that to have a 66 percent chance or better of staying below +2°C, global emissions of carbon dioxide and other greenhouse gases should peak before 2020, the rate of emissions reduction between 2020 and 2050 should be around 3 percent per year, and global emissions in 2050 should be about 50 to 60 percent below their 1990 levels.[57]

These are challenging prescriptions, and many believe they will not be realized, particularly given continued U.S. inaction.[58] Reducing global emissions year after year at 3 percent, as the UNEP urges, is difficult, but it is far more challenging in the context of a growing world economy, which obviously creates huge incentives to increase emissions. If the world economy is growing at 5 percent a year, the carbon intensity of the economy (quantity of emissions released to produce $1 of economic output) would have to decline by 8 percent year after year. That's dauntingly ambitious, but other studies indicate that the rate of emissions reduction will have to be higher than 3 percent a year to stay under the $+2°C$ warming limit.[59] In still another analysis, Tim Jackson in *Prosperity Without Growth* calculates that with normal growth in the well-to-do countries and rapid growth in incomes in the developing world, global carbon intensity would have to fall by 9 to 11 percent every year between now and 2050.[60]

Faced with such numbers, some analysts are concluding that affluent countries will have to reduce their rates of economic growth in order to make growing space available to the developing economies. The rich countries, the United States especially, are already being called upon to reduce emissions by 80 to 90 percent by 2050. An 80 percent reduction over forty years requires U.S. emissions to decline at 4 percent a year. More likely to be needed, a 90 percent reduction over thirty-five years would require a 6.5 percent annual reduction in emissions. If the U.S. economy is growing at 3 to 3.5 percent a year, the carbon intensity of U.S. output will have to decline by at least 7 percent and, more likely, 9 percent each year. Because these rates of carbon intensity decline are implausibly high, the United States will be faced with a tradeoff between continuing with its current growth imperative and doing the right thing for climate protection.

Right now, the United States is the main stumbling block internationally to climate action. If this were to continue, one can foresee other countries taking major retaliatory action of some sort. The years and decades ahead will see the United States faced with a powerful new set of demands requiring far-reaching and difficult change in both domestic and foreign policy: (1) a growing burden stemming from the need to cope with and, as best one can, adapt to climate change, including the need to cope abroad with the inevitable humanitarian and security crises; (2) the need to transform the U.S. energy economy radically and quickly, shifting out of fossil fuels and into renewables and efficiency on a mammoth scale; (3) the imperative of heavily investing both political and financial capital internationally in the effort to find climate solutions that are both effective and equitable in the context of the developing world; and (4) a mounting challenge to the centrality of economic growth in U.S. national life, a challenge that will be dramatically sharpened if climate change is allowed to spin out of control and thus comes to eclipse all other issues, as it easily might.

The scale of the energy transformation needed in the United States and globally is staggering. Here is one estimate: "At the global level, in order to shift away from a world that gets 81 percent of its energy from fossil fuels and to cut emissions of carbon dioxide to just 14 gigatons per year, here is what the International Energy Agency says will have to be built *every year* between now and 2050: 35 coal-fired and 20 gas-fired power plants with carbon capture and storage; 30 nuclear power plants; 12,000 onshore wind turbines paired with 3,600 offshore ones; 45 geothermal power plants; 325 million square meters' worth of photovoltaics; and 55 solar-thermal power plants. That doesn't even include the need to build electric cars and hydrogen fuel cell vehicles in order to shift transportation away from burning gasoline."[61]

Michael Klare has described the challenge the United States faces: "To put things in perspective, fossil fuels now provide about 84 percent and nuclear power about 8.5 percent of America's net energy supply; renewables, including hydropower, provide a mere 8 percent. Although the amount of energy provided by renewables is expected to grow in the years ahead, the United States is projected to need so much more energy under its current path—114.5 quadrillion British thermal units per year in 2035, compared with approximately 100 quadrillion today, that it will need much larger amounts of oil, gas and coal to supply the necessary increase. As a result, says the Energy Department, we will rely more on fossil fuels in 2035 than we do today, and will be emitting greater quantities of carbon dioxide. Clearly, the existing path leads us ever closer to environmental catastrophe. Only by freezing (and eventually reducing) the total amount of energy consumed and reversing the ratio between traditional and alternative fuels can disaster be averted."[62]

The pressure to reduce U.S. reliance on fossil fuels will be alleviated somewhat if carbon capture and storage (CCS) proves viable and timely. CCS involves first capturing carbon dioxide emissions from operating power plants and then, after transport, injecting the carbon dioxide deep into the earth for geologic storage. The process is still in the demonstration stage, and if the process is proven viable and affordable, it could move to commercialization after about 2025. Industry currently estimates that it will increase power plant costs between 40 and 75 percent. The International Energy Agency estimates that with full and rapid deployment, CCS could account for about 20 percent of energy-related emissions reduction by 2050, about the same contribution IEA sees from renewable energy technologies.[63] This must be seen as a best-case scenario. CCS could easily be slower, more expensive, and less important in overall emissions reduction, even assuming demonstration efforts are successful. In short, CCS is not something on which societies can now bank heavily in planning climate protection.[64]

The failure of U.S. climate policy has more to do with domestic politics than international affairs, and it has everything to do with the forty-year failure of U.S. energy policy. Both failures are the result of the great political power of the fossil fuels industry, which has prevented any serious U.S. movement to reduce carbon dioxide emissions.[65] The enormous power of Big Oil and Big Coal in American politics is reflected in the fact that at this late date, with all the focus on renewable energy and all the disasters generated by coal, oil, and gas, federal subsidies to fossil fuels between 2002 and 2008 came to $72 billion; those to renewables only $29 billion, with more than half of that going to corn-based ethanol.[66] Technological advances that have opened up large supplies of shale oil and gas will make the shift away from fossil fuels even more difficult.

With Congress now home to many climate deniers and skeptics, it is worth remembering that there was already ample scientific evidence thirty years ago to spur major climate action. In January 1981, President Carter's Council on Environmental Quality (CEQ) "warned today that national and international energy policies must immediately start addressing the problem of carbon dioxide pollution if major long-range climatic and economic problems were to be avoided." We even knew enough back then to have a rough idea of what was needed: "One recommendation of the [CEQ] report is that agreement be reached by industrialized nations on a safe maximum level for carbon dioxide in the air. It suggested a level 50 percent higher than that of pre-industrial times as an upper limit."[67] The ensuing thirty years of neglect now weigh heavily on us and the world.

A major analysis of where the world stands in addressing climate and other environmental threats has been carried out by a large group of the world's most eminent scientists. Completed in 2009, the analysis, "Planetary Boundaries: Exploring the Safe Operating Space for Humanity," identified nine key boundaries that human society should not cross if it is to avoid "deleterious and even catastrophic consequences." Unfortunately, the study found that human society has already exceeded three of the boundaries—climate change, biodiversity loss, and releases of biologically active nitrogen—and that societies are perilously close to exceeding the boundaries for freshwater use, land deterioration, and ocean acidification.[68] It's time for the United States to get serious about these issues, before it is too late. We have failed so utterly to act at home and to give leadership abroad that the world is firmly on the path to a ruined planet in the lives of today's children.

Part Two   In the Beauty of the Morning

Let none despair. The American character, whatever its shortcomings, abounds in courage, creative energy, and resourcefulness and is bottomed upon the profound conviction that nothing in the world is beyond its power to accomplish.
—ARTHUR M. SCHLESINGER, SR.

There is an America beyond despair, and it is not hard to find. Ask a parent, ask yourself, what America you would like for your grand-children and their children, and the odds are good that in the reply a new America unfolds. Part II explores the terrain of this new America, America the Possible. It undertakes the tricky task of envisioning the better country that is still within our power to reach.

Much as Part I describes the situation in which we find ourselves today as we approach the bottom of the curve on page 12, Part II describes a future to which we can aspire, one we arrive at well along the ascending path to a new America. The key to this transition from today to tomorrow is systemic, transformative change, the subject of Parts III and IV.

5 America the Possible

*A utopian vision arises out of a moral indictment of a set of insti-
tutions or beliefs which have been corrupted. But instead of leading to quietism or despair or nihilism, such a cri de coeur becomes
utopian when it informs a vision of a different world, one with a
moral order remote from that evident in the debased present.*
—JAY WINTER

*The real science of political economy, which has yet to be dis-
tinguished from the bastard science, as medicine from witchcraft,
and astronomy from astrology, is that which teaches nations
to desire and labour for the things that lead to life, and that
which teaches them to scorn and destroy the things that lead to
destruction.* —JOHN RUSKIN

Thoreau enjoined us, "Go confidently in the direction of your
dreams!" But what is the dream of a better America? Any reserva-
tions stemming from the possible presumptions in answering this
question—who is "we," after all? can we even correctly anticipate
future generations' concerns?—should be put to rest by the realization that we are responsible for the consequences of our actions, and
those consequences extend far into the future. As the great biogeolo-
gist Preston Cloud noted in *Cosmos, Earth and Man* in 1978, "We are
prone to dodge the issue of posterity's rights with the complacent

judgment that, after all, no one can foresee the future, and that each generation must therefore look after its own needs as they come along, with whatever means avail. There is some truth to that view, but more escapism. . . . Our knowledge of past events, current trends, biological and societal processes, and natural laws can be brought to bear in attempts to anticipate the future and to exercise some control over it. From such considerations arises a responsibility to posterity that cannot be set aside merely because we cannot see exactly how to fulfill it in all particulars."[1]

There is one sure berth from which to launch an inquiry into the future—one powerfully put by the poet Drew Dellinger:

> it's 3:23 in the morning
> and I'm awake
> because my great great grandchildren
> won't let me sleep
> my great great grandchildren
> ask me in dreams
> what did you do while the planet was plundered?
> what did you do when the earth was unraveling?[2]

We are thus drawn ineluctably to the question: what America should we strive to create? Envisioning the better country that is still within our power to reach is tricky. Of course, it must be a plausible future, and not every future is ours to have. We have effectively closed down certain options. A future without any climate change, for example, is no longer possible. But a beautiful future is still ours if we are willing to struggle for it. It will not come easily, but little that is worth having ever does. If while reading through the following hopes and dreams for my five grandchildren, you begin to think that what I describe is utopian, remember what Victor Hugo wrote in *Les Misérables:* "There is nothing like a dream to create the future. Utopia today, flesh and blood tomorrow."

I will explore this future by following four guideposts that mark the path to a better place. After identifying each guidepost, I will describe the America the Possible to which the guidepost has led us. If you want a timeframe, imagine 2050, four decades away.

Let me preview the four guideposts. In our envisioning of an American future worth striving for, we want, first, to see an America that has successfully climbed out of the basement described in Part I. Here, we want to join with other leading countries on the major issues that define the broad contours of national life. Second, we want to see an America where new values have come to the fore. Third, we want to have provided our progeny safe passage around the potential calamities that might otherwise have consigned them to lives bound in shallows and miseries. And, last, we want for them a place where the quotidian affairs of life provide a setting rich with fellowship and opportunities for exploration and development.

Guidepost 1

First, and most obviously, we want an America where the long list of shortcomings previously reviewed has been successfully addressed. Guidepost 1 thus leads us to basic social justice, real global security, environmental sustainability, true popular sovereignty, and economic democracy.

By 2050 in America the Possible, we will have pursued the transformative changes described in Chapter 1 and marshaled the economic and political resources to remedy the most glaring of today's deficiencies. As a result, family incomes in America will be far more equal, similar to the situation in the Nordic countries and Japan today. Large-scale poverty and income insecurity will be things of the past. Good jobs will be available to all those who want to work. Our health-care and educational systems will be among the best in the world, as will our standing in child welfare and equality of women. Racial and ethnic disparities will be largely eliminated.

Today's big social problems—guns and homicides, drugs and incarceration, white-collar crime and Wall Street high jinks—will be down to acceptable levels. Major national challenges like the national debt, illegal immigration, the future of Social Security, oil imports and the shift to sustainable energy, and environmental and consumer protection will have been addressed wisely. U.S. emissions of carbon dioxide and other greenhouse gases will have been reduced to a tiny fraction of today's.

Internationally, the United States will have assumed the role, in Chalmers Johnson's phrase, of a "normal nation." Military spending will be reduced to a level about like Europe's today; military interventions will be rare and arms sales small. Resources thus freed up will be deployed to join with other nations in addressing climate change and other global environmental threats, nuclear proliferation, world poverty and underdevelopment, and other global challenges. The United States will be a leader in strengthening the institutions of global governance and international regulation, and we will be a member in good standing in the long list of treaties and other international agreements in which we do not now participate.

Politically, implementation of prodemocracy reforms will have saved our politics from corporate control and the power of money, and these reforms will have brought us to an unprecedented level of true popular sovereignty. Moreover, government in America will again be respected for its competence and efficiency. And, yes, taxes will be higher and tax burdens fair and equitable.

Overall, the economy will be governed to ensure broadly shared prosperity and to preserve the integrity and biological richness of the natural world. It will simply be assumed that the priority of economic activity is to sustain human and natural communities. Investment will concentrate in areas with high social and environmental returns, and it will be guided by democratically determined priorities at the national and local levels. Corporations will be under effective public control, and new patterns of business ownership and management—involving workers, communities, governments, and other stakeholders—will be the norm.

This recitation seems idealistic today, but the truth is, we know how to do these things. As elaborated in Part III, our libraries are full of plausible, affordable policy options, budget proposals, and institutional innovations that could realize these and other important objectives. And today's world is full of useful models we can adapt to our circumstances.

Guidepost 2

A second dimension of the world we should hope for and seek for our grandchildren is an America whose values and dominant culture are very different from today's. Guidepost 2 thus leads us to new values, motivations, and habits of thought to infuse and animate American life.

Many have concluded that addressing our many challenges will require the rise of a new consciousness, with different values dominant in American culture. For some, it is a spiritual awakening—a transformation of the human heart. For others it is a more intellectual process of coming to see the world anew and deeply embracing the emerging ethic of the environment and the old ethic of what it means to love thy neighbor as thyself. But for all, the possibility of a sustainable and just future will require major cultural change and a reorientation of what society values and prizes most highly.

Paul Raskin and his Global Scenario Group have developed many scenarios of future conditions, including some that include no fundamental changes in consciousness and values. But without a change in values, all their scenarios run into big trouble. Raskin's team urges a future where society turns "to non-material dimensions of fulfillment . . . the quality of life, the quality of human solidarity and the quality of the earth. . . . Sustainability is the imperative that pushes the new agenda. Desire for a rich quality of life, strong human ties and a resonant connection to nature is the lure that pulls it toward the future."[3] The revolution Raskin and his colleagues envision is primarily a revolution in values and consciousness.

Two of the leading authorities on religion and ecology, Yale's Mary Evelyn Tucker and John Grim, believe that "we are called to a new intergenerational consciousness and conscience" and that "values and ethics, religion and spirituality" are important factors in "transforming human consciousness and behavior for a sustainable future."[4] A deep understanding of science is not antithetical and can also contribute to a new consciousness, as Tucker and Brian Swimme recently demonstrated in their remarkable film *Journey of the Universe*.[5]

What these people and many others are saying is that today's challenges require a rapid evolution to a new consciousness.[6] I would never say that no progress can be made until America's dominant culture has been transformed. But I do believe that we won't get far in addressing our major challenges unless there is a parallel, ongoing transformation in values and culture.

Following Guidepost 2, our dominant culture will have shifted, from today to tomorrow, in the following ways:

- Instead of viewing humanity as something apart from nature, and nature as something to be transcended and dominated, we will see ourselves as part of nature, as offspring of its evolutionary process, as close kin to wild things, and as wholly dependent on its vitality and the services it provides.
- Rather than seeing nature as humanity's resource to exploit as it sees fit for economic and other purposes, we will see the natural world as holding intrinsic value independent of people and having rights that create the duty of ecological stewardship.
- We will no longer discount the future by focusing so intently on the short term, but instead take the long view and recognize our duties to human and natural communities well into the future.
- Instead of today's hyperindividualism and social isolation, we will reward those who foster a powerful sense of community and social solidarity, in all venues from rural to cosmopolitan.
- Violence will no longer be glorified nor wars easily accepted. The spreading of hate and invidious divisions will be frowned on and will no longer be a launching pad for careers in broadcasting.

- Materialism, consumerism, and the primacy of ever-more possessions will give way to a culture that grants priority to family and personal relationships, learning, experiencing nature, service, spirituality, and living within Earth's limits.
- Rather than tolerate gross economic, social, gender, and political inequality, we will demand and work for a high measure of equality in all of these spheres.

Here's an often overlooked fact: We don't need to wait on these changes but can bring them about. "The central conservative truth is that culture, not politics, determines the success of a society," Daniel Patrick Moynihan remarked. "The central liberal truth is that politics can change a culture and save it from itself."[7] More on this in Chapter 8.

We actually know important things about how values and culture can change. One sure path to cultural change is, unfortunately, the cataclysmic event—the crisis—that profoundly challenges prevailing values and delegitimizes the status quo.[8] The Great Depression is the classic example. I think we can be confident that we haven't seen the end of major crises.

Milton Friedman was an accomplished economist and a fierce advocate. I did not often agree with his positions on policy, but he was right to point to the way crises can bring ideas to the fore: "Only a crisis—actual or perceived—produces real change," he wrote. "When that crisis occurs, the actions that are taken depend on the ideas that are lying around. That, I believe, is our basic function: to develop alternatives to existing policies, to keep them alive and available until the politically impossible becomes politically inevitable."[9] As Naomi Klein ably shows in *The Shock Doctrine: The Rise of Disaster Capitalism*, Friedman and his followers have applied his philosophy to aggressively advance far-reaching privatization and unfettered free enterprise.[10] Yet the very measures he advocated are now part of a system that is spawning its own disasters and headed toward its own end.

Two other key factors in cultural change are leadership and social narrative. Harvard's Howard Gardner has written, "Whether they are heads of a nation or senior officials of the United Nations, leaders . . . have enormous potential to change minds . . . and in the process they can change the course of history.

"I have suggested one way to capture the attention of a disparate population: by creating a compelling story, embodying that story in one's own life, and presenting the story in many different formats so that it can eventually topple the counterstories in one's culture. . . . The story must be simple, easy to identify with, emotionally resonant, and evocative of positive experiences."[11]

Bill Moyers, a powerful force for good in our country, has written, "America needs a different story. . . . The leaders and thinkers and activists who honestly tell that story and speak passionately of the moral and religious values it puts in play will be the first political generation since the New Deal to win power back for the people."[12] There is some evidence that Americans are ready for another story. Large majorities of Americans, when polled, express disenchantment with today's lifestyles and offer support for values similar to those urged here.[13]

Another key source of value change is social movements. Social movements are all about consciousness raising, and if successful, they can help usher in a new consciousness. The need for a new social movement in America is a principal subject of Chapter 9. The proliferation of protests in cities across our country in 2011 may have signaled its beginning.

Another way forward to a new consciousness lies with the world's religions. Mary Evelyn Tucker has noted that "no other group of institutions can wield the particular moral authority of the religions."[14] The potential of faith communities is enormous, and they are turning more attention to issues of social justice, peace, and environment, with books like Bob Edgar's *Middle Church* and Jim Wallis's *Soul of Politics* pointing the way.[15] In his 2009 encyclical, "Charity in Truth," Pope Benedict XVI called for a radical rethinking of economic life, the profit motive, and economic disparities.[16] Spiritual awakening to new values and new consciousness can also derive from the arts, literature, philosophy, and science. Consider, for example, the long tradition of "reverence for life" stretching back to the Emperor Ashoka more than 2,200 years ago and forward to Albert Schweitzer, Aldo Leopold, Thomas Berry, E. O. Wilson, Terry Tempest Williams, and others.[17]

Education, of course, can also contribute enormously to cultural change. Here one should include education in the largest sense, embracing not only formal education but also day-to-day and experiential education as well as the fast-developing field of social marketing. Social marketing has had notable successes in moving people away from bad behaviors such as smoking and drunk driving, and its approaches could be applied to these themes as well.

A major and very hopeful path is seeding the landscape with innovative, instructive models. A remarkable and yet undernoticed thing going on in the United States today is the proliferation of innovative models of community revitalization and business enterprise. Local currencies, slow money, state Genuine Progress Indicators, locavores—these are bringing the future into the present in very concrete ways. These actual models will grow in importance as communities search for answers on how the future should look, and they can change minds. Seeing is believing.

In sum, cultural transformation won't be easy, but it's not impossible either.

Guidepost 3

High on any list of our duties to future generations must be the imperative that we keep open for them as many options and choices as possible. That is our generation's gift of freedom. Here, the first order of business is to preserve the possibility of a bright future by preventing any of today's looming disasters from spinning out of control or otherwise becoming calamitous or so overwhelming that they monopolize resources of time, energy, and money, thus foreclosing other options.[18]

What are the biggest threats in this regard? Here is my list:

- severe disruption of global climate
- widespread exhaustion, erosion, and toxification of the planet's natural resources and life-support systems
- militarism and permanent war
- nuclear disaster
- major economic or financial collapse, possibly linked to failing energy supply and soaring prices or an out-of-control worldwide financial sector
- runaway terrorism and resulting loss of civil liberties
- pandemics and antibiotic resistance
- social and cultural decay, including the rise of criminality
- hollowing out of democracy and the dominance of corporatocracy and plutocracy
- something weird from the lab (nanotech? robotics? genetic engineering? a new weapon system? indefinite life extension?)

Much ink has been deployed warning us about these threats, and we must take them very seriously. In America the Possible, these warnings have been taken seriously and the threats avoided. In all of the threats listed, we can already see problems, but we are not yet fated to experience their worst.

Guidepost 4

The final guidepost to the hoped-for future involves what might be called the virtues of necessity. Even with disaster averted, there are still powerful constraints and limits on future options. Yet a great many of these constraints are actually blessings in disguise, or can be. Consider this *New York Times* report from a Transition Town meeting in Idaho: "Transition's approach is adamantly different from that of the survivalists. . . . The movement may begin from a similarly dystopian idea: that cheap oil has recklessly vaulted humanity to a peak of production and consumption. . . . But Transition then takes an almost utopian turn. Rob Hopkins [father of the Transition Town movement] insists that if an entire community faces this stark challenge together, it might be able to design an 'elegant descent' from that peak. We can consciously plot a path into a lower-energy life—a life of walkable villages, local food and artisans and greater intimacy with the natural world—which, on balance, could actually be richer and more enjoyable than what we have now. Transition, Hopkins has written, meets our era's threats with a spirit of 'elation, rather than the guilt, anger and horror' behind most environmental activism. 'Change is inevitable, [Hopkins said,] but this is a change that could be fantastic.'"[19]

In fact, in Guidepost 4, several developments are coming together and are pushing us to nothing less than a new way of living: the imperative of protecting climate and the earth's living systems, the need to adjust to the rise of scarcities in energy and other resources, and the desirability of shifting national priorities to things that truly improve social well-being and happiness. As the bumper sticker says, the important things in life aren't things.

We are now forced to reconsider how we live and work by the realizations that current approaches to environmental management aren't succeeding well at all. If we are going to cope with the big environmental challenges like climate change, deeper changes will be necessary.

The world's leading scientists have repeatedly warned that human societies are already living well beyond planetary means. The Millennium Ecosystem Assessment was a massive four-year effort involving 1,360 scientists and other experts worldwide to assess conditions and trends regarding the world's ecosystems. At the conclusion of this unprecedented effort in 2005, the assessment issued the following statement: "Nearly two thirds of the services provided by nature to humankind are found to be in decline worldwide. In effect, the benefits reaped from our engineering of the planet have been achieved by running down natural capital assets.

"In many cases, it is literally a matter of living on borrowed time. . . .

"Unless we acknowledge the debt and prevent it from growing, we place in jeopardy the dreams of citizens everywhere to rid the world of hunger, extreme poverty, and avoidable disease—as well as increasing the risk of sudden changes to the planet's life-support systems from which even the wealthiest may not be shielded."[20]

The Global Footprint Network has developed the Ecological Footprint for each nation. When summed up, they found that the *global* Ecological Footprint now exceeds the earth's biocapacity, by about 50 percent—a measure of the degree we are not living off nature's interest, but instead are drawing down its capital. "For how long will this be possible?" they ask. "A moderate business-as-usual scenario, based on United Nations projections showing slow, steady growth of economies and populations, suggests that by mid-century, humanity's demand on nature will be twice the biosphere's productive capacity. At this level of ecological deficit, exhaustion of ecological assets and large-scale ecosystem collapse become increasingly likely."[21]

The key point here is that any accurate depiction of a successful America of the future must include a profound commitment to sustaining and restoring environmental quality and to living within the limits of the biosphere. The changes we must make to live within our planetary means will be huge, demanding, and especially difficult for we the "people of plenty," to use David Potter's phrase.[22] Long-standing, even sacrosanct American priorities and major institutions must change if we are to live lightly on the planet and share what's left of it equitably with other countries. Indeed, the imperative of adjusting the scale of economic activity to planetary limits has led some scientists, economists, and others to question the viability of today's growth imperative. After reviewing information like that in Chapter 4 on what will be needed to protect climate and live within ecological limits, a leading British economist, Tim Jackson, concludes that "we have no alternative but to question growth."[23] Chapter 6 explores in more detail the forces leading us to a post-growth future.

Then, there are the emerging constraints on the economy caused by growing scarcities in commodities and natural resources and the resulting rise in their prices, as discussed in the following chapter. Economist Jeff Rubin, in his book *Why Your World Is About to Get a Whole Lot Smaller,* has described some of the consequences of expensive oil: denser communities, smaller motor vehicles, and a return to the frugality until recently associated with the generation that grew up during the Great Depression. "Soon, your food is going to come from a field much closer to home, and the things you buy will probably come from a factory down the road rather than one on the other side of the world. You will almost certainly drive less and walk more and that means you will be shopping and working closer to home."[24] But don't be surprised, Rubin added, if this smaller world in fact ushers in greater enjoyment. Much the same message is captured in the title of Christopher Steiner's 2009 book: *$20 Per Gallon: How the Inevitable Rise in the Price of Gasoline Will Change Our Lives for the Better.*[25]

Many researchers have looked at the combined threats and predicted deeper change still. In his book *Future Scenarios: How Communities Can Adapt to Peak Oil and Climate Change,* David Holmgren develops the view, shared with the Transition Town movement, that energy and climate constraints are so binding that the only viable scenario is what he calls "energy descent," a vision that entails "a relocalization of economies, simplified technology, a ruralization of populations away from very large cities, and a reduction in total population."[26] Yet this view of our possible future is positively idyllic compared with James Howard Kunstler's prognosis in *The Long Emergency:* "I believe that we face a dire and unprecedented period of difficulty in the twenty-first century, but that mankind will survive and continue further into the future—though not without taking some severe losses in the meantime, in population, in life expectancies, in standards of living, in the retention of knowledge and technology, and in decent behavior."[27] And Kunstler is far from alone in his dystopian views.

The lesson here is that one finds a spectrum of opinion about what our energy and environmental challenges have in store for us.

Interestingly, however, these authors stress similar, recurring themes about the direction of change. And among many there is a sense that the changes could be salutary, if we are wise enough.

Finally, there are the growing realizations brought to us primarily by the new field of positive psychology. Studies that compare levels of happiness and life satisfaction among nations at different stages of economic income find that the citizens of wealthier countries do report higher levels of life satisfaction. But the correlation between income and life satisfaction is rather poor, and it is even poorer when factors such as quality of government are statistically controlled. And this positive relationship virtually disappears when one looks only at countries with GDP per capita over $10,000 per year. In short, once a country achieves a moderate level of income, further growth does not significantly improve perceived well-being.[28]

Even more challenging to the idea that well-being increases with higher incomes are extensive time-series data showing that throughout almost the entire post–World War II period, as incomes skyrocketed in the United States and other advanced economies, reported life satisfaction and happiness levels stagnated or even declined slightly.[29] The consistency of this finding across a broad range of societies is impressive. After reviewing the new evidence, Richard Easterlin and Laura Angelescu conclude that "there is no significant relationship between the improvement in happiness and the long-term rate of growth of GDP per capita."[30]

But that is not all. Ed Diener and Martin Seligman, two leaders in positive psychology, note, "Even more disparity [between income and well-being] shows up when ill-being measures are considered. For instance, depression rates have increased 10-fold over the same 50-year period, and rates of anxiety are also rising. . . . There is [also] a decreasing level of social connectedness in society, as evidenced by declining levels of trust in other people and in governmental institutions."[31]

An acute observer of the American scene is psychiatrist Peter Whybrow. In *American Mania*, Whybrow sees a perversion of America's search for happiness: "For many Americans the hallowed search for happiness has been hijacked by a discomforting and frenzied activity. . . . Unwittingly, in our relentless pursuit of happiness we have overshot the target and spawned a manic society with an insatiable appetite for more."[32]

You may have heard the joke: "Those who say money can't buy happiness just don't know where to shop!" But the truth is that the data indicate that money can't buy happiness or satisfaction in life among the more affluent. Study after study show that there is a sharply declining marginal utility to extra income. As Diener and Seligman put it: "Economic growth seems to have topped out in its capacity to produce more well-being in developed nations. . . . Efforts and policies to raise income in wealthy nations are unlikely to increase well-being and might even undermine factors (such as rewarding social relationships or other cherished values) that have higher leverage for producing enhanced well-being."[33]

If incomes are such weak generators of well-being in our more affluent societies, what are the things that really do produce happiness and well-being? The answer is somewhat complicated, but when a founder of the field of positive psychology was asked to state briefly the lessons of positive psychology, his answer was: "Other people."[34] We flourish in a setting of warm, nurturing, and rewarding interpersonal relationships, and within that context we flourish best when we are giving, not getting.

Diener, Seligman, Whybrow, and others depict American society as having gone astray and lost its way. Psychologist David Myers sees this pattern of soaring wealth and shrinking spirit as the "American paradox." He observes that at the beginning of the twenty-first century, Americans found themselves "with big houses and broken homes, high incomes and low morale, secured rights and diminished civility. We were excelling at making a living but too often failing at making a life. We celebrated our prosperity but yearned for purpose. We cherished our freedoms but longed for connection. In an age of plenty, we were feeling spiritual hunger. These facts of life lead us to a startling conclusion: Our becoming better off materially has not made us better off psychologically."[35]

I believe we Americans must take seriously these three sets of considerations in Guidepost 4. Willy-nilly, high energy and commodity prices seem very likely, and eventually we will come to our senses about the need to live within scientifically prescribed environmental boundaries. The lifestyle changes urged by the burgeoning literature on human well-being are the most "discretionary" of the three, but even here the message is beginning to sink in.

If we manage these factors well, Guidepost 4 can lead us to a higher quality of life both individually and socially.[36] Life in America the Possible will tend strongly in these directions:

Relocalization. Economic and social life will be rooted in the community and the region. More production will be local and regional, with shorter, less-complex supply chains, especially but not only in food supply. Enterprises will be more committed to the long-term well-being of employees and the viability of their communities and will be supported by local, complementary currencies and local financial institutions. People will live closer to work, walk more, and travel less. Energy production will be distributed and decentralized, and predominantly renewable. Socially, community bonds will be strong; neighbors and genuine, unpretentious connections important; civic associations and community service groups plentiful; support for teachers and caregivers high. Personal security, tolerance of difference, and empathy will be high. Local governance will stress participatory, direct, and deliberative democracy. Citizens will be seized with the responsibility to manage and extend the commons—the valuable assets that belong to everyone—through community land trusts and otherwise.

New business models. Locally owned businesses, including worker-, customer-, and community-owned firms, will be prominent. So too will hybrid business models such as profit/nonprofit and public/private hybrids. Cooperation will moderate competition. Investments will promote import-substitution. Business incubators will help entrepreneurs with arranging finance, technical assistance, and other support. Enterprises of all types will stress environmental and social responsibility.

Plenitude. Consumerism will be supplanted by the search for abundance in things that truly bring happiness and joy—family, friends, the natural world, meaningful work. Status and recognition will go to those who earn trust and provide needed services to the community. Individuals and communities will enjoy a strong rebirth of re-skilling, crafts, and self-provisioning. Overconsumption will be considered vulgar and will be replaced by new investment in civic culture, natural amenities, ecological restoration, education, and community development.

More equality. Because large inequalities are at the root of so many social and environmental problems, measures will be implemented to ensure much greater equality not only of opportunity but also of outcomes. Because life is simpler, more caring, and less grasping, and people are less status conscious, a fairer sharing of economic resources will be possible. Livelihoods will be secure.

Time regained. Formal work hours will be cut back, freeing up time for family, friends, hobbies, household productions, continuing education, skills development, caregiving, volunteering, sports, outdoor recreation, and participating in the arts. Life will be less frenetic. Frugality and thrift will be prized and wastefulness shunned. Mindfulness and living simply with less clutter will carry the day. As a result, social bonds will strengthen. The overlapping webs of encounter and participation that were once hallmarks of America, a nation of joiners, will have been rebuilt. Trust in each other will be high.

New goods and services. Products will be more durable, versatile, and easy to repair, with components that can be reused or recycled. Applying the principles of industrial ecology, the negative impacts of products throughout their life cycles will be minimized, and production systems will be designed to mimic biological ones, with waste eliminated or becoming a useful input elsewhere. The provision of services will replace the purchase of many goods, and sharing, collaborative consumption, and community ownership will be commonplace. Fewer people will own, and more will prefer to lend and lease.

Resonance with nature. Energy will be used with maximum efficiency. Zero discharge of traditional pollutants, toxics, and greenhouse gases will be the norm. Green chemistry will replace the use of toxics and hazardous substances. Organic farming will eliminate pesticide and herbicide use. Prices will reflect the true environmental costs of the products we consume. Schools will stress environmental education and pursue "no child left inside" programs. Nearby natural areas and zones of high ecological significance will be protected. Environmental restoration and cleanup programs will be focuses of community concerns. There will be a palpable sense that all economic and social activity is nested in the natural world. Biophilic design will bring nature into our buildings and our communities.[37]

Growth off, children on the pedestal. Growth in GDP and its local and regional variants will not be seen as a priority, and GDP will be seen as a misleading measure of well-being and progress. Instead, indicators of community wealth creation—including measures of social and natural capital—will be closely watched. Special attention will be given to children and young people. Their education and receipt of loving care, shelter, good nutrition and health care, and an environment free of toxins and violence will be our measures of how well we're doing as a nation.

Resilience. Society and economy and the enterprises within them will not be too big to understand, appreciate, or manage successfully. A key motivation will be to maintain resilience—the capacity to absorb disturbance and outside shocks without disastrous consequences.

Glocalism. Despite the many ways life will be more local, and in defiance of the resulting temptation to parochialism, Americans will feel a sense of citizenship at larger levels of social and political organization, even at the global level. In particular, there will be a deep appreciation of the need to bring political accountability and democratic control to the many things that can be done only at national and international levels.

I cannot do better than to close with a quote from the remarkable John Maynard Keynes. He was also thinking about possible futures in his 1933 essay "Economic Possibilities for Our Grandchildren." There, he envisioned the day not unlike today when the "economic problem" was solved, at least for the well-to-do countries. Then, he wrote, "For the first time since his creation man will be faced with his real, his permanent problem—how to use his freedom from pressing economic cares, how to occupy [his] leisure . . . how to live wisely and agreeably and well. . . .

"When the accumulation of wealth is no longer of high social importance, there will be great changes in the code of morals. The love of money as a possession . . . will be recognized for what it is, a somewhat disgusting morbidity, one of those semi-criminal, semi-pathological propensities which one hands over with a shudder to the specialists. . . .

"I see us free, therefore, to return to some of the most sure and certain principles of religion and traditional virtue—that avarice is a vice, that the exaction of usury is a misdemeanour, and the love of money is detestable, that those walk most truly in the paths of virtue and sane wisdom who take least thought for the morrow. We shall once more value ends above means and prefer the good to the useful. We shall honour those who can teach us how to pluck the hour and the day virtuously and well, the delightful people who are capable of taking direct enjoyment in things. . . .

"Chiefly, do not let us overestimate the importance of the economic problem, or sacrifice to its supposed necessities other matters of greater and more permanent significance."[38]

To most the life depicted here will seem like a corner of paradise. Others may find the local focus a bit confining. But I believe we can rest assured that Americans will always find ways to keep things exciting, interesting, and amusing. There will be no shortage of challenges in America the Possible.

As e. e. cummings almost said, there's a hell of a good country next door: let's go!

Part Three Transformations

Leave your windows and go out, people of the world,
go into the streets, go into the fields, go into the woods
and along the streams. Go together, go alone.
Say no to the Lords of War which is Money
which is Fire. Say no by saying yes
to the air, to the earth, to the trees,
yes to the grasses, to the rivers, to the birds
and the animals and every living thing, yes
to the small houses, yes to the children. Yes.
—WENDELL BERRY

The key to building a new political economy and, with it, a better tomorrow, is successful pursuit of an ambitious set of interacting, mutually reinforcing transformations that undermine the key features of the current system and replace them with new arrangements needed for a sustaining economy and a successful democracy.

The aim of these transformations is deep, systemic change. That means that many of the proposals are "impractical" and "politically unrealistic." That's true by today's standards but says more about our politics than the proposals themselves. If some of these ideas seem radical today, wait until tomorrow. It will be clear before long that system change is not starry-eyed but the only way forward.

Taken together, the proposals presented in Part III will take us beyond American capitalism as we know it today. Whether we would then have a reinvented capitalism or a new species altogether seems largely definitional. The important thing is how we move to a new system of political economy truly sustaining of people and planet.

6 A Sustaining Post-Growth Economy

The recent spate of disasters has translated into such spectacular profits that many people around the world have come to the same conclusion: the rich and powerful must be deliberately causing the catastrophes so that they can exploit them. . . . The truth is at once less sinister and more dangerous. An economic system that requires constant growth, while bucking almost all serious attempts at environmental regulation, generates a steady stream of disasters all on its own, whether military, ecological or financial.

—NAOMI KLEIN

When I was in school in England, the dean of my college told us when we first arrived that we could walk *on* the grass in the courtyard but not *across* it. That helped me love the English and their language. Here is another good use of prepositions: there are limits *of* growth, and there are limits *to* growth.

The limits *of* growth are worth dwelling on for a moment. Contrary to the constant claims that we need more growth, there is only so much growth can do for us. If economists were true to their trade, they would recognize that there are diminishing returns to growth. Most obviously, the value of income growth declines as one gets richer. An extra $1,000 of income means a lot more to someone making $15,000 a year than to someone making $150,000. Meanwhile, growth at some point also has increasing marginal costs. For example, workers have to put in too many hours, or the climate goes haywire. It follows that for the economy as a whole, we can reach a point where the extra costs of more growth exceed the extra benefits. One should stop growing at that point. Otherwise the country enters the realm of "uneconomic growth," to use Herman Daly's delightful phrase, where the costs of growth exceed the benefits it produces.[1]

America is now experiencing uneconomic growth. If one could measure and add up all the environmental, security, social, and psychological costs that U.S. economic growth generates at this point in our history, and throw in the costs of the lost opportunities occasioned by our growth fetish, they would exceed the benefits of further ramping up what is already the highest GDP per capita of any major economy.[2] I reviewed in Chapter 1 the many ways growth is not delivering for Americans despite the high price we pay for it.

It is time for America to move to post-growth society, where working life, the natural environment, our communities and families, and the public sector are no longer sacrificed for the sake of mere GDP growth; where the illusory promises of ever-more growth no longer provide an excuse for neglecting our country's compelling social needs; and where true citizen democracy is no longer held hostage to the growth imperative.

The case that there are limits *to* growth—crudely, not that we shouldn't grow but that we cannot grow—is based on the perception that we are entering a new age of environmental scarcity and rising prices that will constrain growth.[3] The world economy, having doubled in size three times since 1950, is phenomenally large in comparison with the planetary base that is the setting for all economic activity. It is now consuming the planet's available resources on a scale that rivals their supply while releasing its waste products back into the environment on a scale that greatly affects the major biogeophysical cycles of the planet. Natural resources are becoming increasingly scarce, and the planet's sinks for absorbing waste products are already exhausted in many contexts. According to the Ecological Footprint analysis, Earth would have to be 50 percent larger than it is for today's economy to be environmentally sustainable.[4]

If we now live in a world where the natural resources, ecological services, and environmental sinks needed for economic activity are becoming scarcer across a wide front, we should see prices rising. And indeed we do. As economist Paul Krugman explained in late 2010: "Oil is back above $90 a barrel. Copper and cotton have hit record highs. Wheat and corn prices are way up. Over all, world commodity prices have risen by a quarter in the past six months. . . . What the commodity markets are telling us is that we're living in a finite world, in which the rapid growth of emerging economies is placing pressure on limited supplies of raw materials, pushing up their prices. . . . Also, over the past year, extreme weather—especially severe heat and drought in some important agricultural regions— played an important role in driving up food prices. And, yes, there's every reason to believe that climate change is making such weather episodes more common."[5]

Prices of many things are rising rather rapidly. Add rare earths, lithium, and various non-fuel minerals to Krugman's list.[6] Indeed, investor Jeremy Grantham's index of thirty-three commodities suggests, in his words, a "paradigm shift" from generally declining prices in the twentieth century to sharply rising ones in the twenty-first.[7] If these patterns hold, as seems likely, and we factor in the economic losses due to climate disruption and the higher energy prices due to climate protection policies, it's hard to imagine that economic growth won't be slowed. Moreover, as discussed in Chapter 4, the increasing scarcity of the atmospheric sink for greenhouse gas emissions is going to challenge growth among the affluent countries. Reducing carbon emissions at required rates may not be possible in national economies that are stressing growth maximization.

Richard Heinberg, who has long been one of those calling attention to the peak oil issue, focuses on three factors that have led him to conclude that the old days of steady economic expansion are over: the depletion of important resources, including fossil fuels and minerals; the proliferation of adverse environmental consequences that must be addressed; and the financial disruptions due to both resource scarcity and the mountains of debt that have accumulated in recent years.[8]

After much controversy, the possibility of peak oil in the near future is now accepted by many. Peak oil is the point of maximum production after which production begins to decline. Many hold the view today that oil will peak and begin to decline before 2030,[9] but Daniel Yergin, who probably knows more about the oil business than any person alive, takes a different view. Thanks largely to tar sands oil and other unconventional sources, which would be more expensive and risky environmentally, he sees oil production continuing to climb until about 2030, then leveling off for a couple of decades before beginning a gradual decline after 2050.[10]

Whenever oil output does peak, it is useful to recall the warnings in the "Hirsch Report," *Peaking of World Oil Production,* released by the Department of Energy in 2005. It stated: "The peaking of world oil production presents the U.S. and the world with an unprecedented risk management problem. As peaking is approached, liquid fuel prices and price volatility will increase dramatically, and, without timely mitigation, the economic, social, and political costs will be unprecedented. . . . Peaking will result in dramatically higher oil prices, which will cause protracted economic hardship in the United States and the world. . . . In the developed nations, the problems will be especially serious. In the developing nations peaking problems have the potential to be much worse."[11]

Neither Yergin nor the Hirsch Report gives sufficient weight to constraints needed to protect climate and live within ecological limits.[12] But others have. Three authors whom I admire have recently looked at the growing limits to growth:

Bill McKibben in *Eaarth:* "Now that we're stuck between a played-out rock and a hot place, it's time to think with special clarity about the future. On our new planet growth may be the one big habit we finally must break. . . . To its theologians, collapse is as automatic and involuntary as growth has been to its acolytes. The rest of this book will be devoted to another possibility—that *we might choose instead to try to manage our descent.* That we might aim for a *relatively graceful decline.*"[13]

Stephen Marglin and others in our report to the United Nations: "The growth regime of the past is problematic. . . . Our considered view is that the range of problems the world faces requires nothing less than a civilizational response, a change in how we live, work, and understand. . . . If growth is limited on a planetary scale by the inadequacy of sources of energy or raw materials or the inadequacy of sinks for carbon, nitrogen, and other pollutants, the idea of social justice . . . requires that the claims of the poor, chiefly but not exclusively residing in the South, take precedence over the claims of the rich, who reside mostly in the North."[14]

Thomas Homer-Dixon in *Foreign Policy:* "Within this century, environmental and resource constraints will likely bring global economic growth to a halt. . . . For the 2.7 billion people now living on less than $2 a day, economic growth is essential to satisfying the most basic requirements of human dignity. And in much wealthier societies, people need growth to pay off their debts, support liberty, and maintain civil peace. To produce and sustain this growth, they must expend vast amounts of energy. Yet our best energy source—fossil fuel—is the main thing contributing to climate change, and climate change, if unchecked, will halt growth. We can't live with growth, and we can't live without it. This contradiction is humankind's biggest challenge this century, but as long as conventional wisdom holds that growth can continue forever, it's a challenge we can't possibly address."[15]

So there we have it: the traditional solution that America has invoked for nearly every problem—more economic growth—is in big trouble. Given the limits to and of growth, it's time for America to begin the transition to a post-growth society.

Here's the good news. We already know the types of policies needed toward a sustaining, post-growth economy. It is possible to identify a long list of public policies that would slow GDP growth, thus sparing the environment, while simultaneously improving social and individual well-being. Such policies include shorter workweeks and longer vacations; greater labor protections, including a "living" minimum wage, protection of labor's right to organize, and generous parental leaves; guarantees to part-time workers; a new design for the twenty-first-century corporation, one that embraces recharter-ing, new ownership patterns, and stakeholder primacy rather than shareholder primacy; restrictions on advertising; incentives for local and locally owned production and consumption; strong social and environmental provisions in trade agreements; rigorous environ-mental, health, and consumer protection (including fees or caps on polluting emissions and virgin materials extractions, leading in turn to full incorporation of environmental costs in prices); greater eco-nomic equality with genuinely progressive taxation of the rich (in-cluding a progressive consumption tax) and greater income support for the poor; increased spending on neglected public services; and initiatives to address population growth at home and abroad. Taken together, these policies would undoubtedly slow GDP growth, but quality of life would improve, and that's what matters.

In this mix of policies, Juliet Schor and others have stressed the importance of work time reduction.[16] For example, if productivity gains result in higher hourly wages (a big "if" in recent decades) and work time is reduced correspondingly, personal incomes and over-all economic growth can stabilize while quality of life increases. She points out that workers in Europe put in about three hundred fewer hours each year than Americans.[17]

Of course, even in a post-growth America, many things do in-deed need to grow. We need to grow the number of good jobs and the incomes of poor and working Americans. We need growth in the availability of health care and the efficiency of its delivery; growth in education and training; growth in security against the risks atten-dant to illness, old age, and disability; growth in investment in public infrastructure and in environmental protection; growth in the de-ployment of climate-friendly and other green technologies; growth in the restoration of both ecosystems and local communities; growth in research and development; and growth in international assistance for sustainable, people-centered development for the world's poor. These are among the many areas where public policy needs to ensure that growth occurs.

Jobs and meaningful work top that list because unemployment is so devastating. As I write in 2011, America should be striving to add five hundred thousand new jobs a month, but likely future rates of overall economic growth won't get us near this goal. The availability of jobs, the well-being of people, and the health of communities should not be forced to await the day when GDP growth might somehow deliver them. It is time to shed the view that government provides mainly safety nets and occasional Keynesian stimuli. We must insist that government have an affirmative responsibility to ensure that those seeking decent-paying jobs find them. The surest, and also the most cost-effective, way to that end is direct government spending, investments, and incentives targeted at creating jobs in areas where there is high social benefit, such as modern infrastructure, child and elder care, renewable energy and energy efficiency, environmental and community restoration, local banking, and public works and childhood education, where there is a huge backlog of needs.[18] Creating new jobs in areas of democratically determined priority is certainly better than trying to create jobs by pump priming aggregate economic growth, especially in an era when the macho thing to do in much of business is to shed jobs, not create them. Another path to job creation is reversing the U.S. gung-ho stand on free trade globalization. To keep investment and jobs at home, William Greider urges that Washington "rewrite trade law, tax law, and policies on workforce development and subsidy."[19]

Such policies are an excellent place to begin, but achieving a successful and sustaining post-growth economy may require more dramatic interventions. Many environmental scientists and economists, including many in ecological economics, advocate for a steady-state economy, with continuous technological change, broadly conceived, applied to reduce the environmental burden of the nongrowing GDP. The Center for the Advancement of a Steady State Economy sees such an economy as "a positive alternative to the pursuit of endless economic growth. It is an economy that aims to maintain a stable level of resource consumption and a stable population. It is an economy where energy and resource use are reduced to levels that are within ecological limits, and where the goal of maximizing economic output is replaced by the goal of maximizing quality of life." They isolate its four key features: (1) sustainable scale, or a state in which the economy fits within the planet's ability to provide resources and absorb wastes, (2) fair distribution and equal opportunity, (3) efficient allocation of resources ("taking account of where markets work and where they don't"), and (4) a culture in which the demands for economic growth defer to things that really matter—the health and security of individuals and communities.[20]

To keep the scale of economic activity sustainable, three rules are essential: renewable resources should not be harvested at rates that exceed regeneration rates, the exploitation of nonrenewable resources should not occur at rates that exceed the creation of renewable substitutes, and releases of pollutants should not exceed the assimilative capacities of the ecosystems receiving them nor cause unacceptable consequences for human health.[21]

In *Managing Without Growth*, Canadian economist Peter Victor presents a model of the Canadian economy that illustrates the real possibility of scenarios "over a 30 year time horizon for Canada in which full employment prevails, poverty is essentially eliminated, people enjoy more leisure, greenhouse gas emissions are drastically reduced, and the level of government indebtedness declines, all in the context of low and ultimately no economic growth."[22] In Victor's model, a stiff carbon tax is used to control emissions of the principal greenhouse gas, carbon dioxide; labor productivity gains are taken as increased leisure time; population growth levels off; and unemployment declines due to work-sharing arrangements. The model succeeds in generating these results, however, only if no-growth is phased in over several decades, not imposed immediately. In his discussion of policies needed for the transition to a steady state, Victor mentions caps on emissions, resource-harvesting limits that take into account the environment's assimilative capacity and resource regeneration rates, government social policies to eliminate poverty, reduced work time for employees, and other measures.

In a 2010 article in *Nature*, Victor raises some of the difficult issues that lie ahead. He notes it is already clear that degrowth is needed in key areas, including materials use, fossil energy, and land and water utilization, "so degrowth of national economies may be unavoidable."[23] And he adds: "There is debate about whether capitalism is compatible with steady-state or degrowth economies. A shrinking economy brings a real risk that profit-seeking companies and their shareholders will be disappointed, credit ratings will suffer, the financial system will be in jeopardy, trade will shrink and the whole capitalist system could spiral to a collapse. Whether this would happen remains an open question. [Economist Robert] Solow, for one, sees no reason why capitalism could not survive with slow or even no growth. Others are more skeptical—especially about the survival of capitalism in degrowth societies."[24]

Another leading ecological economist, Tim Jackson, also points to difficult changes that will be needed in a steady-state economy. Lower productivity growth of labor and capital as well as generally lower returns on investment can be expected. "Ultimately," he notes, "this will also mean raising tough questions about the ownership of assets, and the control over the surpluses from those assets."[25]

Some argue that answering these "tough questions" is essential and believe that economic democracy—what Gar Alperovitz calls the "democratization of wealth"[26]—is needed in order to undermine the growth imperative in the private sector, ensure responsible business practices, and focus investment resources on meeting real societal needs.

Many in this school stress the need for far greater worker, consumer, and public ownership and policies to encourage their development. Remember the definition of capitalism: an economic system in which employers—the owners of capital—hire workers to produce goods and services for the owners' profit. Advocates of economic democracy see the beginning of an erosion of this system through new forms of ownership and control. They believe that conscious promotion of these developments can hasten that erosion.[27]

William Greider reports, "At the start of this new century, around 10 million Americans are worker-owners in some 11,000 employee-owned companies."[28] Much of this worker ownership stems from the idea—first put forward in 1958 by Louis Kelso—of employee stock ownership plans, or ESOPs. The ESOP approach resembles a leveraged buyout: employees borrow capital to buy the company's stock, take a controlling position, and pay back the creditors from the profit they earn. Worker ownership in the United States reached $800 billion in 2002, roughly 8 percent of all U.S. corporate stock. Jeff Gates in his pathbreaking book *The Ownership Solution* notes that the ESOP concept is being extended to RESOP (related enterprise share ownership plans), in which employees of smaller companies can gain an ownership stake in larger, more established companies, and to CSOPs (customer stock ownership plans), in which customers acquire a major stake in the operation.[29]

The CSOP is akin to another growing pattern of ownership: the co-op. There are already over thirty thousand co-ops in the United States. Gar Alperovitz has noted, "Roughly 10,000 credit unions (with total assets of over $600 billion) supply financial services to 83 million members; 36 million Americans purchase their electricity from rural electric cooperatives; more than a thousand mutual insurance companies (with more than $80 billion in assets) are owned by their policyholders; and approximately 30 percent of farm products are marketed through cooperatives."[30]

At the grandest level, state and national ownership funds can be established for the benefit of citizens and the environment. These public trusts would operate on fiduciary principles: government-created trustees would hold and conserve the valuable assets of the commons—the things that belong or should belong to all of us, such as natural resources, the atmosphere, and the airwaves—for the benefit of current and future generations. Income could be generated, for example, through the proceeds of natural resource sales or from the auction of carbon dioxide emission rights.[31] Peter Barnes, a leading advocate of these approaches, sees major political gains in them: insulating national assets from politics and predation and building public support for difficult measures like emission fees by returning much of the revenue to all citizens, as is done by the Alaska Permanent Fund with its oil revenues.[32]

Several other groundbreaking patterns are worthy of note here:

- The top one thousand pension funds in the United States own nearly $5 trillion in assets, and at least some of these participants in fiduciary capitalism are becoming more assertive on social and environmental issues.[33]

- Cities and states are becoming owners and direct actors in the business arena by chartering municipal development corporations and providing health services and environmental management. Public (governmental) ownership of commercial enterprises in the United States is more common than generally recognized. Public power utilities, water and transportation systems, the Tennessee Valley Authority (TVA), the Veterans Administration (VA) hospitals, Amtrak, state lotteries, and a growing number of municipal and public-private hybrid corporations are all around us.

- Charities and other nonprofit organizations are getting into business, while "social enterprises" are applying their profits to social aims. The distinction between the for-profit and the not-for-profit sectors is blurring. Well over $60 billion is earned annually by the fourteen thousand largest U.S. nonprofits.[34]

All of these trends offer opportunities for greater local control; more sensitivity to employee, public, and consumer interests; and heightened environmental performance. Collectively, they signal the emergence of a new sector that has the potential to be a countervailing center of power to today's capitalism.[35]

A giant "democratization of capital" step beyond these measures is the proposal developed by Richard Rosen and David Schweickart in a Tellus Institute paper.[36] Their proposal would have almost all investment capital be publicly, not privately, generated and subject to democratic control. Investment funds would come not from the savings of private individuals, but from a flat-rate capital assets tax imposed on all businesses. All of this tax revenue would constitute society's main investment fund and be reinvested in the economy. Some investment funds would be allocated democratically to meet national and local needs, and some would be invested locally through public investment banks that would fund new and existing enterprises operating in a market-based economy.

These ideas, very partially described here, offer ways to have a high degree of democratic control of a society's key investment decisions while preserving market principles for the operation of the economy once those decisions are made. If "we the people" are attentive and wise, these measures have the potential to curtail the abuses, misallocations, "irrational exuberance," and excesses of our current financial system. That, of course, is a big "if."

The difficulty our federal and state governments face in meeting their many obligations without high rates of growth stems largely from politicians' fear of new taxes, even carefully crafted, smart ones. Here, the rich and their allies in Congress and state capitals have played the American people for suckers, and, so far, they have gotten away with it. The incessant antigovernment, anti-tax messaging has so completely carried the day that a huge effort is now required to counter it. Making government a more credible, efficient, and visible servant of the people would certainly help the effort.

7   System Changes

Fundamental change—indeed, radical systemic change—is as common as grass in world history.   —GAR ALPEROVITZ

Making our nation and world fit for our children and grandchildren is a task for marathoners—not sprinters. It is a complex and long-term struggle that must be pursued with both urgency and persistence.   —MARIAN WRIGHT EDELMAN

The overall transition to a new system of political economy, one that routinely promotes a flourishing of people and planet, requires the transformation of key features of American economic and political life that lie at the root of our problems. Some of the ideas presented in this chapter should be pursued even in today's political climate; others haven't a prayer and must await different times. But, taken together, they should dispel the myth that there is no viable alternative to the current order.

Transforming the Market

American public life has been profoundly affected by the rise of market fundamentalism and its shadow, resentment of government. In

1981, in his first inaugural address, Ronald Reagan famously proclaimed that "government is not the solution to our problem, government is the problem," thus marking the beginning of our era. In late 2007, Peter Goodman, then the national economics correspondent at the *New York Times*, wrote, "For more than a quarter-century, the dominant idea guiding economic policy in the United States and much of the globe has been that the market is unfailingly wise. So wise that the proper role for government is to steer clear. . . .

"Adam Smith used the metaphor of the invisible hand to describe how markets should function: With everyone at liberty to pursue self-interest, the market omnisciently distributes goods and capital to maximize the benefits for all. Since the Reagan administration, the idea has weighed in as a veritable holy commandment, with the economist Milton Friedman cast as Moses."[1]

The irony here is that the commercial interests that rail against "government interference in the economy" are in fact heavily dependent on government interference in the economy. All but the most ideologically driven advocates of laissez-faire recognize, at least privately, that Washington's alphabet soup of agencies is needed to provide business with standards and rules of the road essential to successful operations. Even more, business interests now routinely deploy government action as an instrument of private financial gain. When the financial crisis hit in late 2008, it did not take the big banks long to find the flight plan to Washington. It would seem that, for many, promarket, antigovernment ideology is less a philosophy of governing than yet another weapon to be deployed against unwanted government action.

The traditional prescription from economists for making the market serve environmental and social objectives is to "get the prices right" by eliminating perverse subsidies and by using government action to force producers to cover external costs—that is, costs otherwise absorbed not by the producers but by the society at large. The goal of such government action is honest prices. Observers like economist James Galbraith see a need for such prices but conclude that using price signals and market mechanisms exclusively is woefully inadequate given the many failings and shortcomings of markets as they actually exist as well as the tremendous economic and social complexity of most of our major national challenges. Galbraith's prescription for how to inject values such as social justice and environmental protection into the market economy is captured in two words: *planning,* which he admits is favored on a par with leprosy and syphilis, and *standards,* including democratically determined regulatory requirements.

Galbraith is decidedly not talking about central planning of the Soviet variety, but he correctly contends in his book *The Predator State* that planning cannot be avoided: "Planning, properly conceived, deals with the use of today's resources to meet tomorrow's needs. It specifically tackles issues markets cannot solve: the choice of how much in the aggregate to invest (and therefore to save), the directions to be taken by new technology, the question of how much weight and urgency are to be given to environmental issues, the role of education, and of scientific knowledge, and culture. . . . And in the modern world, planning happens: it is what corporations exist to do. The only issue, therefore, is whether the planning function is to be left entirely in the hands of private corporations . . . or whether the government and the larger public are entitled to play a role."[2]

America can succeed only if it develops a powerful capacity to define and execute meaningful plans for dealing with complex challenges such as climate change and energy sector transformation. Yesterday, we planned the New Deal, and we planned how to win World War II. Today, we must plan our way forward on many fronts. Planning requires, above all, competence—competence in government, in the private sector, and in citizens generally. And this competence in turn requires, above all, education and public integrity. Education is essential not just to build the skills needed in today's high-tech economy but also to build a capacious understanding of the world in which we live. Public integrity includes not just integrity at the personal level but also the capacity to elevate the public good over private gain. We won't get far in addressing the challenges we now face unless we are a competent nation with a competent government.

Galbraith's message on standards is "do it directly." For example, "You want higher wages? Raise them. You want more and better jobs? Create them. You want safer food, cleaner air, fewer carbon emissions? Pass laws and establish agencies to achieve this. Enforce the laws, staff the agencies, give them budgets and the mandates that they require to make the changes that we need. Politics may stand in the way, but economics does not. And there is nothing really to lose, except 'free-market' illusions."[3]

Standards operate best in the context of sophisticated planning for desired public outcomes. In environmental regulation, for example, we can identify standards of three types. Each has a place, and each moves the "polluter pays" principle forward.

Regulatory standards can be derived from what can be achieved with available technology or management practices. Here the gold standard is what can be done by applying the very best technology available.

Standards can be based on requiring companies to move to full-cost pricing. Victim compensation schemes do this, as do requirements for environmental cleanup and restoration. Using taxes, charges, or tradable allowances to require despoilers to internalize their external costs also falls into this category, and so does the elimination of unneeded and outdated tax breaks and other subsidies. Here the gold standard is "getting the prices right" through internalization of the actual costs of doing business.

Standards can also be based on what is needed to achieve a prescribed quality of the ambient environment. Here the gold standard is full protection of human health, no harvesting of resources beyond long-term sustainable yields, no release of waste products beyond the environment's assimilative capacities, and full protection of ecosystem structure and function.[4]

Of the three approaches to environmental standard-setting, the last should be the preferred approach for most cases. It will likely drive prices further in the right direction than other approaches, best engage the talents of both scientists and economists, force more technological innovation, and best protect the environment. It will also be best understood by the public.

Whatever approach is taken, however, higher and more honest prices will result. Honest prices will help ensure that people take into account the environmental and social impacts of their purchases, whether they are environmentally conscious or just minding their pocketbooks. But here we encounter the need for Galbraith's planning. High prices are not a problem in and of themselves; they are a problem when people don't have the money to pay them. And in America today half the families are in no position to deal with major increases in gasoline and other prices. Strong environmental regulation will not get very far when so many barely get by and are desperate for jobs and greater income security.[5] Clearly, addressing social and environmental needs must go hand in hand, and that requires foresight and planning. The market can be forced to operate in a matrix that ensures good results for people and planet, but only good governance can create that matrix.

Finally, as Robert Kuttner observes in *Everything for Sale*, we need to reverse the market's "tendency to invade realms where it doesn't belong."[6] There are indeed places the market should not go; there are activities and resources that should not be commodified; there are things that are priceless. We need to protect autonomous spaces, in our lives, in our communities, and in nature, just as Karl Polanyi said. Part of that, as the next section discusses, is to reassert public control over the commons—the assets that rightly belong to all of us.

Transforming the Corporation

Like Caesar, today's corporations bestride the narrow world like a colossus. In 1970 there were seven thousand multinationals; by 2007 there were at least sixty-five thousand that together contributed a quarter of gross world product. Despite the rise of other national economies, international mergers, and footloose companies, the United States is still the capital of the corporate world. A third of the world's three hundred largest companies are U.S. corporations, and corporations account for about 85 percent of U.S. business revenue.[7]

Everyone knows there is a tug-of-war between corporate power and citizen power, and in the day-to-day world of politics, it is hardly an equal match. First, business leaders can exert great power directly in the political process through lobbying and campaign contributions. In 1968 there were fewer than a thousand lobbyists in Washington. Today there are well over ten thousand registered lobbyists. Corporate political action committee (PAC) spending increased almost fifteen-fold over the past three decades, from $15 million in 1974 to $222 million in 2005.[8] Of the one hundred largest lobbying efforts in Washington between 1998 and 2004, ninety-two were corporations and their trade associations. The U.S. Chamber of Commerce was the largest.[9]

Second, corporations can shape the debate. Business owns the media, and even public broadcasting depends significantly on corporate donations. Expensive issue advertising, support for conservative think tanks, and well-funded studies are all tools of the corporate trade. Business leaders sit on nonprofit boards and contribute to their fundraising efforts. Business supports university and other research. Its influence can be strong or subtle, but it is there.

Third, labor can strike, but so can capital. It can leave an area, or refuse to invest there if the "business climate" is not right. As long as regions and nations are hell-bent on attracting investment and growth, and competing with each other in the absence of uniform standards, corporate interests will be served. And those interests usually coincide across companies and industries on core issues. "[Despite] highly visible policy conflicts among rival corporate leaders," William Domhoff argues in the fifth edition of his well-known and provocative book *Who Rules America?*, "the corporate community is cohesive on the policy issues that affect its general welfare, which is often at stake when political challenges are made by organized workers, liberals, or strong environmentalists. . . . [The] combination of economic power, policy expertise, and continuing political success makes the corporate owners and executives a dominant class, not in the sense of complete and absolute power, but in the sense that they have the power to shape the economic and political frameworks within which other groups and classes must operate."[10]

Finally, economic globalization and the rise of the global corporation have both increased corporate power and weakened the ability to control it.

As corporations are at the center of today's political economy and its negative consequences, their transformation must be at the center of building the new operating system needed for a sustaining economy. Fundamental here is revisiting basic issues of corporate purpose and design. A nineteenth-century institution must be transformed to meet twenty-first-century needs.

How should we envision the corporate sector we urgently need? Two major and complementary efforts have been undertaken recently addressed to this question. One has been led by the Tellus Institute and its Corporation 20/20 project. In their 2007 paper "Corporate Design: The Missing Business and Public Policy Issue of Our Time," Marjorie Kelly and Allen White identified six new principles of corporate design:

> Principle 1. "The purpose of the corporation is to harness private interests to serve the public interest." Under this principle, the corporation may be launched to serve private interests, but when those interests conflict with the public interest, the public good will come first and prevail.
> Principle 2. "Corporations shall accrue fair returns for shareholders, but not at the expense of the legitimate interests of other stakeholders." Here, shareholder gains will not be achieved by shifting costs of production onto other stakeholders such as employees, communities, the environment, and future generations.
> Principle 3. "Corporations shall operate sustainably, meeting the needs of the present generation without compromising the ability of future generations to meet their needs."

This principle will call into play measures to defeat the severe "short-termism" that today leads to such bad decisions and bad behavior.

Principle 4. "Corporations shall distribute their wealth equitably among those who contribute to wealth creation." Today's profits are seen as accruing to the corporation's owners, but with an equitable distribution of earnings envisioned here, profits will be shared among employees, the community, and others that directly or indirectly contribute to wealth generation, including society in general.

Principle 5. "Corporations shall be governed in a manner that is participatory, transparent, ethical, and accountable." Participatory governance will require meaningful engagement of all stakeholders in the leadership and management of the corporation, including membership on corporate boards. In Germany and Sweden, for example, employees now select from a third to half of the board members of the larger corporations.

Principle 6. "Corporations shall not infringe on the right of natural persons to govern themselves, nor infringe on other universal human rights." Here, corporations will accept the proposition that government is accountable to the people and the democratic process and will embrace the separation of corporation and state. They will thus support strict regulation of lobbying and campaign finance and protection of human rights at home and abroad.[11]

The other exercise in envisioning the corporation of the future also came to fruition in 2007, when a community of individuals and groups advocating for change issued a remarkable but undernoticed report, "Strategic Corporate Initiative: Toward a Global Citizens' Movement to Bring Corporations Back Under Control." While the Corporation 20/20 effort focused mainly on the internal design of the corporation, the "Strategic Corporate Initiative" placed greater emphasis on the external context in which corporations will operate in the future. Here are some excerpts from its vision of a transformed corporate world:

- Political involvement: "In 20 years, we envision a profound shift in political and civic culture. People will once again put their faith in government as an instrument of community and collective self-governance. Corporations will be driven out of key areas of public life where they currently operate or wield significant and illegitimate influence, including elections, essential services, and other essential functions of government. . . . The 'separation of corporation and state' will be nearly as sacrosanct as the 'separation of church and state.' Corporate rights of speech, equal protection, and due process will have been severely restricted through court decisions. The line between corporations and government will be carefully drawn to prohibit any direct or indirect financial influence on elections or state and local initiatives. Lobbying at the local, state, and federal levels will be limited to invitation only by government bodies."

- Protection of the commons: "Within 20 years, in order to enhance local, national, and global commons, roughly a third to a half of all economic activity on earth would be declared 'no go' zones for global corporations. These zones would cover the ecological commons, community commons like roads, and cultural commons like music and science. In these zones, ownership of the commons would be by hundreds of inspiring public and private institutions, from the local to the global level. In addition, new rules at local, national, and global levels, would force corporations to internalize the costs they have historically externalized. To move from an exploited or degraded commons to a healthy society, we must reclaim our commons, give it standing and protect it. We must change our consciousness to be able to see the commons—and cultivate a 'commons sensibility' that takes offense when it is encroached upon."

- Stakeholder primacy: "The public discourse on economics will no longer be dominated by free market fundamentalism. It will include talk about fair dealing, a moral bottom line, and a moral economy. Building on these values, the nation will address the structural issues keeping corporations tied to short-termism. It will be considered bad form to pay CEOs outsized compensation. It will be considered a violation of fundamental human rights to aggressively fight unions. Corporate boards will have worker and public interest directors, and company purpose will be legally broadened to include fair treatment of employees, the environment, and the community. . . . But stakeholder concerns will no longer be left to voluntary initiatives. Instead, stakeholder well-being will be imbedded in social reports and pay tied to social metrics. It will also be enforced by external mechanism, including social rating used in government purchasing guidelines and capital investment policies, municipal ordinances, capital gains taxes on short-term trades, and periodic corporate charter review."

- Innovative corporate forms: "There will be growing recognition that corporate design—in law, charters, ownership, and governance—is a powerful tool for transforming corporate purpose. A movement for hybrid, community-friendly stakeholder enterprises will take off, with exciting experimentation. . . . Employee ownership will be as widespread as home ownership, thanks to government-chartered financing institutions. Such companies will be seen as representing a new sector beyond government, business, and nonprofits—a 'Fourth Sector' equaling 20 to 30 percent of the business sector. . . . Meanwhile, community-oriented companies . . . will continue to grow, providing new, democratically accountable forms of community development that will increasingly displace corporations. . . . The debate will shift from a strict focus on market rules and [antitrust] policies to considerations about the proper role of markets, where markets must be limited, and the shape of the broader political economy. This will open the door to broader concerns about privatization, community-based ownership, and other democratic forms of economic governance. As a result, economic efficiency will become a secondary consideration to the protection of community rights, respect for environmental limits, and protection of the commons. Natural monopolies might even be accepted, so long as they are managed transparently and in the public interest (e.g. municipal utilities) under strict governmental oversight and regulation."

- Tough rating system: "Our vision is that in 20 years, governments at the local, state, and national levels will provide strong procurement incentives, as well as tax and regulatory incentives, to give an advantage to companies with high social and environmental ratings, and disadvantage those with poor ratings. Social and environmental ratings will be embraced culturally as a new measure of risk and sustainability. As a result, all major pension funds, socially responsible investment funds, foundations, and a large percentage of mutual funds will invest primarily in companies that are highly rated socially, in much the same way they now invest in bonds that are highly rated. This rating system would be based on a reliable, respected process which integrates the UN Principles for Responsible Investment—the best existing internationally recognized rating schemes—as well as new civil society ratings schemes currently in development."[12]

Implicit in the "Strategic Corporate Initiative" report's prescriptions is a pincer approach to corporate change: a top-down strategy to rein in giant corporations while simultaneously building from the bottom up a new world of innovative, public purpose, locally rooted corporate entities that can grow to become the norm.

Regarding the top-down approach, some important proposals mentioned in the "Strategic Corporate Initiative" report have since been further developed and elaborated. One involves strengthening communities to push back against corporate power. The Community Environmental Legal Defense Fund has helped communities with this effort, so that today in Pennsylvania, CELDF's home state, 10 percent of the municipalities have adopted ordinances restricting corporate control of local land, water, and other resources.[13]

Another worthy idea is the chartering of large corporations at both the national and international levels. For America's first hundred years, states issued charters to corporations to achieve specific public purposes. These charters often contained strict limitations on what could be done by the corporations, and charters were for limited duration, so periodic review and renewal were necessary. By contrast, issuing corporate charters today is so lax and easily done that an advocacy group in Virginia, a tobacco state, successfully incorporated a business named "License to Kill, Inc.," whose business was stated to be marketing tobacco products in a way that would kill four hundred thousand Americans annually.[14]

Proposals to revive the chartering process as a means of public control have been urged repeatedly in American history, including proposals such as that made by Theodore Roosevelt to create a federal charter to help regulate the trusts of his day. Charles Cray notes that between 1915 and 1932, at least eight bills related to federal chartering were introduced into Congress. In a 2007 paper for the Tellus Institute, Cray argues that "chartering is one of the best ways to hold corporations directly accountable to the public interest."[15]

Federal charters could be required of all large U.S. corporations, or the process could focus on firms in sectors of high public interest, such as the defense industry, banking and finance, national auditing and bond rating firms, and industries that rely principally on natural resources of the commons, such as water, energy, and broadcasting. Typical charter mandates could include requirements for transparency and disclosure, board of directors approval for all campaign finance and lobbying initiatives, broad stakeholder participation on corporate boards, enhanced shareholder rights, holding directors and top management personally liable for gross negligence and other major failings, as well as a general requirement to serve the public interest. Charters would have sunset provisions, which would prompt periodic reviews in which the public would have a right to participate. Charters could be revoked.

The chartering concept should be extended to the international level, as urged by Allen White in another Tellus Institute paper, "When the World Rules Corporations: Pathway to a Global Corporate Charter."[16] International charters make good sense in light of the rise of global corporations and their global-scale impacts and the incongruence of such transnational entities being licensed to operate at the national, and in the United States even the state, level. Many important issues, such as international norms, accountability, and corporate governance, could be addressed in this context. The United Nations Center for Transnational Corporations proposed an allied idea in the mid-1970s, a Code of Conduct for transnationals, but the agency was subsequently abolished in part due to the ensuing corporate backlash. Ultimately, the global corporation requires international standards protecting labor and the environment, and the various United Nations bodies now struggling with this effort need encouragement and support.

An attractive idea complementary to chartering is offered in Richard Rosen's proposal to apply the model of state public utility regulation beyond the power and water sectors where such regulation is now commonplace. In "How Should the Economy Be Regulated?," Rosen notes that state public utility commissions have the power to approve firm investments, and not merely to set rates, and his proposal focuses on public review and approval of proposed investments: "The focus of each [Industrial Regulatory Board] should be to ensure that appropriate financial investments are made by each industry in a way that mutually reinforces the need to achieve key social and environmental goals over the coming decades, with mitigating climate change chief among these goals. . . . The IRB/PUC model would work in the following way. Whenever a business of significant size wanted to invest more than a specified minimum sum of money (e.g., $10 million) in a new production facility for an existing product type, or to create a new product or service, they would apply to their industry IRB for approval of this investment. . . . If the investment proposal was large and/or controversial, the IRB would determine that formal hearings should be held. This would involve a full-scale review of the evidentiary and policy issues relevant to whether or not the proposal should be approved, with or without modification. It is important to note here that generally the initiative to invest would come from either the relevant private or public corporation, and not from the regulatory body or the government.

Thus, typically, no agency of the government would require that any new investment be made by corporations. However, in other situations, a particular industry IRB might have certain legal responsibilities to achieve certain social goals, such as keeping the electricity system reliable. In such a case, the IRB might need to find an existing public or private corporation that would be willing to make the relevant investments needed to achieve that social goal. If no existing corporation was willing to do so, a new public corporation might need to be established with government financial support to enable this social goal to be achieved. . . . Finally, whether or not major new investments or new products and services are broadly in the 'public interest' should be the guiding 'bottom-line' criterion on which all regulatory decisions are ultimately based."[17]

What about the other approach, the need to build a new corporate sector from the bottom up? Whereas many of the ideas for fundamental change in the nature and operation of existing large corporations must await the political transformation discussed in Part IV, building the new corporate sector has already begun in earnest:

- The American Sustainable Business Council (ASBC), a coalition of business networks and businesses committed to building "a vibrant, just and sustainable economy [through] innovative solutions that will transform our economy and society," brings together over 150,000 business professionals and thirty business networks and organizations.[18]
- The Business Alliance for Local Living Economies, one of the most successful of the ASBC members, convenes over eighty community networks in the United States and Canada representing more than twenty-two thousand independent business members. BALLE's mission is to build and strengthen locally owned independent businesses that function in harmony with local ecosystems, meet the basic needs of all people, support social justice and democracy, and foster strong community life.[19]
- The B-Corporation program ("B" for social benefit) includes a certification scheme for companies that meet high environ-

mental, social, and public accountability standards. As of 2011 there were 422 certified B-Corporations with about $2 billion in annual revenues. By 2011, Maryland, Vermont, New Jersey, and Virginia had adopted Benefit Corporation legislation of the type urged by B-Corporation for corporate charters. Companies incorporating as Benefit Corporations are required to produce social as well as shareholder benefits; to consider how decisions affect their employees, communities, and the environment; and to publicly report their performance using third-party standards.[20]

- The Fourth Sector Network now works to encourage and support the development of new business models—including public-private and for-profit/not-for-profit hybrid organizations—that bring together aspects of the private, public, and nonprofit sectors. These new corporate forms are proliferating rapidly, including hundreds of "social enterprises" that deploy their profits for environmental, social, and community goals.[21]

A common theme in these efforts to build a new corporate sector is the promotion of new patterns of ownership and governance, a key aspect of the democratization of capital discussed previously. Gar Alperovitz and his colleagues at the Democracy Collaborative at the University of Maryland cite the Evergreen Cooperatives in Cleveland as pointing the way: "The Evergreen Cooperatives are linked through a nonprofit corporation, a revolving loan fund and the common goal of rebuilding the economically devastated Greater University Circle neighborhoods. A thoroughly green industrial-scale laundry, a solar installation company and a soon-to-be-opened large-scale commercial greenhouse (capable of producing about 5 million heads of lettuce a year) make up the first of a group of linked co-ops projected to expand in years to come."[22] The Democracy Collaborative also urges the continued growth of community development corporations.[23] There are already more than 4,500 such not-for-profit corporations providing community services like affordable housing, and there are almost five hundred U.S. community development financial institutions now serving markets not well served by conventional private finance.

Marjorie Kelly, author of *The Divine Right of Capital*,[24] has explored several innovative ways that new corporations can achieve these objectives. She points out that ownership, governance, capitalization, and compensation structures can be designed to "seamlessly blend a central social mission with profitable operation." "It is this design," she says, "that enables companies to escape the pressure to maximize short-term profits and instead to fulfill a more fundamental purpose of economic activity: to meet human needs and be of benefit to life." She sees three promising models emerging: "Stakeholder-Owned Companies, which put ownership in the hands of non-financial stakeholders; Mission-Controlled Companies, which separate ownership and profits from control and organizational directions; and Public-Private Hybrids, where profit-driven and mission-driven design elements are combined to create unique structures."[25]

Cooperatives are the leading examples of stakeholder-owned companies. It is often noted that a large number of Americans own stock shares, but even more Americans are members of co-ops. Mission-controlled companies can survive, even if they are large and publicly owned, by having a dual-class share structure with super-voting shares irrevocably in the hands of the keepers of the mission. And in public-private hybrids, a profit-making entity is typically controlled by a government, a not-for-profit organization, or a foundation with a public service mission.

In sum, numerous paths to transformation of the corporation can already be seen, and others will surely come into view.[26] The corporation that offers the best hope for the future is one that prioritizes public benefit over private profit, that is locally rooted and faithful to its employees and its communities, and that ensures these objectives will be met through more democratic patterns of ownership and management. The ownership of capital that is most likely to sustain the world we want for our children and grandchildren is ownership that must live daily with the local consequences of its decisions. Importantly, progress down these paths will be increasingly attractive and necessary as changes and forces discussed elsewhere in this book come more and more to the fore. What becomes of today's corporations, for example, when growth is no longer a priority, when the bloom fades on consumerism's rose, when energy prices require a shift toward localization, and when the demand that corporations cease being part of the problem and become part of the solution becomes irresistible?

Transforming Money and Finance

Money is much more than a neutral means of exchange. The way almost all of it is created—by private banks making loans that give rise to debt that must be repaid with interest—has consequences. Although regulated by government, the creation of money has been privatized, and the decisions about how money is allocated to various purposes is largely in the hands of private financial institutions that are in business to make a profit. The idea that government should be responsible for creating all of the nation's money was abandoned, as was the idea that bank loans should be limited to what depositors put at their disposal.

In recent decades we have also seen the eclipse of banking regulations, leading to a radical concentration of money power in too-big-to-fail banks and Wall Street generally. In 1994, the five largest U.S. banks held 12 percent of total U.S. deposits. By 2009 they held nearly 40 percent. The country's twenty largest banks control almost 60 percent of bank assets.[27] Market concentration is even higher in other banking-type businesses, such as credit cards, debt and equity underwriting, and derivatives trading. Many of our country's earlier leaders warned against such concentration of power in the hands of a financial elite. As Thomas Greco notes in *The End of Money and the Future of Civilization*, "Thomas Jefferson said, 'I sincerely believe . . . that banking establishments are more dangerous than standing armies.'; President James A. Garfield, who had previously been chairman of the Banking Committee in the House of

Representatives, said, 'Whoever controls the money in any country is master of all its legislation and commerce.'"[28] Woodrow Wilson, whose presidency oversaw the creation of the Federal Reserve System, later came to regret its creation. "Even if their action be honest and intended for the public interest," Wilson wrote, the very limitations inherent in such concentration "chill and check and destroy genuine economic freedom."[29]

Today, banks are required to hold deposits that are only a small fraction, perhaps 10 percent, of the loans they make. Anyone who takes on debt is creating new money. Banks do not actually lend money; they create promises to supply money they do not possess. As John Kenneth Galbraith famously observed, "The process by which banks create money is so simple that the mind is repelled. Where anything so important is involved, a deeper mystery seems only decent."[30] Mary Mellor has summed up the resulting situation: "The most important outcome of the dominance of bank issued money is that the supply of money is largely in private hands determined by commercial decisions, while the state retains responsibility for managing and supporting the system, as has become clear through the [2008] financial crisis. While the public collectively bears ultimate responsibility for the failures of the privatized money creation system, there is not direct public influence on the overall direction of how that finance is invested or used."[31] In the United States, the Federal Reserve can powerfully influence the supply and hence the price of money, but private banks decide how much to lend and where to lend it. The capital allocation process has become far removed from institutions that serve the public interest and is instead dominated by institutions and individuals seeking only to maximize profits. Still, the degree to which the U.S. government is on the hook to sustain the banking system was demonstrated in 2008–2010 to the tune of trillions of dollars in loans and guarantees, mostly through the Federal Reserve System.

Lost in all this is the concept of the system of money and finance as an essential public utility for the benefit of society as a whole. The evidence is already abundant that today's system of money and finance cannot deliver a fair and sustaining economy. Just as that system is an integral, essential aspect of the current order, its transformation is an integral, essential aspect of the overall transition to a new economy. MIT's Otto Scharmer has summarized why this transformation is needed: "Today we have a system that accumulates an oversupply of money and capital in areas that produce high financial and low environmental and social returns, while at the same time we have an undersupply of money and capital in areas that serve important societal and community investment needs (high social and low financial returns, such as the education of children in low-income communities). According to McKinsey Global Institute (MGI) the world's financial markets were struggling to find investment opportunities for $167 trillion in global 'liquidity' in 2006. That sum was at an unprecedented level, roughly 3.5 times the aggregate global GDP of $52 trillion. The Deputy Secretary of the U.S. Treasury, Robert Kimmitt, estimated the figure at $190 trillion. That's the situation now: we've got too much money where we don't really need it ($190 trillion seeking high financial and low social returns), and we don't have enough invested where we urgently need it (in the ecological, social, and cultural commons in both the global North and the global South)."[32]

There are numerous visions of money and finance in the new economy. Two of the leading ones are presented here. Many critics, like David Korten, who see money and banking as a system of power, seek a radical rebalancing at the expense of institutions that are large, global, driven to excess by the search for profits and personal financial gain, opaque and cloaked in secrecy, and remotely owned and managed (that is, Wall Street) to institutions that are small enough not only to fail but also to be held accountable by the communities in which they operate, locally rooted and community focused, transparent in their operations, supporting the real economy of goods and services, and managed by people who have to live with the consequences of their decisions (that is, Main Street).

Korten observes that the system we now need "would be remarkably similar to the one that financed the United States victory in World War II, produced an unprecedented period of economic stability and prosperity, made America the world's industrial powerhouse, and created the American middle class—a system that was working well until Wall Street launched its 'financial modernization' experiment."[33]

Drawing on proposals developed by Korten himself, William Greider, the Institute for Policy Studies, the Institute for Local Self-Reliance, and numerous others, Korten and colleagues (myself among them) recommended the following in the 2011 report *How to Liberate America from Wall Street Rule:*

1. Reverse the process of banking consolidation and build a national system of community-based, community-accountable financial institutions devoted to building community wealth. Break up the megabanks and implement tax and regulatory policies that favor appropriate-scale community financial institutions and, in particular, community financial institutions organized as cooperatives or owned by nonprofits devoted to community wealth building.

2. Create a State Partnership Bank in each of the 50 states to serve as a depository for state financial assets. State banks can keep these funds circulating in state by partnering with community development financial institutions on loans to local home buyers and locally owned enterprises engaged in construction, agriculture, industry, and commerce.

3. Restructure the Federal Reserve to limit its responsibility to managing the money supply, subject it to federal oversight and public accountability, and require that all newly created funds be applied to funding public infrastructure. Assign responsibility for the regulation of banks and so called 'shadow banking' institutions to specialized regulatory agencies.

4. Create a Federal Recovery and Reconstruction Bank to finance critical green infrastructure projects designated by Congress. It would be funded with the money that the Federal Reserve creates when it determines a need to expand the money supply. Rather than introducing that money into the economy through Wall Street banks, it would instead be in-

troduced through the Federal Recovery and Reconstruction Bank.

5. Rewrite international trade and investment rules to secure national ownership, self-reliance, and self-determination. Bring international rules into alignment with the foundational assumptions of trade theory that the ownership of productive assets belongs to citizens of the country in which they are located and that trade between nations is balanced. Hold corporations operating in multiple countries accountable for compliance with the laws of each country of operation.

6. Implement appropriate regulatory and fiscal measures to secure the integrity of financial markets and the money/banking system. Such measures properly favor productive investment and render financial speculation and other unproductive financial games illegal and unprofitable.[34]

Two additional initiatives that mesh well with these are the proliferation of complementary currencies—the creation of innovative local currencies that inter alia are particularly well suited to linking unmet community needs with underutilized community resources[35]—and the use of web-based platforms that can directly link buyers and sellers and borrowers and lenders without banks or other intermediaries.[36]

The second proposal for wholesale transformation would, in effect, transfer the creation of money from banks back to government. This step has recently been urged by Herman Daly, and historically by numerous others, and it may be possible to harmonize it with the plan offered by Korten. Daly explains that the transfer of money creation back to government would be accomplished by abandoning today's fractional reserve banking and moving to a 100 percent reserve requirement on demand deposits. Banks would lend time deposits, and the depositor would not have access to the money for the period of the deposit. The lending bank would have to count on new and renewing short-term time deposits and/or on long-term time deposits. These requirements would eliminate the bank's ability to create new money. As needed, government would create new money instead.

Daly explains: "This would put control of the money supply and seigniorage (profit made by the issuer of fiat money) in [the] hands of the government rather than private banks, which would no longer be able to live the alchemist's dream by creating money out of nothing and lending it at interest. All quasi-bank financial institutions should be brought under this rule, regulated as commercial banks subject to 100% reserve requirements. Banks would earn their profit by financial intermediation only, lending savers' money for them (charging a loan rate higher than the rate paid to savings or 'time-account' depositors) and every dollar loaned to a borrower would be a dollar previously saved by a depositor (and *not* available to him during the period of the loan), thereby re-establishing the classical balance between abstinence and investment. With credit limited by saving (abstinence from consumption) there will be less lending and borrowing and it will be done more carefully—no more easy credit to finance the massive purchase of 'assets' that are nothing but bets on dodgy debts. To make up for the decline in bank-created, interest-bearing money, the government can pay some of its expenses by issuing more non-interest-bearing fiat money. However, it can only do this up to a strict limit imposed by inflation. If the government issues more money than the public voluntarily wants to hold, the public will trade it for goods, driving the price level up. As soon as the price index begins to rise the government must print less and tax more. Thus a policy of maintaining a constant price index would govern the internal value of the dollar. The external value of the dollar could be left to freely fluctuating exchange rates."[37] The idea, as Daly notes, is not to nationalize banks but to nationalize money.

Calls for such a system have been made often in U.S. history, but rarely from bankers or those fixated on maximizing growth. Notably, Abraham Lincoln stated the case forcefully in defending his decision to print "greenbacks" to finance the Civil War: "The Government should create, issue and circulate all the currency and credit needed to satisfy the spending power of the Government and the buying power of consumers. . . . The privilege of creating and issuing money is not only the supreme prerogative of Government, but is the Government's greatest creative opportunity. . . . By the adoption of these principles, the long-felt want for a uniform medium will be satisfied. The taxpayers will be saved immense sums of interest. The financing of all public enterprises, and the conduct of the treasury will become matters of practical administration. Money will cease to be master and become the servant of humanity."[38]

When loans cannot exceed funds on deposit, many good things happen or at least become possible. Government could spend money directly on democratically determined priorities like needed infrastructure, and could do so without burdening future generations with government debt. Whatever growth imperative is generated by bank-created debt would be weakened. Speculation and indebtedness would decrease, as would the boom and bust cycles of the current system. Deposits would be secure, and the possibility of collapse of the entire credit pyramid due to the failure of big banks would be eliminated. Money for investment would be a direct transfer of savings as either timed loans or equity. The channeling of both government-created money and savings could be aided by democratically controlled banks operating nationally, regionally, and locally—banks that would respond to social needs rather than the demand for profits. There are many issues to be worked out with this proposal, including integrating it with international finance and with the local banking initiative proposed by Korten, but its advantages make it well worth exploring.

Transforming Social Conditions

This book began by examining the intolerable levels of social decline now afflicting America. Poverty, financial insecurity, and economic inequality have all reclaimed highs not seen for many decades, plunging America to the bottom among our peer countries and spawning a host of pathological social consequences. Central to building a new political economy is the transformation of American society from this sad state to one that is truly fair and equitable, where all people have the opportunity *and* the means to realize their potential, where substantial equality is prized and sought with affirmative action, and where caring for one another with compassion and generosity are hallmarks.

When James Truslow Adams coined the phrase "the American dream" in his 1933 book *The Epic of America,* he used it to refer not to getting rich or even especially to a secure, middle-class lifestyle, though that was part of it, but primarily to something finer: "It is not a dream of motor cars and high wages merely, but a dream of a social order in which each man and each woman shall be able to attain to the fullest stature of which they are innately capable, and be recognized by others for what they are, regardless of the fortuitous circumstances of birth or position."[39] That American Dream is well worth carrying with us into the future.

It is a measure of the political strength of the growth ideology that some of the most passionate advocates of greater fairness in American society have adopted the argument that we need more equality in order to promote more growth.[40] A 2011 report from the Center for American Progress makes the case, albeit tentatively, that inequality is bad for sustained economic growth. Robert Reich in his 2010 book *Aftershock* explains his view that America won't have a sustained economic recovery unless a much larger share of income is directed back to the middle class: "Unless America's middle class receives a fair share, it cannot consume nearly what the nation is capable of producing. . . . The inevitable result is slower economic growth and an economy increasingly susceptible to great booms and terrible busts."[41] These views, of course, upend the traditional understanding—that inequality facilitates and spurs on growth.

At least one line of argument suggests that a more egalitarian society would eventually deemphasize economic growth. Much of the consumer impulse that drives GDP growth depends on what economists call positional goods—the drive to acquire things largely because others have them. Robert Frank explains what that means in an unequal society: Positional "arms races," he notes, "are well illustrated by the familiar metaphor in which everyone stands up to get a better view, yet no one sees any better than before. It is the same with many forms of consumption. . . . Although there is scant evidence that middle-income families in America resent the spending of top earners, they are nonetheless affected by it in tangible ways. Additional spending by the rich shifts the frame of reference that defines what the near rich consider necessary or desirable, so they too spend more. In turn, this shifts the frame of reference for those just below the near rich, and so on, all the way down the income ladder."[42] It seems likely that in a far more equal society, the impulse to consume positional goods would decline, thus creating a tendency for growth to slow.

As far as the argument that those who grow rich in America have earned it and deserve to keep it, this claim is hollow in the extreme. Today's high productivity and economic growth stem largely from the accretion of scientific and technological knowledge, most of which is inherited from the past, as Gar Alperovitz and Lew Daly point out in their remarkable book *Unjust Deserts*. In other words, the greater portion of income and wealth today "comes to us through no effort of our own."[43] As Nobel economist Herbert Simon observed, if "we are very generous with ourselves, I suppose we might claim we 'earned' as much as one fifth of [our income]."[44]

Alperovitz and Daly stress the importance of this analysis for distributive justice: "If most of what we have comes to us from those who came before, we quite literally owe it to ourselves to consider how we as a society wish to use and divide this great and generous gift of the past. When and as we do, we believe Americans are increasingly likely to demand answers to the question of why, specifically, any one person should receive more than any other from the gift of the past—from the large share of current wealth that no one living creates."[45]

Whether inequality promotes or inhibits economic growth, we should pursue a more just and equal society regardless. The grounds for action to dramatically reduce America's vast economic insecurity and inequality are ample: in the pragmatic conclusion of Wilkinson and Pickett's *The Spirit Level* that "most of the important health and social problems of the rich world are more common in more unequal societies"; in the ethics of distributive justice; in the need to be true to our national values as reflected in James Truslow Adams's American Dream; in our innate sense of fairness described by Peter Corning in *The Fair Society;*[46] and in the realization developed by Alperovitz and Daly that today's wealth is largely the product of the knowledge commons inherited from the past by all of us and thus rightly to be shared.

In recent years, America's fraying social fabric has galvanized the attention of progressive communities, and an abundance of well-designed proposals to promote economic security and equity have emerged. Some have laid comprehensive plans for a new war on poverty in America; others have focused on the need for universal health insurance or on the imperative of high-quality and affordable education at all levels; still others have concentrated on a just and fair tax system; and many have focused on creating and even guaranteeing meaningful, living-wage employment opportunities for all those seeking jobs, including revitalizing America's manufacturing base.[47]

These are vital areas for action, but they should be complemented by measures that go to the heart of the matter. First, we have heard for decades that America must keep growing, or, otherwise, we will face the need for income redistribution. Well, for the most part America has kept growing, and the need for redistributive policies has only grown more acute. The growth-instead-of-redistribution argument has failed in practice, and in a world where growth will be increasingly constrained, it also fails in theory. It's time for America to face the need explicitly and directly to redistribute incomes.

One good idea is to place brackets around income levels, with minimum and maximum incomes. Here, as elsewhere, Herman Daly has made the case well: "The civil service, the military, and the university manage with a range of inequality that stays within a factor of 15 or 20. Corporate America has a range of 500 or more. Many industrial nations are below 25. Could we not limit the range to, say, 100, and see how it works?"[48]

Harvard's Howard Gardner has argued that "no single person should be allowed annually to take home more than 100 times as much money as the average worker in a society earns in a year. If the average worker makes $40,000, the top compensated individual may keep $4 million a year. Any income in excess of that amount must be contributed to a charity or returned to the government, either as a general gift, or targeted to a specific line item (ranging from the Department of Veterans Affairs to the National Endowment for the Arts)." He further proposed that no individual would be permitted to pass more than $200 million to his or her heirs, and that any excess must be contributed to charity. "To those who would scream 'foul' to such limits on personal wealth," he concludes, "I would remind them that just 50 years ago, this proposal would have seemed reasonable, even generous."[49]

Another good idea is a reverse income tax, as recommended by Robert Reich in *Aftershock*. Building on the negative income tax idea examined in the 1960s and today's earned income tax credit, he urges that "full-time workers earning $20,000 or less (this and all subsequent outlays are in 2009 dollars) would receive a wage supplement of $15,000. This supplement would decline incrementally up the income scale, to $10,000 for full-time workers earning $30,000; to $5,000 for full-time workers earning $40,000; and then to zero for full-time workers earning $50,000.

"The tax rate for full-time workers with incomes between $50,000 and $90,000—whether the source of those incomes are wages, salaries, or capital gains—would be cut to 10 percent of earnings. The taxes for people with incomes of between $90,000 and $160,000 would be 20 percent, whatever the income source."[50]

Reich would join this support for those at the bottom with higher taxes on the wealthy, generating almost all the income needed to pay for his wage supplements: "In a nation facing a widening chasm between the very rich and everyone else, it is not unreasonable to expect those at the top to pay a higher tax on their incomes, from whatever source (wages, salaries, or capital gains). I propose that people in the top 1 percent, with incomes of more than $410,000, pay a marginal tax of 55 percent; those in the top 2 percent, earning over $260,000, pay a marginal tax of 50 percent; and those earning over $160,000, roughly the top 5 percent, pay 40 percent. These taxes, when added to the modest amounts contributed by taxpayers who earn between $50,000 and $160,000 under my plan, would raise $600 billion more than our current tax system per year."[51]

Another major step forward should be to implement the important proposal put forward by Bruce Ackerman and Anne Alstott in *The Stakeholder Society:* "As a citizen of the United States, each American is entitled to a stake in his country: a one-time grant of eighty thousand dollars as he reaches early adulthood. This stake will be financed by an annual 2 percent tax levied on all the nation's wealth. The tie between wealth-holding and stakeholding expresses a fundamental social responsibility. Every American has an obligation to contribute to a fair starting point for all. Stakeholders are free [to] use their money for any purpose they choose: to start a business or pay for more education, to buy a house or raise a family or save for the future. But they must take responsibility for their choices. Their triumphs and blunders are their own."[52]

Reich and Ackerman are right to focus on the revenue side of their proposals. In the years ahead the federal government should spend more on social and jobs programs, on environmental protection, and on neglected needs abroad. Meanwhile, our annual federal budgetary deficits should be brought down to sustainable levels. Government cannot count on high growth rates to expand the federal coffers. The good news, from the point of view of finding our way forward through this thicket, is that there are many ways to raise new revenues—closing down tax breaks for the rich, shifting taxes from things we want to encourage to things we want to discourage, taxing luxury items, closing corporate tax loopholes, strengthening the estate tax, and moving toward a more progressive tax structure. For example, a 2009 report by John Cavanagh and his colleagues at the Institute for Policy Studies proposed the following plan, which would raise an additional $3 trillion in federal revenues over a five-year period:

1. Repeal tax breaks for households with annual incomes over $250,000: $43 billion per year.
2. Tax financial transactions: $100 billion per year.
3. Eliminate the tax preference for capital gains and dividends: $80 billion per year.
4. Levy a progressive estate tax on large fortunes: $40–60 billion per year.
5. Establish a new higher tax rate on extremely high incomes: $60–70 billion.
6. End overseas tax havens: $100 billion per year.
7. Eliminate subsidies for excessive executive compensation: $18 billion per year.[53]

In short, America is not broke. There is plenty of money; it's just in the wrong places.

Transforming the Measure of Progress

Today's measure of economic activity, Gross Domestic Product, sits in regal enthronement, its quarterly utterances, monetized and quantified to the decimal place, casting judgment, praise, or blame on the mere mortals responsible for its keeping. It does not seem to matter that GDP is simply a gross measure of all activity in the formal economy—good things and bad things, costs and benefits, mere market activity, money changing hands, busyness in the economy—for the bigger it gets, the greater the potential for both private profit and public revenue.

Never mind also that even the creator of its formalisms, Simon Kuznets, warned in his first report to Congress in 1934 that "the welfare of the nation [can] scarcely be inferred from a measurement of national income as defined above" and by 1962 was expressing deeper skepticism: "Distinctions must be kept in mind between quantity and quality of growth, between its costs and return, and between the short and the long run," he wrote. "Goals for 'more' growth should specify more growth of what and for what.'"[54]

Enlightened political leaders have long known how misleading GDP is as a measure of national progress and well-being. In his last major speech, in 1968, Robert Kennedy summoned his great eloquence in aid of dethroning GDP: "Our Gross National Product . . . counts air pollution and cigarette advertising, and ambulances to clear our highways of carnage. It counts special locks for our doors and the jails for the people who break them. It counts the destruction of the redwood and the loss of our natural wonder in chaotic sprawl. It counts napalm and counts nuclear warheads and armored cars for the police to fight the riot in our cities . . . and the television programs which glorify violence in order to sell toys to our children. Yet the Gross National Product does not allow for the health of our children, the quality of their education or the joy of their play. It does not include the beauty of our poetry or the strength of our marriages, the intelligence of our public debate or the integrity of our public officials. It measures neither our wit nor our courage, neither our wisdom nor our learning, neither our compassion nor our devotion to our country, it measures everything, in short, except that which makes life worthwhile. And it can tell us everything about America except why we are proud that we are Americans."[55]

Though it is still very much on the throne, GDP's continued dominance is threatened today. Of all the transitions discussed in this book, the transition from GDP to a fuller, more accurate depiction of where the nation is and is heading may be the closest to a tipping point that can hasten its completion.[56] We can now envision a dashboard of indicators to supplement those that measure economic activity, unemployment, and inflation. That dashboard will be built on the enormous ferment and creativity already under way in the indicators community in governmental bodies, academia, and nongovernmental organizations (NGOs).

Efforts are under way to develop (1) measures of true economic progress that correct and adjust GDP so that we can gauge sustainable economic welfare in society, (2) indicators of objective social welfare such as the status of health, education, and economic security, (3) indexes of environmental conditions and trends, (4) indicators of political conditions and democracy, and (5) measures of subjective well-being such as life satisfaction, happiness, and trust.[57]

Two of these efforts deserve special note; they provide strong and promising models.

The first develops the idea that societies need a monetized measure of sustainable economic welfare—an indicator that corrects the shortcomings of GDP as a measure of social well-being and that can be compared with the movements of GDP and GDP per capita on a regular, quarterly basis. The most important efforts to date have been those developing the Index of Sustainable Economic Welfare (ISEW) and its American offshoot, the Genuine Progress Indicator (GPI). The ISEW begins with national private consumption expenditures and then adjusts that for distributional inequalities. It then adds in nonmarket contributions to welfare, such as unpaid housework, and subtracts out defensive expenditures such as police protection and pollution control, and it also subtracts the depreciation of natural resources and environmental assets.

When adjustments such as these are made for six major industrial economies, the results show a clear pattern.[58] ISEW grows in parallel with GDP for a while, then it begins to flatline or even decline, despite continuing increases in GDP. For each of the countries studied, a threshold was reached beyond which growth no longer improved the quality of life as measured by the ISEW.[59]

The ISEW has continued with improvements under the new label of Genuine Progress Indicator. In the United States, the GPI suggests that Americans on average are no better off today than they were in 1970 even though GDP per capita has grown greatly during that period.[60]

It should be acknowledged that alternative measures like ISEW and GPI employ major methodological and data assumptions that are open to dispute, and to improvement, much like GDP itself. Yet, they build on pioneering work of the best economists, including

James Tobin and William Nordhaus.[61] They are serious efforts—and they do tell us something.

A second model worth pursuing is the composite indicator approach used in the Canadian Index of Well-Being (CIW).[62] The CIW measures well-being in eight domains: health, education, environment, living standards, civic engagement, community vitality, time use, and culture and recreation. In each of these domains, a composite indicator is constructed from a number of component indicators. The composite living standards indicator, for example, is built up from indicators such as the unemployment rate, incidence of low income, median income after taxes, income distribution, and so on. In some of the domains, subjective (polling) data complement these objective measures. The composite indicator for each domain is tracked from 1994 forward, so that the trend is clear. By bundling the eight domains into a single composite index, the CIW aims to give a quick snapshot of whether Canadians' quality of life is getting better or worse.

We tend to get what we measure, and it is vital that we look to indicators that focus on truly important things.

Transforming Consumption

The path to a new political economy leads straight away from consumerism and commercialism to a very different world in which getting and spending, material possessions, and overall consumption have a decidedly circumscribed and modest place in everyday life.

In her insightful book, *A Consumers' Republic,* Lizabeth Cohen documents that American consumerism as we know it did not just happen. It is not something in our genes or human nature, at least not wholly. Referring to the era of postwar prosperity that lasted approximately from 1945 to 1975, she notes that "this period of unprecedented affluence did much more than make Americans a people of plenty. Undergirding the pursuit of plenty was an infrastructure of policies and priorities, what I have dubbed, for shorthand, the Consumers' Republic. In reconstructing the nation after World War II, leaders of business, government, and labor developed a political economy and a political culture that expected a dynamic mass consumption economy not only to deliver prosperity, but also to fulfill American society's loftier aspirations."[63]

A consumer society is one in which consumerism and materialism are central aspects of the dominant culture, where goods and services are acquired not only to satisfy common needs but also to secure identity and meaning. Framing this situation as a matter of consumer sovereignty—where the customer is always right—is misleading. Consumption patterns are powerfully shaped by forces other than preformed individual preferences—forces such as advertising, cultural norms, social pressures, and psychological associations.[64]

Consumerism is not, and should not be confused with, consumption that satisfies essential human needs. Consumerism is the faith that meaning, identity, and significance can be found in material, commodity consumption, which in turn requires money. But since meaning and self-realization cannot be found there, nor basic psychological needs so met, consumers remain unfilled and are driven ever on to seek more possessions, which requires still more money, all of which is well understood by marketers. Richard Layard refers to the "hedonic treadmill" to describe the phenomenon whereby people become habituated to their new incomes and their new toys. "When I get a new home or a new car, I am excited at first. But then I get used to it, and my mood tends to revert to where it was before. . . . Advertisers understand this and invite us to 'feed our addiction' with more and more spending. However, other experiences do not pale in the same way—the time we spend with our family and friends, and the quality and security of our job."[65]

A consumer society is one in which the human tendency to compare ourselves with others is grotesquely exploited. This human tendency to compare ourselves with others has not escaped the attention of humorists. There's the joke about the Russian peasant whose neighbor had a cow while he did not. He had lived a good life, and so God asked how He could help. The peasant replied, "Kill the cow!" Numerous studies confirm that happiness levels depend inversely on one's neighbor's prosperity.[66] People constantly compare themselves with others, and if everyone is better off financially, then no one is any happier. Comparative position is what counts, not absolute income, so rising incomes can leave just as many unhappy comparisons.

Consumerism thus has a doubly negative impact. It is the beating heart of the growth system. Private consumption expenditures in the United States, for example, are about 70 percent of gross domestic product, and consumer spending is the principal driver of the economy and its expansion. When the *Financial Times* observed that "the stamina of shoppers will be crucial for global growth," the emphasis was on consumers serving the economy, not the other way around.[67] Second, consumerism gives rise to a host of social pathologies. On the squirrel wheel of getting and spending, with the longest hours on the job in the OECD, and with both parents often at work, we Americans are neglecting the things that would truly make us better off, including personal relationships and social contact. Ed Diener and Martin Seligman, two leaders in the field of positive psychology, point out, "The quality of people's social relationships is crucial to their well-being. People need supportive, positive relationships and social belonging to sustain well-being."[68]

In *The Loss of Happiness in Market Democracies*, sociologist Robert Lane believes Americans suffer from "a kind of famine of warm interpersonal relations, of easy-to-reach neighbors, of encircling, inclusive memberships, and of solidary family life. There is much evidence that for people lacking in social support of this kind, unemployment has more serious effects, illnesses are more deadly, disappointment with one's children is harder to bear, bouts of depression last longer, and frustration and failed expectations of all kinds are more traumatic."[69]

Our families, friends, and true companionship are thus among consumerism's principal casualties. We have channeled our desires, our insecurities, our need to demonstrate our worth and our success, our wanting to fit in and to stand out, increasingly into material things—into bigger homes, fancier cars, more appliances and gadgets, and branded apparel. But in the process, we're slighting the precious things that no market can provide. We are hollowing out whole areas of life, of individual and social autonomy, of community, and of nature, and, if we don't soon wake up, we will lose the chance to return, to reclaim ourselves, our neglected society, our battered world, because there will be nothing left to reclaim, nothing left to return to.

Amitai Etzioni sees the excesses of consumerism also at the roots of our current economic troubles: "The link to the economic crisis should be obvious. A culture in which the urge to consume dominates the psychology of citizens is a culture in which people will do most anything to acquire the means to consume—working slavish hours, behaving rapaciously in their business pursuits, and even bending the rules in order to maximize their earnings. They will also buy homes beyond their means and think nothing of running up credit-card debt. It therefore seems safe to say that consumerism is, as much as anything else, responsible for the current economic mess."[70]

Cohen also highlighted the ironies inherent in the faith that "a prospering mass consumption economy could foster democracy."[71] What actually happened was we witnessed "a decline in the most critical form of political participation—voting—as more commercialized political salesmanship replaced rank-and-file mobilization through parties." She also notes, "The Consumers' Republic's dependence on unregulated private markets wove inequalities deep into the fabric of prosperity. . . . The deeply entrenched convictions prevailing in the Consumers' Republic that a dynamic, private, mass consumption marketplace could float all boats and that a growing economy made reslicing the economic pie unnecessary predisposed Americans against more redistributive actions."[72]

The creation of the Consumers' Republic represented the triumph of one vision of American life and purpose. But there has always been another American vision, what historian David Shi calls the tradition of "plain living and high thinking," a tradition that began with the Puritans and the Quakers and that provides the tradition on which to build a better America for tomorrow. This tradition that sees America as a republic of virtue has always been in tension with the allure of unfettered purchasing, of America as the venue nonpareil for consumer appetites indulged shamelessly and unapologetically. In his book *The Simple Life,* Shi described how the concept of the simple but good life "has remained an enduring—and elusive—ideal. . . . Its primary attributes include a hostility toward luxury and a suspicion of riches, a reverence for nature and a preference for rural over urban ways of life and work, a desire for personal self-reliance through frugality and diligence, a nostalgia for the past, a commitment to conscientious rather than conspicuous consumption, a privileging of contemplation and creativity, an aesthetic preference for the plain and functional, and a sense of both religious and ecological responsibility for the just uses of the world's resources."[73]

If the creation of American consumerism was a project of the country's political and economic leaders after World War II, as Cohen concludes, it should be possible to build a counter project aimed at something better. Overcoming our bad case of national affluenza is important if America is to achieve a host of goals: reducing its ecological footprint, expanding investment in public goods, bolstering retirement security, reducing corporate power, undermining our growth fetish, expanding civic engagement, focusing resources on vast social and economic disparities at home and abroad, and improving the social and psychological well-being of individuals and families.

Etzioni properly asks what should replace the worship of consumer goods and argues that "the two most obvious candidates to fill this role are communitarian pursuits and transcendental ones." "Communitarianism," he writes, "refers to investing time and energy in relations with the other, including family, friends, and members of one's community. The term also encompasses service to the common good, such as volunteering, national service, and politics. Communitarian life is not centered around altruism but around mutuality, in the sense that deeper and thicker involvement with the other is rewarding to both the recipient and the giver. . . . Transcendental pursuits refer to spiritual activities broadly understood, including religious, contemplative, and artistic ones. . . . Communitarian activities require social skills and communication skills as well as time and personal energy—but, as a rule, minimal material or financial outlays. The same holds for transcendental activities such as prayer, meditation, music, art, sports, adult education, and so on."[74]

Juliet Schor has also offered a path forward, one she calls "plenitude." It has four key features: moderation in hours of work, self-provisioning, environmentally aware consumption, and restoring investments in one another and community. In sum, "work and spend less, create and connect more."[75]

What policy agenda would help move America beyond consumerism? First, there are attractive steps, including some described elsewhere in this book, that would help immensely: eliminating wasteful subsidies and imposing limits on virgin materials entering the economy and on emissions, toxics, and other residuals discharged to the environment; requiring full-cost, honest prices, with border tariffs to protect U.S. producers and workers from unfair foreign competition from countries not fully internalizing costs; imposing a surtax on high-end consumption spending along with various luxury taxes;[76] promoting new for-benefit corporations and corporate transformation generally; providing high-quality public services, infrastructure, and amenities; moving to much greater social and economic equality and security; conducting educational and social marketing campaigns that not only provide accurate information to consumers but also address deeper issues such as the shortcomings of consumerism; promoting sharing, renting, and collaborative consumption instead of owning ("do more, own less, rent the rest");[77] attacking waste and throwaway, made-to-break culture by requiring producers to take back products at the end of their useful lives and to design products for durability, easy repair, and even instructive conversation;[78] imposing tight regulation on "easy credit," predatory lending; and promoting initiatives to shift cultural norms that promote consumerism.[79]

Two additional steps are essential. First, we need to put in place a set of new policies that will eliminate overwork and lead to a shorter work-year. Just as America legislated a forty-hour workweek, we can also legislate a thirty- to thirty-two-hour (or four-day) work-week. A take-back-your-time package of initiatives should also include measures to protect part-time workers and favor work sharing; guarantee longer, paid vacations; restrict the use of overtime; and provide for generous parental and caregiving leaves, worker sabbaticals, graduated retirement, and the option of early retirement.[80] Allied with these measures should be support needed for non-income-generating "leisure" activities (continuing education, hobbies, recreation, family and community activities, politics, volunteering, music, the arts, reading, self-improvement, and so on).

Second, we must put advertising in its place, which should be a small place. Advertising is one of the world's most pernicious businesses. In the United States, advertising expenditures grew from $60 billion a year in 1960 to $260 billion in 2004 (in 2003 dollars), or about half of total world spending on advertising that year. In 1983, at the behest of the Reagan administration, the Federal Communications Commission deregulated advertising to children on television. One year later, the ten best-selling toys all had ties to television programs. Between 1983 and 2011, marketing aimed at children swelled from a $100 million-a-year endeavor to a $17 billion-a-year juggernaut. The average child in the United States today sees twenty thousand commercials annually.[81] Meanwhile, ads have invaded air travel, movie theaters, video games, comic books, postseason bowl games, public schools, universities, clothing, and popular songs. And that's not all: "Wizmark's 'Interactive Urinal Communicator' plays 10-second promotional messages to the 'ever elusive targeted male audience you are constantly aiming for.'"[82] The Internet is the largest segment, but "out-of-home" advertising now exceeds radio, newspaper, and magazine advertising combined. Finally, there is the advent reported in the April 23, 2011, issue of *The Economist* of "gladvertising" and "sadvertising:" "a rather sinister-sounding idea in which billboards with embedded cameras, linked to face-tracking software, detect the mood of each consumer who passes by, and change the advertising on display to suit it."[83]

These folks show us no mercy, and we should return the favor. A good start would be a ban on advertising to children in grade school, as is now done in some Nordic countries and Quebec. We should also severely restrict out-of-home advertising, especially in schools. Vermont has made a strong start with its ban on highway billboards. It should be unlawful to circulate mail-order catalogues except on request. To ensure greater truthfulness and relevancy in advertising, a committee of the corporation's directors should be required to attest to the accuracy and relevance of all claims in major ad campaigns, and accuracy and relevance should be closely policed by the appropriate federal agencies, with fines levied when appropriate. Television and radio should be required to make time available so that the public can challenge advertising pitches and commercialism generally, much as *Adbusters* and others now do. Finally, advertising costs should be disallowed as a business expense for tax purposes.[84]

There is no magic bullet with which to slay consumerism, but measures like these will carry us a good distance toward that goal.

Transforming Communities

It has been said that the nation-state is too big for the little things and too little for the big things. That is true if we think of "big" and "little" in terms of the geographic scale. But the things that happen below the national level are certainly not "little" to most of us. As E. F. Schumacher said in *Small Is Beautiful*, "People can be themselves only in small comprehensible groups."[85] We lead local lives, and the things that happen in our communities—and here I use communities to include our neighborhoods, towns, cities, and regions—are BIG.

And what has been happening locally for some decades now is that many, many American communities are being hollowed out under repeated assaults from the same economic and political forces that have given rise to our other grave challenges. Giant corporations come and go at will, taking good jobs with them and bringing in fast-food and big-box ones. Working families are compelled to move from place to place in search of jobs. States compete for what's left of American manufacturing by offering expensive incentives and enacting anti-union "right-to-work" laws. Tax bases erode and local services, education, and public amenities are cut.

In *Making a Place for Community*, Thad Williamson and his colleagues point to the "decay of civic life and community attachment in the United States," and they worry about our country's failure to respond to these trends: "Indeed, our policies . . . often seem designed explicitly to undermine the economic basis of stable communities. While serious observers know this, few want to confront or alter this reality in a direct fashion. Instead, discussions of how to revitalize community (and communities) too often come with this caveat: We want to rebuild community *without* seriously altering the political and economic policies that contradict this goal. The continued evasion of central political-economic questions is a dead end for those concerned with reconstructing civil and community life in the twenty-first century."[86]

Remarkably, some national leaders in the United States have noticed these trends in community decline and have, in effect, blessed them. The 1980 national commission on *A National Agenda for the Eighties* concluded that "the economic health of our nation's communities ultimately depends on the health of our nation's economy. Federal efforts to revitalize . . . areas through [public policies] . . . concerned principally with the health of specific places will inevitably conflict with efforts to revitalize the larger economy." Instead of policies seeking to sustain communities, the commission urged policy efforts that do "not discourage the deconcentration and dispersals of industry and households," because these trends flow from natural workings of the market.[87] Community, like much else, is sacrificed for the sake of economic growth.

Making a Place for Community documents the high costs of neglect of our communities. First, there is the economic loss when "sunk private and public investments in infrastructure, housing, commercial buildings, education, utilities, and other public goods" are partially abandoned and must be replaced elsewhere. There are also costs to democracy and good governance. As the authors note, "Stable geographic communities . . . provide a natural site for organizing political action across class, race, ethnic, and gender lines and for developing what some have termed 'bridging social capital' that can enhance social cohesion and reduce tension throughout society. . . . Giving up on specific localities as the site of democratic debate and common social action would consign America to becoming an increasingly fragmented society, with its citizens disconnected from both local decision making and larger-order governance structures."

The report further observes that "local democratic governance is compromised (perhaps fatally) in situations where local governments' fiscal prospects (and the health of the local economy in general) are dependent on the decisions of private investors, who may or may not pull out jobs at any time. In such situations democratic choice is sharply circumscribed: Local policy inevitably bends away from many publicly favored policies and toward meeting the needs of mobile capital, as well as those of existing businesses with a strong stake in local land values. . . . When localities are left at the mercy of unrestrained economic forces, local politics either becomes relatively meaningless (lacking sufficient power) or tilts toward the interests of a narrow range of business-oriented constituencies."[88] Without a vital and meaningful local politics, effective links between national and local politics weaken greatly.

Another cost is to social capital. "Membership in civic organizations, social networks, local grassroots organizations, and simple personal relationships are all threatened when economic decline causes members of a community to lose their jobs, experience increased financial and familial stress, and perhaps move away. . . . When the economic underpinnings of a community erode, social networks and institutions—such as families, schools, churches, soccer leagues, and civic organizations—are also weakened, with predictably damaging results."[89]

The "transformation in communities" that is now required to address these problems has two related aspects: first, America needs to shift from widespread loss of community wealth and capital—commercial, social, natural, individual—to widespread gains in community wealth and capital, and second, we need to shift from a predominance of economic globalization to a predominance of economic localization. Central to both shifts will be community self-reliance and anchoring wealth in communities through new ownership and production arrangements that limit capital's mobility. Local self-reliance and rootedness can coexist with larger spheres of commerce. Some envision a "multi-local society" where food, electricity, and most essentials would be locally sourced and distributed. These local centers would be connected with national and global networks of production and distribution following the principles of economic efficiency and subsidiarity (production at the most decentralized level possible), fair trade for all parties, and full-cost pricing.[90] Here again E. F. Schumacher was ahead of his time: "We always need both freedom and order. We need the freedom of lots and lots of small, autonomous units, and, at the same time, the orderliness of large-scale, possibly global, unity and coordination."[91]

There are numerous visions of revitalized community life in America,[92] the one I depict in Chapter 5 among them. Another vision is that of the Democracy Collaborative at the University of Maryland. They are developing a new approach to urban economic regeneration that incorporates many of the ideas discussed previously under "Transforming the Corporation." Their approach includes (1) enlarging alternative patterns of ownership (including employee ownership, worker cooperatives, community development finance, land trusts, social enterprise, and so on); (2) building individual and family assets; (3) linking land-use planning to transportation access, energy use, and affordable housing; (4) linking the emerging green economy to wealth-building strategies; (5) utilizing existing urban assets (particularly anchor institutions like hospitals and universities) to focus their procurement, investment, and other economic activities toward local ends; (6) building community economic development capacity; and (7) focusing special efforts on minorities and other vulnerable groups. They urge that state and federal programs be crafted to support community development and finance corporations, local banks, community land trusts, employee and consumer ownership, local currencies and time dollars, municipal enterprise, and nonprofits in business.[93]

Michael Shuman, the author of *Going Local: Creating Self-Reliant Communities in a Global Age*,[94] has been one of the leaders in the U.S. community revitalization movement and has developed a checklist of measures to gauge community progress (see Box 2). It provides a handy point of reference to identify many dimensions of needed change at the community level, all of which should be furthered with a variety of local, state, and federal initiatives.[95] *Yes! Magazine* has spread the word on a long list of community revitalization measures,[96] and there are many excellent organizations working to support communities in this area.[97]

Transforming Foreign Affairs

The overwhelming predominance of military thinking and spending in the conduct of American foreign affairs has reached the point that even the secretary of defense and the chairman of the Joint Chiefs of Staff have been calling for rebalancing. In 2008, Defense Secretary Robert Gates noted, "It has become clear that America's civilian institutions of diplomacy and development have been chronically undermanned and underfunded for far too long, relative to what we spend on the military."[98] In May 2010, Joint Chiefs Chairman Mike Mullen said, "It's time to invest in other departments, such as homeland security, intelligence and the State Department, whose budget pales compared to massive Pentagon funding." He did not leave it at that. "My fear, quite frankly, is that we aren't moving fast enough in this regard," he said. "U.S. foreign policy is still too dominated

BOX 2 Measuring Community Progress

1. *Local Ownership*—What percentage of jobs in the local economy are in locally owned businesses?

2. *Self-Reliance*—To what extent is the community self-reliant, especially in the basics of food, shelter, energy, and water?

3. *Socially Responsible Business*—to what extent are businesses present across all sectors of the local economy that are achieving high levels of triple-bottom-line success?

4. *Youth*—What's the probability that young people stay in your community once they are graduated from high school (or return to the community after college)? A related question: What's the likelihood that a young person can have fun in your community without breaking the law?

5. *Schools*—What's the probability that members of every age group in your community are increasing the amount of time they spend learning this year, compared to last year?

6. *Entrepreneurship*—What's the likelihood that an entrepreneur in your community, especially a young person, can find the capital, technical assistance, mentorship, and other support that makes it possible for him or her [to] form a small business that he/she is passionate about?

7. *Relationships*—What's the likelihood that every resident knows the names of everyone on his or her block, and that the block throws block parties?

8. *Arts*—To what extent are artists, writers, musicians, and other cultural creatives drawn to live in your community?

9. *Safety Net*—What's the probability that the poorest members of the community find adequate food, shelter, and health care?

10. *Diversity*—To what extent does your community have a rich diversity of races, ethnicities, ages, religions, and political viewpoints?

11. *Aging*—To what extent has the concept of retirement been abolished and replaced by seniors embracing new personal and community missions as they age?

12. *Volunteerism*—What's the probability that a resident has run for office, worked for a government program, or volunteered for a community initiative or an act of civic governance?

13. *Sustainability*—What's the degree to which your community meets its needs, present and future, without impairing the ability of other communities to meet their needs, present and future?

14. *Investment*—What's the percentage of your residents' retirement savings that's invested in local business?

15. *Tourism*—[What's] the degree to which outsiders come to visit in part because they regard you as a model community?

16. *Walkability*—What percentage of your residents can find most of what they need—or work, school, purchasing, and play—within a 10 minute walk from home? What percent of people living in your community work there?

17. *Subsidies*—To what extent is every penny of city money linked to business development invested exclusively in locally owned business?

18. *10% Shift*—What percent of your community's purchasing decisions—including those of consumers, businesses, and procurement agencies—are going to local goods and services?

19. *Celebrations*—To what extent are community events places where solutions to once hopeless problems are shared and celebrated?

20. *Global Self-reliance*—To what extent are you sharing your best practices in achieving all of the above with other communities globally? How much time and money are you spending to help other communities worldwide to achieve the level of self-reliance you seek for yourself?

Source: Michael H. Shuman, "20 Measures for a Successful Local Living Economy," *Business Alliance for Local Living Economies*, March 31, 2011. See www.livingeconomies .org.

by the military, too dependent upon the generals and admirals who lead our major overseas commands and not enough on the State Department."[99]

One indication of how much we rely on the military is the recommendation in a 2011 report of the Center for a New American Security. After commending the Obama administration for proposing to actually reduce the Pentagon's base budget (by 1.2 percent), the report continues: *"Since the politics of defense spending may paralyze Congress and the White House over the next 22 months, the impetus for further reform must come from DOD.* Pentagon leaders—including the next secretary of defense—should do more in the months ahead to address two budgetary challenges that threaten U.S. national security: the Pentagon's need to further streamline its operations and America's growing debt."[100] I don't doubt that the report's assessment is accurate, but it is sad.

The problem of imbalance in U.S. national security spending has been forcefully brought out in the regular reports of the Task Force on a Unified Security Budget sponsored by the Institute for Policy Studies and the Center for American Progress. The authors break U.S. security spending into three categories: "offense" (that is, military spending) has held steady in recent years at 87 percent, "prevention" (that is, spending on development and humanitarian aid, nonproliferation, climate and energy, diplomatic initiatives, peace building, and so on) at 5 percent, and "defense" (spending on Homeland Security) at 8 percent.[101]

The United States now spends easily in excess of $1 trillion annually on all these aspects of national security. Some deficit hawks have already targeted the military budget, but rebalancing within security spending is at least as important as budgetary restraint.[102] Recall the list in Chapter 3 of twenty international challenges the United States now faces. America can't contribute meaningfully to addressing these threats on the cheap, so it will be important not only to reduce military spending but also to reallocate a large portion of the "savings" to meeting the so-called unconventional security threats. Major reductions in military spending can be accomplished by troop reductions, canceling unneeded weapons systems, base closings, cutting back on outsourcing and contractors, terminating old wars, and avoiding new ones.

Of course, such changes in spending are unlikely without a host of other changes. For starters, we must build a much broader and more thoughtful understanding of the real long-term threats facing our country, including forging a different concept of national security and a new understanding of the role of the military. Ironically, perhaps, the most cogent recent statement on real security in America comes from two active military officers, Captain Wayne Porter of the Navy and Colonel Mark Mykleby of the Marine Corps. In their 2011 "National Strategic Narrative," they argue that "prosperity without security is unsustainable. Security is a state of mind, as much as it is a physical aspect of our environment. For Americans, security is very closely related to freedom, because security represents freedom from anxiety and external threat, freedom from disease and poverty, freedom from tyranny and oppression, freedom of expression but also freedom from hurtful ideologies, prejudice and violations of human rights. Security cannot be safeguarded by borders or natural barriers; freedom cannot be secured by locks or by force alone. In our complex, interdependent, and constantly changing global environment, security is not achievable for one nation or by one people alone; rather it must be recognized as a common interest among all peoples."[103]

Porter and Mykleby urge three national investment priorities as essential to America's long-term security: our children and especially their education, security that focuses on national "development and diplomacy" rather than solely on "defense and protectionism," and America's natural resources and environment. They worry that our security today and tomorrow is threatened by "the decline of rural economies, joblessness, the dramatic increase in urbanization, an increasing demand for energy, migration of populations and shifting demographics, the rise of grey and black markets, the phenomenon of extremism and anti-modernism, the effects of global climate change, the spread of pandemics and lack of access to adequate health services, and an increasing dependency on cyber networks."[104]

Taking a similar view of the real meaning of security, Andrew Bacevich describes the proper new role for the U.S. military within this framework. From President Truman to President Obama, Bacevich sees the U.S. military posture as a product of a "sacred trinity": "An abiding conviction that the minimum essentials of international peace and order require the United States to maintain a *global military presence*, to configure its forces for *global power projection*, and to counter existing or anticipated threats by relying on a policy of *global interventionism*." In their stead, Bacevich urges a new set of Washington rules: "*First, the purpose of the U.S. military is not to combat evil or remake the world, but to defend the United States and its most vital interests. . . .* The United States should maintain only those forces required to accomplish [this] core mission. *Second, the primary duty station of the American soldier is in America.* Just as the U.S. military should not be a global police force, so too it should not be a global occupation force. . . . *Third, consistent with the Just War tradition, the United States should employ force only as a last resort and only in self-defense.*"[105]

William Pfaff has similarly urged what he calls a "noninterventionist American foreign policy" in lieu of the current effort to assert American values and economic interests simultaneously around the world. Such a noninterventionist approach would "curtail nonessential external commitments and support multilateral methods and forums for dealing with international problems and crises, to the extent that this is useful. It would redefine its national security strategy narrowly so as to make its priorities the protection of the American polity and its constitutional government, and its security against military threat. It would reduce military expenditures to levels commensurate with the actual problems of the contemporary world and not the hypothetical threats of science fiction. It would regard nonstate threats of subversion and terrorism as primarily matters for the criminal police and other civilian agencies of security."[106]

Article I, Section 8, of the U.S. Constitution provides that "the Congress shall have Power To . . . provide for the common defense . . . To declare War . . . [and] To raise and support Armies." The Constitution establishes the president as "Commander in Chief of the Army and Navy" (Article II, Section 2). If civilian, democratic control of the military is to be meaningful, the wall of secrecy that surrounds military and security affairs, and prevents a knowledgeable citizenry from developing, should be breached and means found to encourage robust public debate.[107] Congress and the courts should interpret the War Power meaningfully and enforce it strictly. Legislation should be passed requiring a waiting period between military service and appointment to high federal office. And the pattern of relying on military solutions to problems that should be dealt with otherwise should be halted.

Finally, Congress must be pressed to act to rein in the imperial presidency that reached its zenith with President George W. Bush and that continues today with President Obama. In *Unchecked and Unbalanced: Presidential Power in a Time of Terror*, Fritz Schwarz and Aziz Huq decry the Bush administration's "plunge into torture, its lawless spying and its lock-up of innocents." "Executive unilateralism," they write, "not only undermines the delicate balance of our Constitution, but also lessens our human liberties and hurts vital counterterrorism campaigns. . . . Torture policy, extraordinary rendition, warrantless domestic spying, indefinite presidential lockup: the executive branch developed all of these tactics without Congress's knowledge and with total disregard for statutory prohibitions."[108]

Their conclusion is that "Congress must act . . . by enacting meaningful limiting legislation and by holding effective oversight hearings," but they caution that "Congress will change its ways when voters start demanding that it fulfill its constitutional mandate."[109]

Schwarz and Huq also urge Congress to implement the 9/11 Commission's call "for new framework statutes for intelligence agencies, laws that laid down clear responsibilities and, by implication, imposed clear limits on intelligence work. . . . Congress has failed to match the rapid growth of intelligence agencies with a legal infrastructure for supervising and restraining those agencies." And they point out that "effective national security policy also demands far more openness. Unregulated secrecy hides error and bureaucratic failure from public sight. . . . Secrecy is necessary on occasion. But it often makes us less safe. Legislators (and the public) are disabled from meaningful debate when the executive branch conceals vital changes in law and policy."[110] Schwarz and Huq conclude by observing, "At the beginning of the chain of democratic responsibility stand the people."[111] That, of course, points to the big question: What are we the people going to do? It's time to turn to that question.[112]

Part Four   Writing Free of an Old Skin

I half expect him to tend his trees
with aspirin and soup, the gardener
who finds in destruction
the very reason to carry on;
who would look at the ruins
of Eden and tell the hovering angel
to put down his sword,
there was work to be done.
——LINDA PASTAN

Reflect for a moment on the magnitude of the national challenges reviewed in Part I. Federal and state governments should be addressing each of these major challenges in a determined, long-term way:

- Launch a new War on Poverty aimed at lifting a sixth of our citizens out of poverty;
- Initiate programs to rebuild the middle class and to ensure economic security for families with modest incomes;
- Deploy genuinely progressive taxes and other measures to raise revenues and close the gap in incomes between rich and poor;

- Create an outstanding health care system that delivers outcomes as good as those common in Europe and at costs common in Europe;
- Support educational initiatives that restore American students to the top ranks internationally;
- Lower unemployment and underemployment rates to satisfactory levels, guaranteeing decent-paying jobs to all who want to participate in the labor force;
- Move the United States to the front ranks internationally in child welfare, including meaningful parental leaves and paid holidays and dramatic reductions in child abuse and in advertising targeting children;
- Provide incentives to rebuild social capital in America, including the revitalization of declining cities, encouraging American companies to stay rooted in their communities, providing compassionate care for those who need it, recreating the "nation of joiners," and countering the rise of hate groups;
- Deal responsibly and sensitively with illegal immigration;
- Shift away from policies that encourage consumerism and toward those that encourage long-term public and private investment in R & D, green technology, the industries of the future, infrastructure, environmental restoration, and community development;
- Regulate Wall Street to eliminate systemic risks and protect investors, while building up a system of community-based financial institutions;
- Promote gun control, challenge America's gun culture, and address America's top rank in homicides;
- Address drug abuse, both legal and illegal, and correct policies that have led to America having the world's highest incarceration rate;
- Establish a monetary measure of sustainable economic welfare that is published quarterly along with GDP, and create a new system of indicators to gauge national progress;
- Reduce federal budgetary deficits and U.S. international indebtedness to sustainable levels;

- Rethink America's approach to terrorism and find ways to be more effective while unwinding the post-9/11 buildup of a huge and secretive homeland security apparatus;
- Reduce the military budget, the huge arms industry, and the network of military bases abroad and rethink the real threats to America's national security, the training and arming of foreign military forces, the use of private contractors, and overreliance on the military generally;
- Join with other countries in efforts to greatly strengthen international capabilities to counter neglected "unconventional" threats like the spread of infectious diseases, transnational organized crime, climate change and other global environmental challenges, humanitarian emergencies, world poverty, and human rights abuses;
- Implement comprehensive national energy and climate policies that will simultaneously reduce oil imports and greenhouse gas emissions, and boost energy efficiency and renewable energy;
- Prepare for resource shortages, escalating commodity and resource prices, and for the need to deemphasize economic growth as a central pillar of national economic, budgetary, and security policy;
- Build true citizen sovereignty and political equality as well as the transparency, honesty, accountability, competence, and civility of American government and politics.

This list frames a daunting agenda, even without addressing directly the imperative of deeper change in Part III. Such an agenda obviously requires farsighted, strong, and effective government leadership and action. Inevitably, then, the drive to respond to these challenges leads to the political arena, where a vital, muscular democracy steered by an informed and engaged citizenry is needed. That's the democracy we need, but, unfortunately, it is not the democracy we have. Given the number and seriousness of these challenges, even a well-intentioned and highly capable government would have difficulty. But, of course, it is worse than that. Right now, Washington isn't even seriously trying to address most of these challenges. It is unimaginable that American politics as we know it will deliver the responses needed.

Most of the transformations examined in Part III and even most of the proposals for reform offered by progressives in Washington today will not be possible without a new politics in America. Part IV is about building a new democratic reality.

8 Realizing Democracy

This country, with its institutions, belongs to the people who inhabit it. . . . Why should there not be a patient confidence in the ultimate judgment of the people? Is there any better or equal hope in the world? —ABRAHAM LINCOLN

The majority of the plain people will day in and day out make fewer mistakes in governing themselves than any smaller body of men will make in trying to govern them.
—THEODORE ROOSEVELT

Among the prescriptions for America's future, the imperative of building a new politics in our country stands out as especially urgent. Today's rancorous political debates cannot sustain the change in priorities that the country badly needs. The path to a better America leads inevitably through the thicket of political reform.

The conventional diagnosis is that our national politics, and the governance it yields, are now dysfunctional, with Washington beset by polarization and gridlock and thus broken and unable to perform. Our two major parties are indeed polarized today in a way not seen in modern times, particularly as the Republican Party has veered sharply to the right.[1] And it is certainly true that Washington is failing our country across a wide front.

A sign of things to come occurred as early as 1948 when Strom Thurmond, angered by the Democratic Party's initial embrace of the civil rights cause, led the Dixiecrats and the Deep South states out of the Democratic column in that year's presidential election. The ideological divide between the parties deepened in earnest when President Lyndon Johnson signed civil rights legislation in the mid-1960s. After that, conservative white Southerners began joining the once-hated Party of Reconstruction, and shifted it steadily to the right.

Meanwhile, a growing social "permissiveness" and other challenges to traditional values have spurred the rise of social conservatives in general and the religious right in particular. The American right has had, as Allan Lichtman describes in *White Protestant Nation*, "an enduring appeal to Americans seeking the clarity and comfort of absolute moral codes, clear standards of right and wrong, swift and certain penalties for transgressors, and established lines of authority in public and family life."[2]

By the late twentieth century, Lichtman explains, "conservatives had gained an edge on liberals in critical aspects of political organizing and mobilization." Lichtman notes that the right "used appeals to 'family values' and 'personal responsibility' to recapture the moral high ground that the left had occupied during the era of the civil rights struggle." The right also made more organized use of media technologies "to circumvent what was perceived to be a liberally biased media establishment" and "outpaced the left in developing a richer network of partisan think tanks and advocacy groups outside the party structure."[3]

As a result of these trends, the philosophical differences between Republicans and Democrats clarified and sharpened. But as political scientists Jacob Hacker and Paul Pierson note in *Off Center*, the change has not been symmetrical: "Though the rise in polarization is undeniable, the conventional lament misses crucial aspects of the change. It suggests a transformation that is somehow equal on both sides, as if the two parties had run away from each other at the same speed. In fact . . . the move from the center has been spearheaded and driven by the Republican Party. Over the same era in which conservatives have risen to power, they have moved further and further from the political center."[4]

The resulting gridlock is not neutral, Hacker and Pierson note, "it is corrosive. . . . Rather, stalemate in Washington leads to a slow and steady deterioration of governance."[5]

But our national political condition is actually more dire than the diagnosis of gridlock suggests. If one reviews the past several decades, one sees that Washington has in fact been highly successful and even efficient at serving certain interests and objectives. For example, Washington has successfully shepherded a vast transfer of our national income from the middle class to the very rich. Washington has also been adept at saying "no" to many progressive initiatives, a pattern that Hacker and Pierson note was well under way before the 1980 election of Ronald Reagan, an event typically regarded as pivotal. In 1977 and 1978, Hacker and Pierson observe, Congress effectively stalled and outright killed progress many times: "Tax reform: defeated. A new consumer protection agency: defeated. Election Day voter registration: scuttled before reaching the floor of the House. Health-care reform: defeated. A proposal to tie the minimum wage to the average manufacturing wage to prevent its erosion: defeated. An overhaul of outdated labor relations laws: successfully filibustered in the Senate."[6] Faced with such a list, one is left staring at the ironic truth of President Reagan's famous statement, "Government is not the solution to our problem, government is the problem." In recent years, government has indeed been a big part of what ails us.[7]

Central to the story of our rotten politics is growing economic inequality and the influence of money in our policy-making process. The authors brought together by political analysts Lawrence Jacobs and Theda Skocpol document in *Inequality and American Democracy* a vicious cycle: income disparities shift political access and influence to wealthy constituencies and businesses, which further erodes the potential of the democratic process to act to correct the growing income disparities.[8] If plutocracy describes a system wherein the wealthy enjoy a greatly disproportionate influence in government, and if corporatocracy is a political state in which large corporations have massive power in government, America is now teetering on the verge of full-blown plutocracy and corporatocracy, in substance if not in form.[9] Great concentrations of wealth and power throw up formidable obstacles to progressive reforms that try to challenge our winner-take-all economy. Hacker and Pierson correctly note that "business coalitions, Wall Street lobbyists, medical industry players . . . are fully cognizant of the massive stakes involved, and they are battle-ready after years of training."[10]

There is a vast and bloated lobbying industry devoted to swaying government policy to better serve big business and foreign governments. In his book *So Damn Much Money*, Bob Kaiser, former managing editor at *The Washington Post*, carries his story of "the triumph of lobbying and the corrosion of American government" up through 2007, when, he observes, "The political culture of Washington, which was also the political culture of the United States, had been deteriorating for decades." He links our political decline to the rise of lobbyists, the growing importance of money, the revolving door between politics and business interests, and the declining competence of those in government. By 2007, he writes, "Washington . . . was the center of a vast industry devoted to influencing the American government on behalf of big business, small business, foreign governments, and the multitude of interests and interest groups comprised by the modern United States." And he notes, "The United States government was routinely ineffectual or incompetent. It did not attract many of the best and brightest young Americans."[11]

Similar to Kaiser, James Galbraith blames the rise of what he calls "the predator state," defined as one in which "the systematic abuse of public institutions for private profit or, equivalently, the systematic undermining of public protections for the benefit of private clients" prevails. Galbraith cites "the practice of turning regulatory agencies over to business lobbies, the privatization of national security and the attempted privatization of Social Security, the design of initiatives in Medicare to benefit drug companies, and trade agreements to benefit corporate agriculture at the expense of subsistence farmers in the Third World. In each case, what we see is . . . a predator's drive to divert public resources to clients and friends."[12]

Longtime Washington observer William Greider, in his book *The Soul of Capitalism*, expresses a deep skepticism that today's politics can address the major problems. He writes, "If an activist president set out with good intentions to rewire the engine of capitalism—to alter its operating values or reorganize the terms for employment and investment or tamper with other important features—the initiative would very likely be chewed to pieces by the politics."[13] Robert Kuttner's arresting tale of the first years of the Obama presidency, *A Presidency in Peril*, carries this story forward.[14]

Yet, the intense difficulty of political reform in this climate only underscores the need for it. At stake is nothing less than the prospect for both near-term reforms and the longer-term transformations required. As Michael Waldman, director of one of the key reform groups, the Brennan Center for Justice, has said, "Progressives have to grapple with this central truth—we can't solve the country's problems if we don't fix the systems of democracy."[15] So nothing is more important in America today than prodemocracy reforms aimed at real citizen sovereignty—a government truly of the people, by the people, and for the people. The antidote to creeping corporatocracy and plutocracy in America is a strong, muscular American democracy.

Faith in democracy rests on three principles—principles aptly described by Robert Dahl, the dean of American political science. First is the principle of political equality of all citizens. The second is that government must consider every citizen's interests equally. Finally, the painful lessons of history demonstrate what can happen when certain groups are excluded from full citizenship on the basis of gender, skin color, and lack of property, and suffer keenly as a result. Dahl believes these principles "are at the foundation of democratic governance, provide its legitimacy, and render it, with all its defects, superior to all feasible nondemocratic alternatives."[16]

A foundation of democracy is the principle that all citizens should have a right to participate as equals in the process of governing. All should have the right to vote, have access to relevant information, speak up, associate with others, and participate. Votes should count equally, the majority should prevail subject to respect for basic rights, and the issues thus determined should be the important ones society faces. These are ideals by which America's situation as well as our political reform agenda should be judged.

The good news is that many progressives are experiencing re-kindled hope for prodemocracy reforms. In a powerful essay, Ka-trina vanden Heuvel, editor of *The Nation*, writes, "If we are to finally transcend our downsized politics of excluded alternatives, progressives will have to drive a bold agenda to invigorate democracy at home and capture greater power for the people."[17] Bob Edgar, president of Common Cause, sees an "opportunity to reinvent American democracy in ways that will break the stranglehold of big money, enable us to tackle the enormous challenges of the 21st century, and give Americans the open, honest, and accountable government we deserve."[18] Former conservative Republican Congressman Mickey Edwards has offered a persuasive agenda to "strengthen the democratic process" and "turn our political system on its head, so that people, not parties, control our government."[19]

It is of utmost importance, however, that our efforts at political reform evade the traps of short-term, crisis-driven thinking (such as the half-measures pursued in the wake of the problem-plagued 2000 presidential election). In such instances, proposals are offered to address a few of the more egregious shortcomings exposed by the crisis, but as congressional debate slogs on, both public and political attention wanes and Washington's lobbying establishment, the main beneficiary of the status quo, is happy to let the political reform agenda sink back to its usual second- or third-order priority status. It is vital that prodemocracy reforms remain a top priority for all progressive communities, and that these reforms be pursued consistently through a well-conceived, determined, and ongoing campaign that mobilizes the many strengths of its constituent groups. Environmentalists, consumer advocates, labor unions, antipoverty groups, and those advocating for social justice, good jobs, a smaller military, financial industry reform, health care reform, support of education, and community development—all have a role to play and much to gain by joining forces with those whose primary mission is political reform.

Also, election reform alone, as important as it is, is not sufficient. As Larry Marx observes in his contribution to "Revitalizing Democracy," an excellent 2009 special report of *The American Prospect*,[20] democracy "includes the executive branch as well as the civil-rights movement; poll workers and voting machines as well as the maldistribution of opportunity created by the allotment of wealth; lobbyists' and corporations' influence over public policy as well as civil-society institutions based in communities, labor unions, and identity- or issue-based groups. . . . Shared governance and deliberative democracy can improve governmental decisions and ensure popular satisfaction with outcomes; card-check elections for unions and other labor-law reforms can empower workers; changes in the tax code would facilitate community organizing."[21]

Marx's mention of deliberative democracy is important. As Stuart Comstock-Gay and Joe Goldman point out in their *American Prospect* article, democracy has often in recent years been defined too narrowly and in terms of elections and exercising the right to suffrage. They argue for a true participatory democracy "where people help make the decisions that affect their lives beyond Election Day." "Today, these two concepts are often separated. They are the subject of different reform communities, different legislative efforts, different constituencies. But to invigorate democracy, they must be coupled. . . . About 20 years ago, a new movement emerged to celebrate, cultivate, and articulate public engagement in the governance process. Scholars and civic reformers variously refer to this movement as deliberative democracy, public participation, civic renewal, community building, or collaborative governance."[22]

While most efforts toward nurturing direct, deliberative democracy have occurred at the local level, interesting proposals have been offered to bring it to the national level. For example, Bruce Ackerman and James S. Fishkin have proposed "Deliberation Day—a new national holiday. It will be held two weeks before major national elections. Registered voters will be called together in neighborhood meeting places, in small groups of fifteen, and larger groups of five hundred, to discuss the central issues raised by the campaign. Each deliberator will be paid $150 for the day's work of citizenship. To allow the rest of the workaday world to proceed, the holiday will be a two-day affair, and every citizen will have the right to take one day off to deliberate on the choices facing the nation."[23] In their vision of Deliberation Day, all of the spin doctors, pollsters, and fundraisers that clog our democratic system would have to modulate their methods to suit "a better informed public."

Pointing to many local successes with deliberative democracy, Ackerman and Fishkin conclude that such sessions need not and do not devolve into chaos or erupt into brawls more suitable for bar rooms, as many cynics predict. Instead "they reveal that ordinary citizens are remarkably good at productive interchange—hearing out spokespersons for different sides, and changing their minds on the basis of new arguments and evidence. Ordinary men and women *can* function successfully as citizens."[24]

Fritz Schwarz of the Brennan Center has stressed another democratic imperative: a well-informed citizenry and its handmaiden, open and honest government. Schwarz fears that a growing culture of secrecy and deception in government threatens our democracy: "While some secrets are legitimate, many actions during the Cold War and after the 9/11 attacks were kept secret not to *protect America* but to keep embarrassing and improper information *from Americans.* For example, among the secrets I helped bring to light as Chief Counsel for a Senate Committee, the FBI tried to coerce Martin Luther King to commit suicide; the CIA hired the Mafia to kill Cuba's Fidel Castro; and, for thirty years, the National Security Agency obtained copies of every telegram leaving the United States. And then, during the Bush-Cheney Administration, many policies, such as torture, were adopted and implemented in secret." In our secrecy culture, Schwarz argues, more and more is made secret and secrets are kept for far too long. Such a culture is "inconsistent with democracy's premise. How can voters judge their leaders' character and their country's conduct when so much is hidden? America is becoming, I fear, *a democracy in the dark.*"[25]

The essential complement to making government truly democratic is making it truly competent. We are now long into a process where civil servants have been denigrated and essential government functions underfunded and outsourced while the rolls of political appointees to agency positions have mounted. It's time to stop this erosion and begin the process of building governance capacities capable of coping with today's challenges.

Election Reform: One Person, One Vote

A good place to begin an agenda for realizing democracy is getting far more Americans registered and voting. Voter turnout in presidential elections increased steadily over the 1996–2008 period, but even in the highly energized election of 2008, only about 60 percent of eligible voters went to the polls. Roughly a third of eligible voters in the United States have not even registered to vote. In typical "off-year" or midterm national elections, less than 40 percent of eligible Americans vote.

The most ambitious and also the best way to increase voter registration is to make registration the default position. Upon reaching the age of eighteen, citizens would be automatically registered, as is common in advanced democracies. State governments would shoulder the responsibility for maintaining voter lists, informing voters of their rights and options, including the possibility of opting out of registration and the fact that they would not have to re-register if they moved within the state.[26] The next best alternative to making registration the default position is to implement election-day registration. Already in practice in some states, EDR could be extended by Congress to cover all federal elections.

Once more people are registered, voting itself can be made easier in several ways: the opportunity of early voting should be extended;

election day should be made a national holiday; ballots should be simpler, with less potential for confusion; and the disgraceful but nonetheless widespread practices of discouraging and suppressing voting through intimidation and other deceptive practices should be prohibited and penalized.

The actual process of voting and tallying election results is also in need of thorough overhaul. The United States needs a national elections commission that, as elections expert Steven Hill and others have urged, would be charged with providing and monitoring impartial, nonpartisan, and well-trained election officials; with certifying and testing voting machines that generate voter-verified paper trails that serve as the official ballots for recounts and audits; and generally with maintaining the integrity of the voting process.[27]

Of course, making votes and their outcomes important enough for the voters to care is an integral part of this puzzle. Overcoming voter apathy is hard when there are so many "safe" seats in Congress as well as so many safe, as opposed to swing, states. More generally, we want votes not only to count, but to count equally. In the process, reforms aimed at these objectives should help overcome partisan polarization and gridlock and give opportunities for many new groups to gain access to the levers of power.

The Electoral College is a ripe target for reform. The current arrangement—wherein states have electoral votes equal to the number of congressional districts plus two ("representing" each state's two senators)—means that citizens' votes in small states are worth more than votes elsewhere. Steven Hill points out that eleven traditionally Republican western and mountain states combined have roughly the same population as New York and Massachusetts combined, but in the 2000 presidential election, those eleven states had nine more electoral votes, enough to give victory to George W. Bush.[28]

Ideally, a constitutional amendment would provide for direct election of the president. But as long as that remains a bridge too far, some important interim steps can be taken. The most important would be actions taken by state legislatures to assign all of the state's electoral votes to the candidate that won the national popular vote for president, but only if and when a coalition of states holding at least 270 total electoral votes, the number needed to win in the Electoral College, had enacted similar commitments. By 2011, nine states—including California, Hawaii, Illinois, Maryland, New Jersey, Washington, and Massachusetts—have made such pledges.[29] Together they account for about half of those 270 electoral votes.

Short of that, state legislatures could agree to what is called instant runoff voting (IRV), in which voters rank their preferences among the candidates. Low-scoring candidates—often third-party candidates—are eliminated in the vote counting, and their voters' second choices are added to those that remain until one candidate has a majority. Under this system, no one's vote is "wasted" and the state's electoral votes would be cast for a candidate that won the majority of the vote, not a mere plurality. In 2000, nine states gave all of their electoral votes to a presidential candidate that had not won a majority of the popular vote. When Ross Perot ran as an independent in 1992, fully forty-nine states were won by a candidate lacking a popular majority.[30] (Importantly, IRV can also be used to maximize voter input in all races at the local, state, and federal levels.)

Another proposal for bringing more democracy to the election of president involves substantially enlarging the number of congressional districts, now stuck at 435 members. If the membership of the House of Representatives were expanded to, say, 650 members, not only would Electoral College outcomes more closely resemble the popular vote, but the relationship between members of the Congress and their constituents could potentially be closer.[31] Remember also that the U.S. population continues to grow.

Reform of our current system of primary elections is also needed. There are many possibilities here.[32] The most ambitious would be to have what is called a "nonpartisan blanket primary"—that is, a single national primary listing all presidential candidates, regardless of party, on a single ballot with all voters free to vote. Voters would preferentially rank the candidates, and, using IRV, the two winning candidates would go on to the general election. Mickey Edwards urges this approach.[33] In 2010, with Proposition 14, California adopted such an approach for elections other than presidential elections, and the Supreme Court has given a similar arrangement in the state of Washington the green light. It will be informative to see how it works. In the meanwhile, structured open primaries, in which registered independents can vote in either major party's primary, should be expanded to more states. Right now, about half the states have closed primaries, where only voters registered with a party can vote in its primary, so candidates must appeal to the party's "base" and not more broadly. One very good idea is for each party to have a series of perhaps four or five regional "super Tuesdays" rather than the disorganized and scattered system we have today, wherein Iowa and New Hampshire and other early primary states hold much sway over the remainder of campaign season.

Up to this point I've left partisan gerrymandering of congressional districts out of the discussion, though, as Hacker and Pierson note, the practice has acquired surprising sophistication and ruthlessness in recent years. Here the needed reform is to have district lines drawn by independent, nonpartisan commissions. Voting is cheapened when district lines are drawn to predetermine election outcomes.[34]

Another voting distortion occurs from the simple fact of winner-take-all elections. "Losers" get nothing in such a system, though they may have garnered a substantial share of the popular vote. European governments eliminate this perversion with various proportional representation systems. Roughly, if a minority party gets 20 percent of the vote, for example, that party gets 20 percent of parliament seats. Nothing in the U.S. Constitution prescribes single-member congressional districts, so we could have proportional representation in the United States, either through a set of statewide at-large seats or through multimember districts. Illinois used a system of multimember districts until 1980, when the practice was eliminated almost by accident. Steven Hill and others believe it worked well, so experimenting with it again makes sense.[35]

Short of proportional representation, instant runoff voting, discussed earlier, at least gives a say to those voters whose candidates were eliminated early on. IRV also encourages leading party candidates to appeal to third-party voters. Similarly, fusion voting allows a minority party to list as its candidate on the ballot the candidate of another party. Fusion voting thus allows third parties to bargain with the two major parties for the best representation it can get. With fusion, the Green Party, for example, would not be a "spoiler" in national elections but could bring its voting power to bear on shaping the positions of Democrats or Republicans. Katrina vanden Heuvel explains the benefits: "Fusion allows two or more parties to nominate the same candidate on separate ballot lines. That simple change permits people to vote their values without 'wasting' their vote or supporting 'spoilers.' The positive experience of New York's Working Families Party in the past decade shows you can build a viable minority party this way. And fusion has also helped progressives focus on the challenge of building majorities in a winner-take-all system. These options would dramatically open our electoral system to more choices, ensuring the representation of diverse views instead of seeing them co-opted or suppressed by the 'least worst' options presented by the duopoly."[36] Unfortunately, the duopoly—our two major parties—has felt so threatened by fusion politics that they have stopped it in all but about eight states.

Lastly, there's the U.S. Senate, an anachronistic product of the Constitutional Convention's Great Compromise. Senators from states representing a mere 17 percent of our total, fifty-state population have the power to pass or kill any proposed federal legislation. Given the way filibusters are now managed under Senate Rule 22, senators representing a mere 11 percent of the U.S. population can exercise effective control over legislation, at least in theory. (Of course, the math requires Wyoming and Vermont senators to agree, which today they seldom do!)

While I personally benefit from Vermont's outsized influence on national affairs, I have no doubt that the Great Compromise is not the best means to the best possible country. Short of a constitutional amendment revisiting the Great Compromise, there is another, difficult, way to inject more democracy into the Senate: large states could subdivide into two or more smaller ones.[37] And within the

Senate, procedures should be changed to put time limits on filibusters and to give greater leadership to senators who represent larger populations.[38]

Campaign Finance: Money Talks

News Report from the Future: A funny thing happened on the way to plutocracy. Just when it seemed that big-money donors, aided and abetted by the Supreme Court, were on the verge of a final takeover of American politics, prodemocracy advocates changed tack, found a new way forward, and saved American elections. The key to their success was shifting the emphasis of campaign finance reform to advocate for an ingenious combination of small-donor contributions and public funding of elections—nothing less than democratization of campaign finance itself. This new approach, supplemented by related efforts to make money less important, achieved its first big success in the 2016 presidential race and led to the widely admired system we take for granted today.

Fanciful? I don't think so. The Fair Elections Now Act, introduced in Congress in April 2011, embodies this approach for congressional elections and has numerous cosponsors in the House and Senate. A 2009 public opinion survey conducted jointly by Democratic and Republican pollsters found that Americans support a publicly funded Fair Elections system by an overwhelming margin of 67 percent to 20 percent.[39] Numerous states, including Connecticut, Arizona, Maine, and others, have pursued the approach with good results. Candidates who participated in state "clean" or "fair" election programs similar to Fair Elections Now hold over half of the legislative seats in Arizona, 85 percent in Maine, and 75 percent in Connecticut.[40]

Significantly, the Fair Elections Now Act approach is backed not only by all of the dedicated advocacy groups that have for years led the fight on political reform but also by a broad coalition of environmental, consumer, business, religious, labor, and civil rights organizations, as well as an impressive and bipartisan list of former U.S. senators, including Bill Bradley, Bob Kerrey, Warren Rudman, Alan Simpson, and Tim Wirth.[41]

Mark Schmitt explains what's behind this sea change in approach in his elegant essay on "small-donor democracy." First, the 2008 election revealed that the campaign-finance regulatory regime had collapsed and that small-donor fundraising was viable, thanks to on-line payment systems that made contributing to a political campaign as hassle-free as completing an online purchase. This led to "an entirely new set of assumptions about money in politics." The authors of the existing campaign finance laws assumed that only when candidates were unable to draw on soft-money contributions from corporations and unions, or caps were placed on large donations, would candidates seek out the donor who had only $25 to give, and that the donor with only $25 to give was, perhaps, too cynical about the process even to part with that $25. "These are the assumptions of 1996," Schmitt explains, "when only half a million or so people were involved in politics as contributors and when political participation was at its lowest level ever. . . . We now know two things we didn't know then: Small donors can be drawn to politics, and large sums of money in politics and engaged, participatory democracy are not incompatible; money can, in fact, be an essential form of expression that deepens participation. That is, money, positive engagement with politics and government, and participation can, in certain circumstances, form a virtuous circle."[42]

All of us have a stake in the continued success and expansion of this new approach. The alternative is an orgy of promiscuous embraces between money and power. As longtime *New York Times* reporter Linda Greenhouse put it, "Taken as a whole, the campaign finance picture is beyond dreary."[43] Or, as Michael Waldman concluded, "Our campaign finance system is arguably the worst in the Western world."[44]

How bad is bad? First, there is what Bob Kaiser refers to as "so damn much money." The total amount spent on all federal races in 1996 was $2.1 billion. By 2008, a mere twelve years later, it had grown to a record $5.3 billion. This money comes from a tiny sliver of the U.S. population. In 2008, more than 80 percent of the contributions to federal campaigns came from 1 percent of the population; 60 percent came from only 0.1 percent. Five business sectors accounted for almost half of 2008 campaign contributions. In descending order, they were finance, insurance, and real estate—or FIRE, as insiders say—lawyers and lobbyists, health care, communications, and energy and transportation. Labor unions accounted for only 3 percent of total contributions.[45]

The 2010 elections set a new record for midterm election spending, and the funding patterns just noted for 2008 continued. But one change was the rapid rise of independent expenditure campaigns financed by unlimited and often undisclosed private donations. Reflecting on these results, Dan Weeks, president of Americans for Campaign Reform, noted, "In the aftermath of a Supreme Court decision undercutting decades' worth of campaign finance regulation, we're seeing more and more money from fewer and fewer people flooding campaigns. Anyone who believes that privately financed elections are about representation and free speech, not access and influence, has simply not looked at the data."[46]

So where does all this money go? By a five-to-one margin it goes to incumbents. Given the 80 to 90 percent rate at which incumbents are reelected, and the statistical analysis showing that above a threshold, more funding on average does not improve reelection chances, one can legitimately ask why industry groups feel led to make such generous contributions. The answer appears to be that industry groups give money to members of the congressional committees that are supposed to regulate them or have the power to award them government contracts and tax benefits.[47] As they say, you pay to play.

Special-interest campaign contributions buy access and influence. Consider the deregulation of U.S. banking and finance that brought about the deep economic troubles that have already spanned four years. Between 1990 and 2008, the FIRE brigade lavished $2 billion on federal campaigns. Nine of the ten top House member recipients of Wall Street largess in 2008 served on the Financial Services or Ways and Means committees. Almost all of these top recipients were incumbents.[48]

As campaign costs escalate like an arms race, politicians have begun spending a third of their time raising money, and Democrats and Republicans alike welcome special-interest contributions. Representative Barney Frank, a good and honest Congressman who like so many others before and alongside him has found his committee position helpful, once said, "We are the only people in the world required by law to take large amounts of money from strangers and then act as if it has no effect on our behavior."[49]

No less an authority than former senator Alan Simpson has explained what's going on: "Today, it is those well-funded, but narrowly construed, special interests that provide the lion's share of campaign funds—and exercise undue influence in tax and spending matters as a result. Consider the conflicting incentives in our electoral system. On the demand side, politicians require millions of dollars to win and keep their seats. Those who do not have a fortune of their own must turn to private citizens and groups able to contribute large amounts to campaigns. On the supply side, those with the means and incentive to fund political campaigns frequently have a specific special interest quite apart from the needs of ordinary Americans. Private campaign contributions facilitate this unhealthy alliance—creating, in many cases, a clear conflict of interest that undermines fiscal responsibility."[50]

The labyrinthine terrain of campaign finance law, regulation, and practice is so complicated that not many people can find their way around it. Its inhabitants are in constant battles before the often-feckless Federal Elections Commission or in the courts, struggling over what can and cannot be done under campaign law's numerous ways of getting and spending money in and around campaigns.[51] But for our purposes the most important features of this landscape are a troubling series of Supreme Court decisions.

The Supreme Court, having affirmed (more than once) that corporations are legal personages entitled to various constitutional protections, and further that money spent by corporations on political campaigns is a form of speech protected by the First Amendment, has created huge holes in federal campaign law. In early 2010 it ruled five to four in *Citizens United v. FEC* that corporations (and unions) have a right to spend unlimited sums on television commercials and other speech specifically supporting or opposing particular candidates, provided only that they do so in a way that's not coordinated with the candidate's formal campaign. *Citizens United* thus has opened wide the floodgate, allowing the unlimited flow of funds from the corporation's own treasury—that is, the shareholders' money—into campaigns and given rise to the so-called Super PACs that have already begun to blanket the airwaves with endless negative political ads. As Ronald Dworkin and others have noted, the decision unleashes vast new resources that can undermine the quality of political debate during elections and thus the conditions for the public to make an informed choice.[52]

There are several ways to address the many problems created by *Citizens United*. Most importantly, amending the Constitution to roll back *Citizens United* and to deprive corporations of constitutional personhood would be highly desirable.[53] Or Congress could regulate the impact of the Supreme Court's decision, as Democrats tried unsuccessfully to do in 2010 with the Democracy Is Strengthened by Casting Light On Spending in Elections (DISCLOSE) Act proposals.[54] Requiring disclosure of who is funding an advertisement could help. Two other attractive ideas for regulation are, first, to require that corporate boards or even shareholders approve all campaign spending initiatives and, second, to require that the rule against coordinating ads with the campaign be interpreted and enforced very strictly, as is not the case today. There is also the possibility that the Court itself will reverse the *Citizens United* decision, perhaps if a new justice replacing one of the five in the current majority were appointed.

But a new and all-encompassing approach is needed.[55] As mentioned, the core of this new approach is the Fair Elections Now Act proposal that would fund congressional elections through a mix of small contributions and public funding. Here is how it would work, using races for House of Representatives seats as the example: To

qualify to participate, candidates must agree to accept only donations of $100 or less throughout the election, and they must receive at
least 1,500 such gifts from citizens within their home districts total-
ing at least $50,000. Thus qualified, candidates would receive public
funding of two types: (1) Fair Election funding in the primary and,
if they win, in the general election; the bill introduced in Congress
in 2011 split 40 percent for the primary and 60 percent for the general election, the total for House races set at $1,125,000; (2) $5 in Fair
Election funds for each $1 raised in small donations, thus providing a
powerful incentive to mobilize. Candidates could raise an unlimited
amount of small-donor contributions, but funding from Fair Election funds would be capped at a reasonable level. The legislation
would replace spending limits with contribution limits as a condition
for eligibility for receipt of public funds. A sister legislative proposal
to update and strengthen public and small-donor funding of presidential elections was introduced in 2010.

Some believe that the Internet and the advent of so-called smart-
phone payments will bring about an automatic increase in the small
donation pattern that President Obama set in the 2008 election. That
year, Obama received contributions from more than three million
people, and a big share of his funding was raised from individuals
who gave less than $200. But, in fact, there was a sharp dropoff in
small contributions in 2010. While some of this drop is predictable, it
does suggest that a system that sustains small-donor democracy still
needs to be built.

The proposed legislation also contains important provisions to
make money less important overall. Participating Senate candidates
would receive a 20 percent cut off the lowest broadcast rates, and
in the general election receive a $100,000 media voucher for each
House district in the state.

Several measures complementary to this basic scheme have been
proposed, including:

- expanding broadband capacity throughout the nation and
  making it cheaper;

- ensuring that all carriers and service providers offer full access to political speech, at rates offered to the most favored commercial customers;
- instituting a system of tax credits and tax rebates for small-donor contributions;[56]
- banning lobbyists from fundraising and bundling contributions for federal candidates;
- severing the link between internal fundraising quotas among members of Congress and key committee assignments;[57]
- requiring broadcasters to provide candidates with a minimum amount of free air time as a condition of receiving their federal licenses;[58] and
- implementing the Ackerman-Fishkin "Deliberation Day" described earlier.

This new approach is aimed not at limiting the role of the wealthy few, but rather at enhancing the role of the many. It would help neutralize the power of big money in our democracy, greatly enhancing the possibility of our gaining more elected officials who are not beholden to special interests. It would ensure that big money is not a precondition to seeking public office. It would enable more highly qualified candidates to run and ensure that voters have more meaningful choices. It would strengthen accountability to the voters rather than obligations to the special interests. It would increase citizen participation in politics and help restore the public's waning confidence in government. It would free up huge swathes of officials' time to do the business for which they are elected. And by fostering more diversity and debate, it would address the deplorably low level of public discourse during election season.

The Bigger Picture: Public Issue Campaigns

Reforming the way votes are taken and weighed and the way elections are financed are vital steps but not enough. Elections occur, and then there is the morning after. Elections are but one of numerous factors in a complicated process that determines what American government actually accomplishes. These factors span the distance from the broad contours of public opinion to the detailed rules of congressional procedure. All along the way, lobbying is in the picture.

The Center for Responsive Politics reports that total lobbying spending in Washington jumped from $1.4 billion in 1998 to $3.5 billion in 2010, with thirteen thousand registered lobbyists active that year. The big spenders during this period were the financial, health, communications, and energy sectors, each running up over $3 billion in lobbying expenses.[59] While ExxonMobil spent $5.7 million on campaign contributions in the 2001–2010 period, it spent $138 million on lobbying expenses. Similarly, Chevron spent $2.5 million on campaigns but $63 million on lobbying.[60] The pattern is certainly not restricted to the oil industry.

In *Kabuki Democracy,* Eric Alterman concludes, "If America is to ameliorate its current democratic dysfunction anytime soon, then merely electing better candidates to Congress is not going to be enough. We need a system that has fairer rules, that diminishes the role of money, and that encourages politicians and journalists to honestly investigate and portray the realities they actually observe, thereby reducing the distorting lenses of finance, ideology, and ignorance. And yet these items rarely feature on any progressive agenda."[61]

In their sobering analysis in *Winner-Take-All Politics,* Jacob Hacker and Paul Pierson suggest an approach that looks beyond elections to political reform that diminishes the terrific advantages of the privileged. "The aims should be threefold: to reduce the capacity of entrenched elites to block needed reform; to facilitate broader participation among those whose voices are currently drowned out; and to encourage the development of groups that can provide a continuing, organized capacity to mobilize middle-class voters and monitor government and politics on their behalf. Of these three pillars, the last is the most important—and the most difficult to construct."[62]

In today's Washington, a common vehicle for securing the policy outcome one wants is the issue campaign. Issue campaigns are launched by business groups, public interest nonprofits, or other groups, and can be aimed at getting Congress or the administration to act affirmatively or not to act at all.

A full-blown issue campaign begins with a game plan for getting the desired result. Such a strategy could call for public opinion polling, with special attention paid to the way questions are phrased, as phrasing certainly affects the answers obtained. The issue campaign can also include focus groups and employ framing experts and other consultants that will help shape "messaging" for maximum impact. It can involve massive media buys to mold opinion as well as grassroots mobilization efforts, often called "Astroturfing" because many such efforts are hardly spontaneous manifestations. At the core of it all stand Washington's "K Street" lobbyists, who can flood the Capitol with offers to be "helpful," briefcases full of analyses and issue papers, legislative language, and more, not to mention reminders of how the congressperson's district might benefit from deciding on the issue along the lines he or she has proposed. Meanwhile, campaign contributions recently received lurk in the background. Campaigning for policy outcomes can be highly public or proceed quietly, as behind the scenes as possible.

The biggest lobbying client by far from 1998 to 2011 was the Chamber of Commerce, which has campaigned relentlessly to block federal action on climate change. In 2008, according to an *Energy and Environment News* analysis, the Chamber received a third of its support from only nineteen supporters, and it spent heavily on political activism. It spent $1.2 million on a company that helped generate phone calls, e-mails, and letters to Congress in support of Chamber policy positions. The company reported that on the Chamber's behalf, "petitions, videos, surveys, polls and live response feeds were all employed to engage people and convert them to 'activists.'" Another half million dollars was spent on testing messages with focus groups.[63]

In the issue campaigns on federal climate legislation, almost everybody with a stake in the outcome pulled out all the stops. Ad wars were launched in 2008, with major buys by the Environmental Defense Fund urging action ("Tell Senators Levin and Stabenow to vote

YES on the Climate Security Act") and the Club for Growth opposing the legislation, claiming it would lead to "major job losses, new taxes, and increased energy costs" ("Call Senator Lamar Alexander and tell him to vote NO").[64] Other major players that year were the American Petroleum Institute and the American Coalition for Clean Coal Electricity, which together spent $115 million on issue advertising, grassroots outreach, and other pro-oil and pro-coal communications. These expenditures were in addition to the $15 million the two groups spent on lobbying Congress that year.[65] Altogether, in 2008 the energy industry spent $225 million on lobbying the federal government. Environmental groups spent $11 million, twenty times less.[66] By mid-2009 there were 1,150 registered lobbyists at work in Washington on climate legislation.[67] Climate legislation died in the Senate in the summer of 2009.

The efforts of the Koch brothers, David and Charles, to kill the Climate Security Act have attracted considerable attention, thanks in part to Jane Mayer's *New Yorker* article "Covert Operations."[68] The Koch brothers own Koch Industries, a hundred-billion-dollars-a-year conglomerate that inter alia owns oil refineries in several states and some four thousand miles of pipeline. Mayer reports: "In a study released this spring, the University of Massachusetts at Amherst's Political Economy Research Institute named Koch Industries one of the top ten air polluters in the United States. And Greenpeace issued a report identifying the company as a 'kingpin of climate science denial.' The report showed that, from 2005 to 2008, the Kochs vastly outdid ExxonMobil in giving money to organizations fighting legislation related to climate change, underwriting a huge network of foundations, think tanks, and political front groups. Indeed, the brothers have funded opposition campaigns against so many Obama Administration policies—from health-care reform to the economic-stimulus program—that, in political circles, their ideological network is known as the Kochtopus."[69]

Greenpeace has since updated its report on the Kochs, noting that of the eleven freshman senators who publicly question settled climate science, ten had received 2010 campaign contributions from

Koch Industries, and eight had signed the Americans for Prosperity "No Climate Tax Pledge," aimed at obstructing policy solutions to climate change. "Of the 38 freshman Representatives who deny climate science," Greenpeace reported, "22 received Koch PAC funding in 2010, and all 38 signed the AFP pledge."[70]

The election reforms discussed earlier would, of course, help this depressing situation, but those changes need to be complemented with reforms in other areas. Together, they offer the prospect of injecting the system with a large dose of democracy.

Lobbying reform. The Honest Leadership and Open Government Act passed in 2007 did many positive things. It restricted gifts to members of Congress and put some constraints on the revolving door that leads from congressional employment to top-paying jobs as Washington lobbyists. There are several ways the act should be improved, however.[71] Most important is a ban on registered lobbyists engaging in campaign fundraising. Connecticut enacted such a ban in 2005.[72] Lobbyists should also be required to register regardless of how much time they spend on influence work, and required also to report which members of Congress they meet with. "Strategic consulting" for congressional offices should be classified as lobbying. Congressional staffs should be professionalized, enlarged, and paid better in order to reduce dependence on lobbyists' information and analysis. The offices serving Congress, like the Congressional Research Service and the General Accountability Office, should be strengthened for these same reasons, and the Office of Technology Assessment brought back. Appropriate restrictions should be placed on the lobbying activities of large government contractors. Even stricter revolving-door provisions should also be adopted. Senators and congresspeople and senior congressional staff should all be prohibited from lobbying Congress for several years after leaving Capitol Hill, and President Obama's tough Executive Order effectively closing the revolving door for presidential appointees should be made permanent through legislation, with new provisions extending the ban on lobbying into the subsequent administration.

Disclosing issue campaigns. Individuals and organizations (whether business, trade association, or nonprofit) should be required to disclose expenditures pursuant to major issue campaigns aimed at affecting federal legislation or agency decisions. There are already federal laws requiring disclosure of lobbying expenditures; this would extend that disclosure requirement. Also, the sponsors behind public issue ads should be required to identify themselves in those ads.

Reforming Congress's rules. Books like Thomas Mann and Norman Ornstein's *The Broken Branch* provide excellent roadmaps to reforming the rules under which the House and Senate operate.[73] Two of the most important changes would be (1) elimination of the Senate practice of allowing senators to place "holds" on legislative actions and nominations and (2) modification of the filibuster rule so that the required number of votes to invoke cloture—that is, to proceed with the business at hand—would decline from sixty to fifty-one over a relatively short period. This change would preserve a determined minority's ability to slow things up and call attention to their concerns, while also preserving the Senate's ability to function as a majoritarian body.[74] Another needed reform would put a stop to self-dealing by members of Congress by prohibiting members from participating in decisions where they have a financial interest and from acting on insider information not available to the public.

Undoing regulatory capture. The tendency for regulatory agencies to become too sympathetic to and ultimately be "captured" by those they are supposed to regulate has been observed and deplored for many decades. The Minerals Management Service essentially failed to effectively regulate offshore drilling, thus contributing to the Deepwater Horizon disaster in the Gulf of Mexico. This in turn led senators Sheldon Whitehouse and Sherrod Brown to propose that we "allow our top national law office, the Attorney General of the United States, to step in and clean house whenever an agency or element of government is no longer credibly independent of the industry it is intended to regulate."[75] Upon finding a disorderly house, the attorney general would have the authority to take personnel actions, dictate interim procedures, and audit permits and contracts to ensure they were not affected by improper corporate influence.

Building bridging organizations. Several factors have contributed to a situation wherein average Americans lack access to sophisticated capacity to raise and analyze issues, integrate interests into effective coalitions, and bring their combined weight to bear in politics. In two of the most important books on contemporary American politics, *Off Center* and *Winner-Take-All Politics,* Jacob Hacker and Paul Pierson persuasively argue that a big part of the problem has been the decline of large membership organizations, especially labor unions, that once provided a bridge between average Americans and the complicated and, for normal people, impenetrable process of governing a supersized nation.[76]

It follows that, moving forward, the progressive agenda must give priority to tilting the collective bargaining rules back in favor of what were once held to be the inalienable rights of the working man and woman. Beyond the labor movement, many see hope in "digital democracy"—deploying the power of the Internet and social networking to inform, organize, and mobilize citizen action. MoveOn has certainly done this, and the movement-building work now under way to Rebuild the Dream (www.rebuildthedream.com) is another good example. Generally, a powerful synergy should be created, as Mark Schmitt suggests, between small-donor Internet fundraising, on the one hand, and growing citizen participation in political arenas beyond election campaigns on the other. Several of the innovations urged earlier can, of course, help strengthen fledgling bridging institutions. For example, fusion politics and proportional representation could assist and stabilize effective third parties and third-party-type organizations.

Reforming the media. In his devastating critique of democracy in America today, *Does American Democracy Still Work?,* Alan Wolfe describes what he sees as major deficits in our politics. One important deficit is the decline of institutions that remain outside partisan politics. Among the areas where he sees problems (for example, growing ideological bias and partisanship) are the courts, attitudes about science, what was once called the American Establishment, and most of all, the media. Wolfe posits that we pay a price for the waning of powerful institutions that don't come saddled with political agendas. "The single most important political contribution that disinterested groups make to democracy is their ability to call a stop to politics," he writes. "Yet in the new politics of democracy, nearly every one of the institutions America once counted on to stand above contending political and economic forces is finding it more difficult to do so."[77]

Wolfe sees three developments as having led to the decline in the once-proud tradition of major media outlets delivering hard news to mass audiences: "corporate acquisitions that enabled non-media companies to own media outlets; deregulation on the part of the Federal Communications Commission that reduced the need for 'prestige' broadcasting; and the rise of competition from cable networks." In the aftermath of these changes, the three major networks decided to tailor their news broadcasts to suit public tastes—or what they perceived the public to want. These developments, coupled with the rise of the Internet and its news aggregators and bloggers, has led to what Cass Sunstein has called "the Daily Me"—people get the news they want, both because it is catered to them and because they seek it. The Daily Me in fact has many positive features. Part of my Daily Me is the remarkable Amy Goodman and her program "Democracy Now!," which I access thanks to Free Speech TV. The insightful Thom Hartman is also there, and together they provide accounts of current events largely absent in the network news. But the Daily Me can also mean that the possibility of a widely shared, fact-based understanding of issues is diminished and that an individual's outlook on events is routinely reinforced and rarely challenged.

There are other problems. Extreme media consolidation has led to a situation where six major companies now control most of the media in America. Disney owns 227 radio stations, ten television stations, ABC, *Discover* magazine, TouchStone Pictures, Miramax, Pixar, and the History, Lifetime, and A & E channels. Since 1995 the number of independently owned television stations has declined by

40 percent. Fewer and more powerful owners have influence over the viewpoints that get aired, and on who gets hired to report and edit the news. Media giants have less interest in local news and more interest in reducing costs through cutting staff and teams of investigative journalists, and they have more opportunities to do so. A tougher line at the Federal Communications Commission, antitrust enforcement, and new legislation could roll back this concentration of media power, as Freepress.org, Common Cause, and other prodemocracy media advocates have urged.[78]

In *The Death and Life of American Journalism*, John Nichols and Robert McChesney address specifically the decline of newspapers and the profession of journalism.[79] "The implications are clear: if our policy-makers do nothing, if 'business as usual' prevails, we face a future where there will be relatively few paid journalists working in competing newsrooms with editors, fact-checkers, travel budgets and institutional support. Vast areas of public life and government activity will take place in the dark," they argue.[80] The *State of the Media* report for 2010 estimated that newsrooms shrank by one-fourth in the preceding three years. Newspapers have been hit by declining ad revenue and circulation, but Nichols and McChesney also blame "the phenomenon of media corporations maximizing profits by turning newsrooms into 'profit centers,' lowering quality and generally trivializing journalism. . . . The Internet, by making news free online and steering advertisers elsewhere, merely accelerated a long-term process and made it irreversible. Unless we grasp the structural roots of the problem, we will fail to generate viable structural solutions. By ignoring the public-good nature of journalism and the roots of the current crisis, too many contemporary observers continue to fantasize that it is just a matter of time before a new generation of entrepreneurs creates a financially viable model of journalism using digital technologies."[81] They make a persuasive case that the lasting solution is to return to the days when American government subsidized journalism. They point to the experience elsewhere: the top six nations on *The Economist*'s Democracy Index have generous journalism subsidies.[82] Public trusts and other arrangements could put funding beyond politics. Complementary initiatives should strengthen support for public broadcasting. A 2007 Roper poll found that for the fourth straight year, the Public Broadcasting System (PBS) was ranked first in public confidence.[83]

Another area requiring vigilance is ensuring that the Internet remains available to enhance democracy. To these ends, Common Cause and others have called for strict protection of network neutrality and the promotion of community broadband networks.[84]

A prodemocracy agenda like the one described here must move to top priority. Such an agenda should draw support from Americans across most of the political spectrum. For those of a progressive bent, it is now vital that they come together, regardless of their particular concerns, to promote prodemocracy reforms by building a powerful movement for political change.

9   The Movement

Perhaps a new spirit is rising among us. If it is, let us trace its movement well and pray that our own inner being may be sensitive to its guidance, for we are deeply in need of a new way beyond the darkness that seems so close around us.

—MARTIN LUTHER KING, JR.

When considering what's needed in the process of change, one question leads to another. Like babushka dolls, there is always another one revealed. But here is the ultimate one as far as this book and I are concerned: How do progressives begin to drive real change? The short answer is that we need to build a powerful progressive movement. In today's America, progressive ideas are unlikely to be turned into action unless they are pushed relentlessly by citizen demand. The more serious the change sought, the louder the demand must be.

This reality has been stressed by many of our most perceptive observers. *Washington Post* columnist Harold Meyerson wrote in 2010, "If there's a common feature to the political landscapes in which Carter, Clinton and now Obama were compelled to work, it's the absence of a vibrant left movement. . . . In America, major liberal reforms require not just liberal governments, but autonomous, vibrant mass movements, usually led by activists who stand at or beyond liberalism's left fringe."[1] Leading community activist and head of the Center for Community Change Deepak Bhargava, reflecting in 2010 on President Obama's record, observed, "The main lesson we should draw from the last year and from American history is that it takes social movements that exhibit intensity, tenacity, and imagination to get big things done in our country. . . . Strategies relying on insider influence are incapable of delivering large-scale change."[2]

Successful movements for serious change are launched in protest against key features of the established order. They are nurtured on outrage at the severe injustice being perpetrated, the core values being threatened, and the future prospects that are unfolding. And they insist that power concede to their demands. Here, one is reminded of Frederick Douglass's famous 1857 statement about the challenge to slavery: "If there is no struggle there is no progress. Those who profess to favor freedom and yet deprecate agitation are men who want crops without plowing up the ground. They want rain without thunder and lightning. They want the ocean without the awful roar of its many waters. The struggle may be a moral one, or it may be a physical one, or it may be both moral and physical, but it must be a struggle. Power concedes nothing without a demand. It never did and it never will."[3] If progressives hope to succeed, then the movement must capture the spirit of Frederick Douglass.

Throughout this book I have made reference to the various progressive communities. Note the plural. What does not exist yet, and what must now be built with urgency, is a unified progressive community.

When I was dean of Yale's environment school, I was fortunate to have two very bright and thoughtful students, Jeni Krencicki and Dahvi Wilson, spend the better part of 2006 researching and trying to understand why progressives were losing to conservatives across a broad front. In the end, they concluded that progressives suffered from "strategic deficit disorder." They stated the matter very plainly: "Elites within the Progressive movement have failed to develop comprehensive strategies to gain influence and lasting power in American politics over the past several decades. No unified Progressive identity has been developed. Nor have there been any concerted efforts to institutionalize coordination among the various Progressive groups. Instead, strategists have relied on traditional methods of maintaining a loosely connected structure of autonomous activists and organizations. . . . This failure to adapt has reduced the ability of Progressive elites to prevent infighting within the movement and to ensure a high degree of message discipline. Think tank leaders, organizational heads, grassroots organizers, politicians, and Progressive media outlets have neglected to construct an infrastructure capable of developing and promulgating clear policy objectives and strategic messages. They have not invested in the development of training programs to shape their scattering of activists into a cadre of strong messengers. They have proven weak at engaging new constituencies, uninterested in creating any kind of movement larger than a single campaign, and reluctant to adapt to a quickly changing political context."[4]

Netroots leaders Jerome Armstrong and Markos Moulitsas Zúniga reach much the same conclusion: "Members of each group—environmentalists, pro-choice activists, civil libertarians, plaintiffs' attorneys, and so on—promote their agenda above all others and show little or no understanding of the larger progressive values they share with the other groups. And so the whole is never greater than the sum of its parts."[5] *Grist*'s perceptive blogger David Roberts has similarly stressed the need for a unifying narrative among progressives: "We need a new story about the world progressives are trying to build, what they're fighting for, their grand vision of history's direction."[6] Without a coherent progressive message and more powerful progressive movement, it is no wonder that progressive politicians in Washington so often seem lost and feckless.

Wilson and Krencicki noted in 2006 that efforts were under way to address the deficiencies they found. Numerous ad hoc coalitions among progressives have arisen, most often to prevent serious rollbacks in federal programs. Longtime progressive leader Betsy Taylor calls attention to the promising emergence by 2008 of broader efforts such as the Democracy Alliance, America Votes, Center for Progressive Leadership, Campaign for Stronger Democracy, and

Netroots Nation.[7] These efforts and others mentioned below are building the needed progressive infrastructure. Still, Taylor reports, "If we are to build the kind of movement that can not only play defense but actually propel a new vision for our nation, we must try anew to build bridges and deepen our connections across issues and constituencies."[8]

Let's explore, as an example, the gap that now separates two major progressive communities, the liberals focused on issues like social justice, worker rights, and jobs, and my tribe of environmentalists. Many of us, I think, bestride the uneasy gap that separates the two. We have a foot in both camps, and if a pollster asked us, we would say "yes" to liberal and "yes" to environmentalist. Progressive souls in Congress generally support both causes. But between the people and the Congress, organized groups typically advocate for the two causes separately and on their own. That's true of the progressive community as a whole.

There's much less silo-ing on the right, where the typical think tank or advocacy group will address everything from stripping the Environmental Protection Agency of its power to address climate change to ensuring minimal taxes on capital gains.

Clearly, the walls separating social justice liberals and environmentalists must be breached. This progressive fusion is essential, first of all, because both groups are stronger if they support each other. That should be sufficient reason, given the formidable forces both face. But there are deeper realities to consider beyond mere alliance.

For their part, environmentalists need to see that real progress on their issues will remain elusive unless the liberal agenda of social justice and political reform is steadily realized. In a land of pervasive economic insecurity and stark inequality like ours, American environmentalists will keep losing. In such a land, the economic will continue to trump the environmental, and environmentalists will continue to live in a strange place where they can save the planet only if it helps the economy.

Environmentalists need for liberals to succeed, but what about the opposite? Do liberal groups that fight for social and political improvements need for environmentalists to succeed? They do. For example, environmentalists' success in the areas of climate and energy would usher in an era of much-needed growth in the green jobs sector. Also, the new rights-based approach to environmental protection is embracing liberal themes like the right to food and water, the right to cultural survival, and more.

But I would like to stress the liberal stake in environmentalism at a deeper level.

Consider a world in which environmentalists continue to lose on the big issues like climate change. Such a world would be an increasingly nasty place. A world where environmentalists fail is a world of food and clean water shortages, rising sea levels, more and regular heat waves, fires, floods, storms, droughts, and other so-called natural disasters. It is a world of deforestation, desertification, and biotic impoverishment, one choked with pollution and toxins, and suffering from energy shortages and unpleasant surprises. Such a world is not one wherein the concerns of the poor and the powerless or even the average Joe and Jane are likely to fare well.

In recent years, military experts and others have warned repeatedly that climate disruption could lead to humanitarian emergencies, climate refugees, conflicts over water and other resources, failed states, extreme North-South tensions, and any number of further threats to international security and stability. At a minimum, one can conclude that the liberal program—the agenda of democracy, peace, human rights, and social justice—is threatened by unfolding environmental trends. We know that in times of great stress and loss, societies can tend to illiberal "solutions." Liberals need to appreciate how serious and near-term the environmental threats actually are because political and social systems are threatened by climate change, not just ecological ones. Liberals need to recognize that these environmental threats are much too serious to leave to the environmentalists alone.

Once liberals and environmentalists agree they need each other, they need to initiate a serious dialogue on the still-divisive issue of economic growth. More generally, they need to develop a common platform. The two communities need to find a way to champion the goals that liberals see growth as supporting—notably the creation of good jobs—while still accepting the underlying reality that GDP growth in America today isn't delivering on its intended purpose of bettering human lives and that it is, meanwhile, at the root of the emerging climate crisis. A common platform would embrace a profound commitment to social justice, job creation, and environmental protection; a sustained challenge to consumerism and commercialism and the lifestyles they offer; a healthy skepticism of growth mania and a democratic redefinition of what society should be striving to grow; a challenge to corporate dominance and a redefinition of the corporation and its goals; a commitment to an array of prodemocracy reforms in campaign finance, elections, the regulation of lobbying; and much more. A common agenda would also include an ambitious set of new national indicators beyond GDP to inform us of the true quality of life in America.

Coming together is important because all progressive causes face the same reality. We live and work in a system of political economy that cares profoundly about profit and growth and about international power and prestige. It cares about society and the natural world in which it operates primarily to the extent that it is required by law to do so. The progressive mandate is to inject values of justice, democracy, sustainability, and peace into this system. Our best hope for doing this is thus a fusion of those concerned about environment, social justice, true democracy, and peace into one powerful progressive force. We have to recognize that we are all communities of a shared fate. We will rise or fall together, so we'd better get together (see Box 3).

As noted, this process has begun. In addition to the efforts previously mentioned, there are U.S. policy centers whose work spans many progressive causes. The Institute for Policy Studies, Demos, the Center for American Progress, the Campaign for America's Future, the Tellus Institute, and the Progressive Ideas Network come to mind.[9] Preparing the Corporate Strategic Initiative report described in Chapter 7 created synergy among a wide array of individuals and organizations that focus on corporate reform and, in the

BOX 3 **All Together Now:**
Some Areas with Progressive Communities
Active in American Public Affairs

Consumer protection

Political reform

Media reform

Environmental protection

Employment and wages

Antipoverty and equity

Education

Health care

Retirement and income security

Banking and finance reform

Social services and caregiving

Criminal justice

Drug reform

Immigration reform

Animal rights and humane
treatment

Civil rights and liberties

Cities and communities

Corporate reform

Tax reform

Housing

Energy

Agriculture

Science and technology

Transportation

Foreign policy

International development and
justice

Peace and security

Trade

Human rights

International institutions and
governance

Population

Globalization

Labor

Business

Investors

Farmworkers

Minorities

Faith communities

Women

Lesbian, gay, bisexual, and
transgender people

Children

Youth and students

Philanthropy

Seniors

Teachers

Universities and research centers

process, provided a template for collaboration that should be applied in a dozen areas. Efforts like the Blue-Green Alliance and the Apollo Alliance are linking environmental and labor interests, especially around the theme of green jobs.[10] The New Economics Institute, the New Economy Working Group, and the New Economy Network are bringing groups together around many of the themes discussed in this book.[11] MoveOn has proved to be a powerful and durable avenue for progressive action on both policy issues and elections.[12]

Highly promising is the 2011 launch of the American Dream Movement led by MoveOn and the new group that Van Jones has created, Rebuild the Dream. In one of its first actions, the American Dream Movement has framed a Contract for the American Dream, a platform that includes many progressive themes: jobs, clean energy, good schools, health care, labor rights, Social Security, tax fairness, Wall Street reform, peace, and clean and fair elections.[13] The effort is learning a bit from the Tea Party, which, whatever its fate, created an open-source brand that brought together many of the right's libertarian-leaning, antigovernment members and small groups. Not tied to a single individual or led by a central organizational structure, the Tea Party is bound together by determination to cut government spending and to use participation in the electoral process to do it. (Tea Party members, by the way, are right that today's government in Washington is a big problem; they are wrong in not seeing that government can and must be a big part of the solution. Many of its members—frustrated middle-class Americans who have much to gain from good government programs—thus mistakenly lend their weight to those whose great wealth insulates them from the need for government.) And now we have the hope-inspiring developments launched in late 2011 by Occupy Wall Street and carried forward in scores of U.S. cities. The Occupy protests encompass a broad range of grievances. They were preceded by a series of direct action protests against banks and others organized by US Uncut using social networking sites Facebook and Twitter. Internationally, thanks to the work of Bill McKibben and 350.org and other groups around the world, a climate justice movement that fuses a wide variety of progressive causes is gaining strength.[14] The World Social Forum on a regular basis convenes individuals and organizations spanning almost the entire range of progressive concerns. And The Widening Circle campaign of the Tellus Institute and others is bringing together an impressive coalition of international efforts aimed at building a global citizens movement.[15]

An invigorated American progressive movement will also be built on gathered momentum in electoral politics. A big mistake has been made by many progressive groups, including the environmental community where I have worked for several decades. The miscalculation has been to neglect electoral politics, which has played second fiddle (at best) to public education, lobbying, litigating, and working with federal agencies. Progressives now must come together to build a mighty force in electoral politics, strengthening the efforts of America Votes, State Voices, and others.[16] The 2008 Obama campaign shows what can be done. For the progressive movement to secure a powerful place in American politics will require grassroots organizing, strengthening groups working at the state and community levels, reaching out to broaden membership, and developing motivational messages and moral appeals. It will also require building party-like organizations, creating political action committees (PACs), and fielding candidates. As Betsy Taylor puts it, "Our electoral machine must get more horsepower if we hope to succeed."[17]

The language we use and the messages we seek to convey are integral to political success. I can see clearly now that we environmentalists have been too wonkish and too focused on technical fixes. We have not developed the capacity to speak in a language that aims straight at the American heart, resonates with both core moral values and common aspirations, and projects a positive and compelling vision. Throughout my forty-odd years in the environmental community, public discourse on environment has been dominated by lawyers, scientists, and economists. Now we need to hear more from the preachers, the poets, the psychologists, and the philosophers.

Our message must be founded on hope and honest possibility. Alex Steffen of worldchanging.com describes well their importance in sustaining movements: "Cynicism is often seen as a rebellious attitude in Western popular culture, but in reality, our cynicism advances the desires of the powerful. . . . When no one believes there might be a better solution, those who benefit from the status quo are safe. When no one believes in the possibility of action, apathy becomes an insurmountable obstacle to reform. But when people have some intelligent reasons to believe that a better future can be built, that better solutions are available, and that action is possible, their power to act out of their highest principles is unleashed. . . . History attests that if we can show people a better future, we can build movements that will change the world."[18]

An invigorated American progressive movement will be built in communities. Former House Speaker Tip O'Neill famously said, "all politics is local," and a progressive movement must stress building locally, from the bottom up. We all live local lives, and if more and more people are to become engaged politically, engaging them locally is imperative. Most of the promising things happening in America today are happening at the community level, so the case is compelling for linking progressive initiatives at the local level into building a national progressive movement. This is community action melded into a national strategy.[19]

An invigorated American progressive movement will likewise turn its eyes toward the world.[20] There are at least three reasons for the American progressive movement to consider itself sister to similar movements in other countries and, indeed, as part of a global citizens movement. We have, first of all, a lot to learn from other countries. Progressives in Europe and many other places are having more success than American progressives.[21] Close knowledge of what's succeeding abroad as well as personal contacts with progressive leaders abroad can help us make a stronger case at home. Second, progressive groups can draw inspiration from each other. Being part of something bigger and international is empowering for all, and the United States has too often been insular, nurturing a bad, go-it-alone attitude. Finally and most importantly, there is the huge international agenda on which nationally based progressive communities must collaborate—topics like the UN-sponsored climate treaty negotiations, cooperation in support of sustainable human development in the poorer countries, and much more.

An invigorated American progressive movement will help people identify the true victims and villains. Movements gather strength when people realize that they are being victimized and that there are many others in the same boat. Of course it helps when they are also able to identify those responsible for their plight—the villains of the story. Many on the right, like House Majority Leader Eric Cantor, work with consummate cynicism to raise the specter of "class warfare" when, for example, efforts are launched to tax the rich a bit more. With admirable candor, Warren Buffett, an advocate for fairer taxes, has said, "There's class warfare, all right, but it's my class, the rich class, that's making war, and we're winning."[22] In 1936, Harold Laswell wrote *Politics: Who Gets What, When, and How.* He declared that "the study of politics is the study of influence and the influential . . . the influential are those who get the most of what there is to get. . . . Those who get the most are elite; the rest are mass."[23] Today, the elite have gotten about all there is to get, and the great mass of people have gotten the shaft. Progressives need to get a lot better at telling true stories about what's really going on. Consider the multiple scandals and scams inside the whole housing mortgage business, including the millions of victims of the foreclosure crisis. Equally bad are the ways average Americans suffer from acts of corporate greed that are perfectly legal.

An invigorated American progressive movement must also embrace the accumulated knowledge that generations of thoughtful scholars have made possible. With the right seemingly disavowing good science at every turn, it is doubly important that progressives draw heavily on the contributions of our impressive scientific community. The scientific content of public policy issues is increasing steadily, and progressives won't be leading in the right directions without such an embrace. Also, while progressives should encourage both appeals to moral values and kicking up a ruckus, it remains important to ground campaigns in solid analysis, accurate history, and facts. They go together well. As Stephen Colbert has quipped, "The facts have a well-known liberal bias."

In the end, achieving meaningful changes will require a rebirth of marches, protests, demonstrations, direct action, and nonviolent civil disobedience.[24] Leading thinkers on social movements see four roles for social activists, typically with different people in the different roles. Bill Moyer and his colleagues have described these four roles ably: "Social movement activists need first to be seen by the public as responsible *citizens*. They must win the respect and, ultimately, the acceptance of the majority of ordinary citizens in order for their movements to succeed. Consequently, citizen activists need to say 'Yes!' to those fundamental principles, values, and symbols of a good society that are also accepted by the general public. At the same time, activists must be *rebels* who say a loud 'No!' and protest social conditions and institutional policies and practices that violate core societal values and principles. Activists need to be *change agents* who work to educate, organize, and involve the general public to actively oppose present policies and seek positive, constructive solutions. Finally, activists must also be *reformers* who work with the official political and judicial structures to incorporate solutions into new laws and the policies and practices of society's public and private institutions."[25]

Here we are focusing on the rebels. Rebels dramatize issues, show the depth of concern, attract public and media attention, build sympathetic support, and put issues on the agenda. No one who followed recent events in Egypt or at the Wisconsin State House, or who remembers the civil rights and antiwar protests of the 1960s and 1970s, can doubt their importance. "There are no structures or institutions left that have not been contaminated or destroyed by corporations," author and social critic Chris Hedges reminds us. "And this means it is up to us. Civil disobedience, which will entail hardship and suffering, which will be long and difficult, which at its core means self-sacrifice, is the only mechanism left."[26] Those words ring true to those who have worked for decades to elicit a meaningful response to the existential threat of climate change and who find, after all the effort, only ashes.

There are historical circumstances that require the birth of this progressive movement. The widespread persistence of relative poverty at home and absolute poverty abroad, the emerging exhaustion of the planet's renewable and nonrenewable resources, the impossibility of ongoing exponential growth on a finite planet, the destruction of the climate regime that has nurtured human civilization, the drift to militarism and endless war—these warn us that business as usual is not an option. America the Possible awaits us—if we are prepared to struggle, to put it all on the line. I have argued here that the day will come when large numbers of Americans will conclude, with the Howard Beale character in the film *Network*, "I'm mad as hell and I'm not going to take this anymore!" The progressive movement must not only be ready for that day, it must also hasten its arrival.

Here is a good passage on which to end, from the poet Seamus Heaney.[27]

> History says, *Don't hope*
> *On this side of the grave.*
> But then, once in a lifetime
> The longed-for tidal wave
> Of justice can rise up,
> And hope and history rhyme.

Full of hope, it is time to rise up and make history.

Notes

Preface

1. See generally the Occupy website, www.occupytogether.org. See also Sarah van Gelder et al., eds., *This Changes Everything: Occupy Wall Street and the 99% Movement* (San Francisco: Berrett-Koehler, 2011); Nathan Schneider, "From Occupy Wall Street to Occupy Everywhere," *The Nation*, October 31, 2011, 13; Michael Greenberg, "Zuccotti Park: What Future," *The New York Review of Books*, December 8, 2011, 12 (noting that many of the Occupy Wall Street protesters resist traditional politics); and Christopher Ketcham, "The New Populists," *The American Prospect*, January/February 2012, 11.

2. Dee Hock, *Birth of the Chaordic Age* (San Francisco: Berrett-Koehler, 1999), 3.

3. David Suzuki, *The Legacy* (Vancouver: Greystone Books, 2010), 3.

4. Gar Alperovitz, "The New-Economy Movement," *The Nation*, June 13, 2011, 20.

5. "Charter Agreement," New Economy Network, February 9, 2010, http://www.new economynetwork.org/about/about-us/new-economy-network-charter-agreement/.

6. See New Economy Network, www.neweconomynetwork.org; New Economics Institute, www.neweconomicsinstitute.org; New Economy Working Group, www.new economyworkinggroup.org; Institute for Policy Studies, www.ips-dc.org; Demos, www.demos.org; Democracy Collaborative at the University of Maryland, www.democracycollaborative.org; *Yes! Magazine*, www.yesmagazine.org; Center for a New American Dream, www.newdream.org; Capital Institute, www.capitalinstitute.org; *Solutions* journal, www.thesolutionsjournal.com; Tellus Institute, www.tellus.org; Business Alliance for Local Living Economies, www.livingeconomies.org; American Sustainable Business Council, www.asbcouncil.org; and Fourth Sector Network, www.fourthsector.net.

Chapter 1. Manifesto

1. These international comparisons are drawn from OECD, *OECD Factbook 2010* (Paris: OECD, 2010); OECD, *OECD Factbook 2009* (Paris: OECD, 2009); OECD, *Society at a Glance 2011* (Paris: OECD, 2011); *UN Development Programme Human Development Report 2011* (New York: UNDP, 2011); Sarah Burd-Sharps et al., *The Measure of America: American Human Development Report 2008–2009* (New York: Columbia University

Press, 2008); Kristen Lewis and Sarah Burd-Sharps, *The Measure of America, 2010–2011* (New York: New York University Press, 2010); Charles M. Blow, "America's Most Vulnerable," *New York Times,* December 11, 2010, A19, and "Empire at the End of Decadence," *New York Times,* February 18, 2011; Sam Dillon, "Top Test Scores from Shanghai Stun Educators," *New York Times,* December 7, 2010; Richard Wilkinson and Kate Pickett, *The Spirit Level: Why Greater Equality Makes Societies Stronger* (New York: Bloomsbury Press, 2009); *Environmental Performance Index 2012,* www.epi.yale.edu; and "Ecological Footprint Atlas 2010," Global Footprint Network, October 13, 2010, http://www.footprintnetwork.org/images/uploads/Ecological_Footprint_Atlas_ 2010.pdf. For a few indicators such as social mobility, complete country data are not available. U.S. social spending on the disadvantaged is mid-range if private social spending is included.

Huge progress has been made on several fronts in the United States, these negative trends notwithstanding. Between 1960 and 2005, life expectancy grew from seventy to seventy-eight years; the proportion of the population with a high school diploma grew from 41 percent to 84 percent, and the proportion of those with a bachelor's degree grew from 8 percent to 27 percent. See Burd-Sharps et al., *The Measure of America, 2008–2009, 29.*

2. See generally Andrew Glyn, *Capitalism Unleashed: Finance, Globalization and Welfare* (Oxford: Oxford University Press, 2006). President Roosevelt's Second Bill of Rights is discussed in Norton Garfinkle, *The American Dream vs. the Gospel of Wealth* (New Haven: Yale University Press, 2006), 118–121. Garfinkle also discusses the history of the 1980s rebirth of the laissez-faire doctrine of old and the shift of focus from employment to aggregate GDP growth as the main measure of economic health. Garfinkle, *The American Dream,* 144–162. See also William vanden Heuvel, "Eleanor Roosevelt and Her Greatest Achievement," www.theinterdependent.org, Fall 2008, 29; and William Greider, "The Future of the American Dream," *The Nation,* May 25, 2009, 11.

3. Paul A. Samuelson and William D. Nordhaus, *Macroeconomics,* 17th ed. (Boston: McGraw-Hill Irwin, 2001), 409.

4. Robert Dallek, *The Lost Peace: Leadership in a Time of Horror and Hope, 1945–1953* (New York: HarperCollins, 2010). See also Derek Leebaert, *The Fifty-Year Wound: The True Price of America's Cold War Victory* (Boston: Little, Brown, 2002); William Pfaff, *The Irony of Manifest Destiny: The Tragedy of America's Foreign Policy* (New York: Walker, 2010); Andrew Bacevich, *American Empire: The Realities and Consequences of U.S. Diplomacy* (Cambridge, MA: Harvard University Press, 2002); and James Carroll, *House of War* (Boston: Houghton Mifflin, 2006).

5. See generally Samuel Bowles et al., *Understanding Capitalism: Competition, Command, and Change* (New York: Oxford University Press, 2005). See also Peter A. Hall and David Soskice, eds., *Varieties of Capitalism* (Oxford: Oxford University Press, 2001); Colin Cronch and Wolfgang Streeck, *Political Economy of Modern Capitalism* (London: Sage, 1997); and David Harvey, *The Enigma of Capital* (Oxford: Oxford University Press, 2010).

6. See Tim Jackson, *Prosperity Without Growth: Economics of a Finite Planet* (London: Earthscan, 2009); Peter Victor, *Managing Without Growth* (Northampton, MA: Edward Elgar, 2008); Stephen Spratt et al., *The Great Transition* (London: New Economics Foundation, 2009); Peter Brown and Geoffrey Garver, *Right Relationship: Building a*

Whole Earth Economy (San Francisco: Berrett-Koehler, 2009); Herman E. Daly, *Beyond Growth* (Boston: Beacon Press, 1996) (to whom we are all indebted); Clive Hamilton, *Growth Fetish* (London: Pluto Press, 2004); David C. Korten, *Agenda for a New Economy* (San Francisco: Berrett-Koehler, 2010); and Andrew Simms et al., *Growth Isn't Possible: Why We Need a New Economic Direction* (London: New Economics Foundation, 2010). See also Robert Costanza, "Stewardship for a 'Full' World," *Current History*, January 2008, 30; and R. Beddoe et al., "Overcoming Systemic Roadblocks to Sustainability: The Evolutionary Redesign of Worldviews, Institutions and Technologies," *Proceedings of the National Academy of Sciences* 106 (2009): 2483–2489. And see John de Graaf and Dave Batker, "What's the Economy for, Anyway?" at www.bullfrogfilms.com. The challenge to growth is not new. See, e.g., E. J. Mishan, *The Cost of Economic Growth* (Harmondsworth, U.K.: Penguin, 1969); Donella Meadows et al., *The Limits to Growth* (New York: Signet, 1972); Herman E. Daly, ed., *Toward a Steady-State Economy* (San Francisco: W. H. Freeman, 1973); and Fred Hirsch, *Social Limits to Growth* (Cambridge, MA: Harvard University Press, 1976).

7. Thomas L. Friedman, *The Lexus and the Olive Tree* (New York: Anchor, 2000).

8. "Calling Corporate Social Responsibility to Account," Trucost, London, United Kingdom, May 7, 2010; Sarah Terry Cobo, "The Environmental Costs of Doing Business Could Erase a Third of Corporations' Profits," AlterNet, March 23, 2010, http://www.alternet.org/story/146050.

9. Karl Polanyi, *The Great Transformation: The Political and Economic Origins of Our Time* (Boston: Beacon Press, 1944), 3, 73, 131.

10. See generally Medard Gabel and Henry Bruner, *Global Inc.: An Atlas of the Multinational Corporation* (New York: New Press, 2003), 2–3. See also John Cavanagh et al., *Alternatives to Economic Globalization* (San Francisco: Berrett-Koehler, 2002); and Richard J. Barnet and Ronald E. Muller, *Global Reach* (New York: Simon and Schuster, 1974).

11. Juliet Schor, *The Overworked American: The Unexpected Decline of Leisure* (New York: Basic Books, 1992). See James Gustave Speth, *The Bridge at the Edge of the World: Capitalism, the Environment, and Crossing from Crisis to Sustainability* (New Haven: Yale University Press, 2008), 126–164, and the works cited there. See also Benjamin R. Barber, *Consumed* (New York: Norton, 2007); and The Worldwatch Institute, *State of the World 2010: Transforming Cultures, from Consumerism to Sustainability* (New York: Norton, 2010).

12. See Chapter 3. On soft power, see Joseph S. Nye, Jr., *Soft Power: The Means to Success in World Politics* (New York: Public Affairs, 2004).

13. David Korten, *How to Liberate America from Wall Street Rule*, A Report of the New Economy Working Group, July 2011. See www.neweconomyworkinggroup.org. There are numerous interesting books on the subject of money and finance. See, e.g., Mike Nickerson, *Life, Money and Illusion* (Lanark, ON: Seven Generations, 2006); Thomas H. Greco, Jr., *The End of Money and the Future of Civilization* (White River Junction, VT: Chelsea Green, 2009); Bernard Lietaer, *The Future of Money* (New York: Random House, 2002); and Ellen Hodgson Brown, *The Web of Debt* (Baton Rouge: Third Millennium Press, 2008). See also Korten, *Agenda for a New Economy;* and Woody Tasch, *Slow Money* (White River Junction, VT: Chelsea Green, 2008). See also the discussions on the site of The Capital Institute, www.capitalinstitute.org.

14. See Rainforest Action Network, www.ran.org. See also Nick Mathiason, "Banks Attacked for Failure to Meet Equator Principles on Environment," *The Guardian*, January 14, 2010, http://www.guardian.co.uk/business/2010/jan/14/equator-principles-banks-environment-campaigners.

15. William Greider, *The Soul of Capitalism: Opening Paths to a Moral Economy* (New York: Simon and Schuster, 2003), 32.

16. Richard A. Rosen et al., *Global Scenarios for the Century Ahead: Searching for Sustainability* (Boston: Tellus Institute, 2010), 3–4, 14. See also Spratt et al., *The Great Transition;* and Paul D. Raskin, "World Lines: A Framework for Exploring Global Pathways," *Ecological Economics* 65 (2008): 461.

17. See James Gustave Speth, "Towards a New Economy and a New Politics," *Solutions* no. 5, May 28, 2010, http://www.thesolutionsjournal.com/node/619; Costanza, "Stewardship for a 'Full' World," 30–35; and William E. Rees, "Achieving Sustainability," *Journal of Planning Literature* 9, no. 4 (May 1995): 343. Two important statements of the need for a new economic paradigm are Brown and Garver, *Right Relationship*, and Korten, *Agenda for a New Economy*. See also Robert H. Frank, *The Darwin Economy* (Princeton, NJ: Princeton University Press, 2011) (arguing that there can be no presumption that market competition promotes the public good).

18. Societal collapses have occurred throughout history. See, e.g., Joseph A. Tainter, *The Collapse of Complex Societies* (Cambridge: Cambridge University Press, 1988); and Jared Diamond, *Collapse: How Societies Choose to Fail or Succeed* (New York: Viking, 2005). But as Paul Raskin has stressed, the point of crisis can also open possibilities for profound improvement: "Past structures drive the present into an uncertain future; human vision and action pull the present toward imagined futures. Through the interaction between determination and choice, systems can bifurcate into distinctly different states. . . . Similarly, our planetary system can branch discontinuously into alternate global trajectories. In these decades of transition, we have amplified influence on the kind of world that consolidates out of the turbulence of change. We will squander this moral responsibility and pragmatic opportunity if collectively we are too complacent, too cynical, and too timid. We can seize it with a richness of vision and boldness of action." Paul D. Raskin, "Planetary Praxis," in Stephen R. Kellert and James Gustave Speth, eds., *The Coming Transformation* (New Haven: Yale School of Forestry and Environmental Studies, 2009), 130.

   Immanuel Wallerstein, the father of World System Analysis, believes, "The first [premise] is that historical systems, like all systems, have finite lives. They have beginnings, a long development, and finally, as they move far from equilibrium and reach points of bifurcation, a demise. . . . The modern world-system, as a historical system, has entered into a terminal crisis and is unlikely to exist in fifty years." Immanuel Wallerstein, *The End of the World as We Know It* (Minneapolis: University of Minnesota Press, 1999), 1.

19. See note 18, Chapter 5. Regarding postapocalypse fiction, see, e.g., Jim Crace, *The Pesthouse* (New York: Vintage, 2007); James Howard Kunstler, *World Made by Hand* (New York: Grove Press, 2008); Margaret Atwood, *Oryx and Crake* (New York: Anchor, 2003) and *The Year of the Flood* (New York: Anchor, 2009); Cormac McCarthy, *The Road* (New York: Vintage, 2007); and Nick Harkaway, *The Gone-Away World* (New York: Vintage, 2008).

20. Rebecca Solnit, *Hope in the Dark* (New York: Penguin, 2006), 164.

21. See Gar Alperovitz, *America Beyond Capitalism* (Hoboken, NJ: John Wiley, 2005), 1–5. David Harvey's analysis is instructive. "Can the capitalist class reproduce its power in the face of the raft of economic, social, political and geopolitical and environmental difficulties? Again, the answer is a resounding 'Yes it can.' This will, however, require the mass of the people to give generously of the fruits of their labour to those in power, to surrender many of their rights and their hard-won asset values (in everything from housing to pension rights) and to suffer environmental degradations galore, to say nothing of serial reductions in their living standards which will mean starvation for many of those already struggling to survive at rock bottom. . . . Conventional mantras regarding the perfectibility of humanity with the help of free markets and free trade, private property and personal responsibility and low taxes and minimalist state involvement in social provision sound increasingly hollow. A crisis of legitimacy looms." Harvey, *The Enigma of Capital*, 215–217.

22. See, e.g., Raskin, "World Lines: A Framework for Exploring Global Pathways," 461–470; and Thomas Homer-Dixon, "One Panarchic Future," *World Watch*, March/April 2009, 8, and "When Wise Words Are Not Enough," *Nature* 458 (2009): 284–285.

23. John Maynard Keynes, "Economic Possibilities for Our Grandchildren," in Keynes, *Essays in Persuasion* (1933; repr. New York: Norton, 1963), 365–373.

Chapter 2. Society at the Breaking Point

1. U.S. Census Bureau, *Current Population Survey, 1960 to 2011 Annual Social and Economic Supplements*, http://www.census.gov/prod/2011pubs/p60-239.pdf.

2. U.S. Census Bureau, "Income, Poverty and Health Insurance Coverage in the United States: 2010," news release, September 13, 2011.

3. The U.S. Census Bureau's Supplemental Poverty Measure for 2010 is at http://www.census.gov/newsroom/releases/pdf/2011-11-07_spm1_slides.pdf.

4. Tony Pugh, "U.S. Economy Leaving Record Numbers in Severe Poverty," *McClatchy Newspapers*, February 22, 2007.

5. Charles M. Blow, "Suffer the Little Children," *New York Times*, December 24, 2010 (citing UNICEF, *Child Poverty in Perspective: An Overview of Child Well-Being in Rich Countries* 6 [2007], http://www.unicef-irc.org/publications/pdf/rc7_eng.pdf); National Center for Children in Poverty, *Who Are America's Poor Children?*, http://www.nccp.org/publications/pdf/text_1001.pdf; Center for American Progress, *From Poverty to Prosperity*, April 2007, 11, http://www.americanprogress.org/issues/2007/04/pdf/poverty_report.pdf; and Sabrina Tavernise, "Soaring Poverty Cast Spotlight on 'Lost Decade,'" *New York Times*, September 13, 2011.

6. Mica Panic, "Child Poverty Exposes the Anglo-American Model, " *Financial Times*, April 2, 2007, 13. See also Nicholas Bakalar, "Researchers Link Deaths to Social Ills," *New York Times*, July 4, 2011.

7. "Hunger and Food Stamps," editorial, *New York Times*, May 13, 2007, 11.

8. Jason DeParle, "Hunger in U.S. at a 14-Year High," *New York Times*, November 17, 2009. About forty-six million Americans use food stamps on any given day. See Lizzy Ratner, "Food Stamps vs. Poverty," *The Nation*, January 2, 2012, 12.

9. Barbara Ehrenreich, "Is It Now a Crime to Be Poor?" *New York Times*, August 9, 2009.

10. Center for American Progress, *From Poverty to Prosperity*, 11.

11. OECD, *OECD Factbook, 2009* (Paris: OECD, 2009), 287.

12. Jacob S. Hacker, *The Great Risk Shift* (New York: Oxford University Press, 2006, 2008), xv.

13. Hacker, *The Great Risk Shift*, Chapter 1.

14. Jennifer Wheary et al., *By a Thread: The New Experience of America's Middle Class* (New York: Demos, 2007), 7. See also Motoko Rich, "Economic Insecurity," *New York Times*, November 22, 2011.

15. Sarah Burd-Sharps, *The Measure of America: The American Human Development Report, 2008–2009* (New York: Columbia University Press, 2008), 129.

16. "Nearly Half of Americans Are 'Financially Fragile,'" *Wall Street Journal*, May 23, 2011; and Motoko Rich, "Many Low-Wage Jobs Seen as Failing to Meet Basic Needs," *New York Times*, March 31, 2011. See also Peter Gosselin, *High Wire: The Precarious Financial Lives of American Families* (New York: Basic Books, 2008).

17. Richard Eskow, "By the Time You Read This: Why the Mortgage Crisis Dwarfs Almost Everything Else," Campaign for America's Future, March 31, 2011, http://www.ourfuture.org/blog-entry/2011031331/time-you-read-why-mortgage-crisis-dwarfs-almost-everything.

18. James K. Galbraith, "Attack on the Middle Class!" *Mother Jones*, November/December 2010, 27; Richard McCormack, "The Plight of American Manufacturing," *The American Prospect*, January/February 2010, A2; and Michael Snyder, "Ten Signs That Our Nation Is Becoming Poorer," AlterNet, January 4, 2011, http://www.alternet.org/story/149405.

19. David Wessel, "U.S. Firms Keen to Add Foreign Jobs," *Wall Street Journal*, November 22, 2011.

20. See Emmanuel Saez's website, University of California, Berkeley, http://www.econ.berkeley.edu/~saez/TabFig2008.xls. See also "One Nation, Divisible," *The Economist*, November 20, 2010, 33; Bill Moyers, "Welcome to the Plutocracy!," Address at Boston University, October 29, 2010, http://archive.truthout.org/bill-moyers-money-fights-hard-and-it-fights-dirty64766. See also Sabrina Tavernise, "Soaring Poverty Casts Spotlight on 'Lost Decade,'" *New York Times*, September 13, 2011, reporting that median income of male full-time workers fell about $1,000 between 1973 and 2010.

21. Jason DeParle et al., "Older, Suburban and Struggling, 'Near Poor' Startle the Census," *New York Times*, November 18, 2011; and "Bordering on Poverty," *New York Times*, November 18, 2011.

22. Motoko Rich, "Jobs Report Offers a Mixed Bag, but Little Comfort," *New York Times*, February 4, 2011; "The Jobs Crisis," editorial, *New York Times*, September 3, 2011; Michael Lind, "That Sound You Hear Is the Social Fabric About to Snap," Salon.com, October 19, 2009, http://www.salon.com/opinion/feature/2009/10/19/jobs/print.html.

23. Andy Kroll, "How the McEconomy Bombed the American Worker," TomDispatch.com, May 8, 2011, http://www.tomdispatch.com/blog/175389.

24. Steven Hill, *Europe's Promise: Why the European Way Is the Best Hope in an Insecure Age* (Berkeley: University of California Press, 2010), 101, 121.

25. OECD, *Society at a Glance 2009* (Paris: OECD, 2009), 97.

26. "In the Shadow of Prosperity," *The Economist*, January 20, 2007, 32.

27. Eduardo Porter, "A Bridge Over the Atlantic, in Labor Policy," *New York Times*, April 1, 2007, 5.

28. Paul Krugman, "Learning from Europe," *New York Times*, January 11, 2010.

29. Economic Policy Institute, *The State of Working America 2006/2007* (Ithaca, NY: Cornell University Press, 2007), 146.

30. Economic Policy Institute, *The State of Working America 2011*, updated December 3, 2010, http://www.stateofworkingamerica.org/charts/view/82.

31. Robert Pear, "Top Income Earners Doubled Share of Nation's Income, Study Finds," *New York Times*, October 25, 2011.

32. Robert Reich, "Inequality in America and What to Do About It," *The Nation*, July 19–26, 2010, 13. Income shares at the top declined somewhat with the recession that began in 2008, but much of that decline has been regained.

33. John Cavanagh and Chuck Collins, "The New Inequality," *The Nation*, June 30, 2008, 11.

34. G. William Domhoff, "Wealth, Income and Power," July 2011, http://sociology.ucsc.edu/whorulesamerica/power/wealth.html.

35. Nicholas D. Kristof, "Our Banana Republic," *New York Times*, November 6, 2010. See also Peter Whoriskey, "Income Gap Widens as CEO's Thrive," *Washington Post*, reprinted in *Valley News*, June 26, 2011, C1.

36. Chuck Collins et al., "Shifting Responsibility: How 50 Years of Tax Cuts Benefited the Wealthiest Americans," Wealth for the Common Good, April 7, 2010, http://wealthforcommongood.org/shifting-responsibility/.

37. Richard Wilkinson and Kate Pickett, *The Spirit Level: Why Greater Equality Makes Societies Stronger* (New York: Bloomsbury Press, 2009), 173.

38. Wilkinson and Pickett, *The Spirit Level*, 174.

39. Wilkinson and Pickett, *The Spirit Level*, 159–160. See also Jason DeParle, "Harder for Americans to Rise from Lower Rungs," *New York Times*, January 4, 2012.

40. Jacob Hacker and Paul Pierson, *Winner-Take-All Politics: How Washington Made the Rich Richer—and Turned Its Back on the Middle Class* (New York: Simon and Schuster, 2010). See also Robert Lieberman, "Why the Rich Are Getting Richer," *Foreign Affairs*, January/February 2011, 155.

41. Reich, "Inequality in America and What to Do About It," 14.

42. Robert D. Putnam et al., *Better Together: Restoring the American Community* (New York: Simon and Schuster, 2003), 4. See also Robert D. Putnam, *Bowling Alone* (New York: Simon and Schuster, 2000).

43. Shankar Vedantam, "Study: Social Isolation Up," *Washington Post*, reprinted in *(Charleston, SC) Post and Courier*, June 24, 2006, 6 A.

44. Putnam, *Bowling Alone*, 139–140.

45. Ben Schott, "Who Do You Think We Are?" *New York Times*, February 25, 2007, 15.

46. Eric M. Uslaner, *The Moral Foundations of Trust* (Cambridge: Cambridge University Press, 2002), 33, 181.

47. Bruce Judson, *It Could Happen Here: America on the Brink* (New York: HarperCollins, 2009), 171.

48. Laura MacInnis, "U.S. Most Armed Country with 90 Guns per 100 People," Reuters, August 28, 2007.

49. Bob Herbert, "A Flood Tide of Murder," *New York Times*, January 10, 2010.

50. "Empathy: College Students Don't Have as Much as They Used To," University of Michigan Institute for Social Research, May 27, 2010.

51. John Fritze, "Medical Expenses Have 'Very Steep Rate of Growth,'" *USA Today*, February 4, 2010, 6A.

52. Editorial, "Bleak News on Health Insurance," *New York Times*, September 14, 2011.

53. Michael Mandel, "What's Really Propping Up the Economy," *Business Week*, September 25, 2006, 55.

54. Sam Dillon, "Top Test Scores from Shanghai Stun Educators," *New York Times*, December 7, 2010.

55. Amanda Ripley, "Your Child Left Behind," *The Atlantic*, December 2010, 94.

56. Michael E. Porter, "Why America Needs an Economic Strategy," *Business Week*, November 10, 2008, 42; Tamar Lewin, "Once a Leader, U.S. Lags in College Degrees," *New York Times*, July 23, 2010.

57. Burd-Sharps, *The Measure of America, 2008–2009*, 108.

58. See, e.g., John Hechinger, "U.S. Students Lacking History Knowledge Test Shows," *Valley News*, June 15, 2011; and Winnie Hu, "Geography Report Card Finds Students Lagging," *New York Times*, July 19, 2011.

59. Sharon Otterman, "Most New York Students Are Not College Ready," *New York Times*, February 7, 2011.

60. Motoko Rich, "Jobs Report Offers a Mixed Bag, but Little Comfort," *New York Times*, February 4, 2011; "The Trap," *The Economist*, January 16, 2010, 32.

61. Bill Marsh, "Jobless, Sleepless, Hopeless," *New York Times*, September 6, 2009; Michael Luo and Megan Thee-Brenan, "Poll Reveals Trauma of Joblessness in U.S.," *New York Times*, December 15, 2009.

62. Motoko Rich, "For the Unemployed Over 50, Fears of Never Working Again," *New York Times*, September 19, 2010.

63. Harold Meyerson, "Employers Profit as Workers Languish," *Washington Post*, reprinted in *Valley News*, September 8, 2010, A 6; Simon Johnson, "Employment vs. Corporate Profit," *New York Times*, January 17, 2011; Catherine Rampell, "U.S. Economic Growth Bounces Back to Rate Seen Before Recession," *New York Times*, January 29, 2011, B 1; Motoko Rich, "Weighing Costs, Companies Favor Temporary Help," *New York Times*, December 19, 2010.

64. Paul Krugman, "Defining Prosperity Down," *New York Times*, August 1, 2010.

65. Charles M. Blow, "America's Most Vulnerable," *New York Times*, December 11, 2010, based on UNICEF, *The Children Left Behind* (New York: UNICEF, 2010).

66. Marque-Luisa Miringoff and Sandra Opdycke, *America's Social Health* (Armonk, NY: M. E. Sharpe, 2008), 221. Better reporting is likely also involved here.

67. "In Numbers," *The Atlantic*, January/February 2010, 57.

68. Richard Louv, *Last Child in the Woods* (Chapel Hill, NC: Algonquin Books, 2005). See also Stephen R. Kellert, *Building for Life* (Washington, DC: Island Press, 2005), 9–89.

69. Timothy Eagan, "The Rise of Shrinking-Vacation Syndrome," *New York Times*, August 20, 2006.

70. Charles M. Blow, "Suffer the Little Children," *New York Times*, December 24, 2010.

71. Burd-Sharps et al., *The Measure of America, 2008–2009*, 142.

72. Peter Goodman, "Despite Signs of Recovery, Chronic Joblessness Rises," *New York Times*, February 21, 2010; Peter Coy, "The Lost Generation," *Business Week*, October 19, 2009, 33; Lizzy Ratner, "Generation Recession," *The Nation*, November 23, 2009, 23.

73. Terrance Heath, "The Black Unemployment Epidemic, Part 1," OurFuture.org, May 12, 2011, http://www.ourfuture.org/blog-entry/2011051913/black-unemployment-epidemic-pt-1.

74. Burd-Sharps et al., *The Measure of America, 2008–2009*, 142. See generally "Mass Incarceration in America," *American Prospect*, January/February 2010.

75. See the articles in "Special Report: State of Denial," *New Scientist*, May 15, 2010, 35–45.

76. Jerry Coyne, "Selling Science," *Science* 325 (2009): 678–679.

77. Gillian Tett, "Why Has America Fallen Out of Love with Science?" *Financial Times*, November 26, 2011, 8.

78. Coyne, "Selling Science," 678.

79. Naomi Oreskes and Erik M. Conway, *Merchants of Doubt* (New York: Bloomsbury Press, 2010), 6, 267. See also James Hoggan, *Climate Cover-Up* (Vancouver: Greystone Books, 2009); and Howard Friel, *The Lomborg Deception* (New Haven: Yale University Press, 2010). And see Al Gore, "Climate of Denial," *Rolling Stone*, June 7–21, 2011, 76; Thomas L. Friedman, "Is It Weird Enough Yet?" *New York Times*, September 13, 2011; and Editorial, "In the Land of Denial," *New York Times*, September 6, 2011. See generally Chris Mooney and Sheril Kirshenbaum, *Unscientific America* (New York: Basic Books, 2009); and Chris Mooney, *The Republican War on Science* (New York: Basic Books, 2005).

80. Mark Buchanan, "Gimme Money, That's What I Want," *New Scientist*, March 21, 2009, 27. See also Paul Sullivan, "Net Worth, Self-Worth and How We Look at Money," *New York Times*, May 6, 2011.

81. Barbara Ehrenreich, *This Land Is Their Land* (New York: Henry Holt, 2008), 4.

82. See Jerry W. Markham, *A Financial History of Modern U.S. Corporate Scandals* (Armonk, NY: M. E. Sharpe, 2005); and Judith Warner, "Dysregulation Nation," *New York Times Magazine*, June 20, 2010, 11. See also James Stewart, *Tangled Webs: How False Statements Are Undermining America* (New York: Penguin, 2011); Rick Perlstein, "Fact-Free Nation," *Mother Jones*, May/June 2011, 25; and Harriet Fraad, "American Depressions," *Tikkum*, January/February 2010. On insider trading, see "Tipping the Scales," *The Economist*, October 15, 2011, 83. Interestingly, catastrophes like floods, bombings, and earthquakes seem to reconstitute community. See Rebecca Solnit, *A Paradise Built in Hell* (New York: Viking, 2009).

83. David Callahan, "The Moral Market," DemocracyJournal.org, Summer 2009, 51–52, http://www.democracyjournal.org/13/6690.php?page=all.

84. "Confronting the Monster," *The Economist*, November 20, 2010, 29.

85. Mark Lander, "Chinese Savings Helped Inflate American Bubble," *New York Times*, December 26, 2008.

Chapter 3. The Weight of the World

1. Leslie H. Gelb, "GDP Now Matters More Than Force," *Foreign Affairs*, November/December 2010, 38. See also Michael Mandelbaum, *The Case for Goliath: How America*

Acts as the World's Government in the Twenty-first Century (New York: Public Affairs, 2005).

2. The books on this theme are legion. For example, see Paul Kennedy, *The Rise and Fall of the Great Powers* (New York: Vintage, 1989); Andrew J. Bacevich, *American Empire: The Realities and Consequences of U.S. Diplomacy* (Cambridge, MA: Harvard University Press, 2002); Niall Ferguson, *Colossus* (New York: Penguin, 2004); Jim Garrison, *America as Empire* (San Francisco: Berrett-Koehler, 2004); Amitai Etzioni, *From Empire to Community* (New York: Palgrave MacMillan, 2004); Richard A. Falk, *The Declining World Order* (London: Routledge, 2004); Alice H. Amsden, *Escape from Empire* (Cambridge, MA: MIT Press, 2007); Tom Engelhardt, ed., *The World According to Tom Dispatch* (New York: Verso, 2008); David P. Calleo, *Follies of Power* (Cambridge: Cambridge University Press, 2009); William Pfaff, *The Irony of Manifest Destiny: The Tragedy of America's Foreign Policy* (New York: Walker, 2010); Dilip Hiro, *After Empire* (New York: Nation Books, 2010); Chalmers Johnson, *Dismantling the Empire* (New York: Henry Holt, 2010); and Richard H. Immerman, *Empire for Liberty* (Princeton, NJ: Princeton University Press, 2010).

3. See http://www.sipri.org/research/armaments/milex/factsheet2010.

4. Chris Hellman, "$1.2 Trillion: The Real National Security Budget No One Wants You to Know About," March 1, 2011, http://www.alternet.org/story/150086; and Robert Higgs, "Defense Spending Is Much Greater Than You Think," The Independent Institute, April 17, 2010, http//blog.independent.org/2010/04/17/defense-spending-is-much-greater-than-you-think.

5. Discretionary spending here is federal spending after entitlements and interest on the debt are subtracted.

6. This estimate, by the Watson Institute for International Studies at Brown University, is reported in *The American Prospect*, September 2011, 31. See also Joseph E. Stiglitz and Linda J. Bilmers, *The Three Trillion Dollar War* (New York: Norton, 2008).

7. Nick Turse, "Empire of Bases 2.0," TomDispatch.com, January 9, 2011, http://www.tomdispatch.com/blog/175338. See also Andrew J. Bacevich, *Washington Rules: America's Path to Permanent War* (New York: Henry Holt, 2010), 25–26.

8. Thom Shanker, "Despite Slump, U.S. Role as Top Arms Supplier Grows," *New York Times*, September 7, 2009.

9. Tom Engelhardt, "A World Made by War," TomDispatch.com, October 17, 2010, http://www.tomdispatch.com/blog/175308.

10. William Hartung, *Prophets of War: Lockheed Martin and the Making of the Military Industrial Complex* (New York: Nation Books, 2011).

11. Andrew J. Bacevich, "The Tyranny of Defense, Inc.," *The Atlantic*, January/February 2011, 79.

12. Dana Priest and William M. Arkin, "A Hidden World, Growing Beyond Control," *Washington Post*, July 19, 2010.

13. Dana Priest and William M. Arkin, "Monitoring America," *Washington Post*, December 20, 2010. See also Ginger Thompson and Scott Shane, "Cables Portray Expanded Reach of Drug Agency," *New York Times*, December 25, 2010.

14. William Pfaff, "Manufacturing Insecurity: How Militarism Endangers America," *Foreign Affairs*, November/December 2010, 133.

15. Chalmers Johnson, *Blowback* (New York: Henry Holt, 2000), *The Sorrows of Empire* (New York: Henry Holt, 2004), and *Nemesis* (New York: Henry Holt, 2007).

16. Johnson, *Nemesis*, 3.

17. Johnson, *Nemesis*, 6–7.

18. Johnson, *The Sorrows of Empire*, 39–65. William Astore points out that militarism is broader than jackboots and kamikazes and describes as well "a situation in which a country's civil society and political culture are permeated to the point of dominance by military attitudes and values." William Astore, "The Militarization of America," AlterNet, June 14, 2011, http://www.alternet.org/story/151291/the_militarization_of_america%3A_how_the_military_mindset_is_permeating_our_political_culture_and_society.

19. Nicholas D. Kristof, "The Big (Military) Taboo," *New York Times*, December 26, 2010, 16.

20. Pfaff, "Manufacturing Insecurity," 140.

21. Michael T. Klare, *Resource Wars: The New Landscape of Global Conflict* (New York: Henry Holt, 2001); Diane Raines Ward, *Water Wars: Drought, Flood, Folly, and the Politics of Thirst* (New York: Penguin Putnam, 2002); and Gwynne Dyer, *Climate Wars: The Fight for Survival as the World Overheats* (Oxford: Oneworld, 2010).

22. Johnson, *Nemesis;* Garry Wills, *Bomb Power: The Modern Presidency and the National Security State* (New York: Penguin, 2010).

23. Chalmers Johnson, "Empire vs. Democracy," TomPaine.com, January 31, 2007, http://www.tompaine.com/print/empire_vs_democracy.php. On the "imperial presidency" and its future, see Bruce Ackerman, *The Decline and Fall of the American Republic* (Cambridge, MA: Harvard University Press, 2010); and Frederick A. O. Schwarz, Jr., and Aziz Z. Huq, *Unchecked and Unbalanced: Presidential Power in a Time of Terror* (New York: New Press, 2007).

24. David K. Shipler, *The Rights of the People* (New York: Alfred A. Knopf, 2011). See also "Backward at the FBI," *New York Times*, June 19, 2011, Sunday Opinion, 7; and Jonathan Turley, "America Can No Longer Claim to Be the Land of the Free," *Washington Post*, reprinted in *Valley News*, January 29, 2012, F3.

25. Chris Hedges, "The Disease of Permanent War," Truthdig, May 18, 2009, http://www.truthdig.com/report/item/20090518_the_disease_of_permanent_war. See also Jane Mayer, *The Dark Side: The Inside Story of How the War on Terror Turned into a War on American Ideals* (New York: Doubleday, 2008); and Jeremy Scahill, *Blackwater: The Rise of the World's Most Powerful Mercenary Army* (New York: Nation Books, 2007).

26. Chalmers Johnson, "It's the Beginning of the End for the American Empire," AlterNet, August 17, 2010, http://www.alternet.org/story/147880.

27. Pfaff, "Manufacturing Insecurity," 140.

28. See, e.g., Michael Mandelbaum, *The Frugal Superpower* (New York: PublicAffairs, 2010); Gelb, "GDP Now Matters More Than Force"; Roger C. Altman and Richard N. Haass, "American Profligacy and American Power," *Foreign Affairs*, November/December 2010.

29. Gelb, "GDP Now Matters More Than Force," 35–37.

30. Mandelbaum, *The Frugal Superpower*, 30.

31. James Gustave Speth, *Red Sky at Morning: America and the Crisis of the Global Environment* (New Haven: Yale University Press, 2004), 110–111.

32. Robert Gates, "Helping Others Defend Themselves," *Foreign Affairs*, May/June 2010.

33. See generally Population Action International, *Why Population Matters* (Washington, DC: Population Action International, 2011). See also Juliet Eilperin, "Population Growth Taxing Planet's Resources," *Washington Post*, October 23, 2011.

34. National Intelligence Council, *Global Trends 2015*, December 2000, 27–28, http://www.cia.gov/cia/publications/globaltrends2015/index.html. See also Misha Glenny, *McMafia: A Journey Through the Global Criminal Underworld* (New York: Knopf, 2008).

35. Rosaleen Duffy, "Your Role in Wildlife Crime," *New Scientist*, September 11, 2010, 28; "Bluefin Tuna Decline Fueled by $4 Billion Black Market," *Yale Environment 360*, November 8, 2010.

36. "No Stopping Them," *The Economist*, February 5, 2011, 69.

37. See Ken Ellingwood and Brian Bennett, "High-Profile Panel Urges Non-Criminal Approach to World Drug Policy," *Los Angeles Times*, June 1, 2011; Jimmy Carter, "Call Off the Drug War," *New York Times*, June 17, 2011, A31; Charles M. Blow, "Drug Bust," *New York Times*, June 10, 2011; "At Last, a Border Crackdown," editorial, *New York Times*, December 24, 2010; Jorge G. Castaneda, "What's Spanish for Quagmire?" *Foreign Policy*, January/February 2010, 78; Sam Quinones, "State of War," *Foreign Policy*, March/April 2009, 77; and James C. McKinley, Jr., and Marc Lacey, "Along the U.S.-Mexico Border, a Torrent of Illicit Cash," *New York Times*, December 26, 2009.

38. Mandelbaum, *The Frugal Superpower*, 7.

Chapter 4. Running Out of Planet

1. J. R. McNeill, *Something New Under the Sun: An Environmental History of the Twentieth-Century World* (New York: Norton, 2000), 334–336.

2. I have covered this territory in two books, in 2004 and 2008. James Gustave Speth, *Red Sky at Morning: America and the Crisis of the Global Environment* (New Haven: Yale University Press, 2004) and *The Bridge at the Edge of the World: Capitalism, the Environment, and Crossing from Crisis to Sustainability* (New Haven: Yale University Press, 2008). There are many excellent books on our environmental challenges. See, e.g., Paul Ehrlich and Anne Ehrlich, *One with Nineveh* (Washington, DC: Island Press, 2004); Lester R. Brown, *Plan B 4.0* (New York: Norton, 2009); Ross Gelbspan, *Boiling Point* (New York: Basic Books, 2004); Dianne Dumanoski, *The End of the Long Summer* (New York: Crown, 2009); Al Gore, *Our Choice* (Emmaus, PA: Rodale, 2009); Paul Gilding, *The Great Disruption* (New York: Bloomsbury, 2011); and Larry J. Schweiger, *Last Chance* (Golden, CO: Fulcrum, 2009). On the climate threat, see particularly David W. Orr, *Down to the Wire* (New York: Oxford University Press, 2009); Mark Hertsgaard, *Hot* (New York: Houghton Mifflin, 2011); and James Hansen, *Storms of My Grandchildren* (New York: Bloomsbury, 2010).

3. Millennium Ecosystem Assessment (MEA), *Ecosystems and Human Well-Being: Synthesis* (Washington, DC: Island Press, 2005), 31–32.

4. Food and Agriculture Organization, *Global Forest Resources Assessment 2005* (Rome: FAO, 2006), 20. Focusing on net change in forest area in South America, Central Amer-

ica, Africa, and South and Southeast Asia, the total forest area lost per year is about twenty-eight million acres between 2000 and 2005.

5. MEA, *Ecosystems and Human Well-Being: Synthesis*, 2; MEA, *Ecosystems and Human Well-Being*, vol. 1: *Current State and Trends* (Washington, DC: Island Press, 2005), 14–15. See also N. C. Duke et al., "A World Without Mangroves?" *Science* 317 (2007): 41–42. And see Carmen Revenga et al., *Pilot Analysis of Global Ecosystems: Freshwater Systems* (Washington, DC: WRI, 2000), 3, 21–22; World Resources Institute et al., *World Resources, 2000–2001* (Washington, DC: WRI, 2000), 72, 107; Lauretta Burke et al., *Pilot Analysis of Global Ecosystems: Coastal Ecosystems* (Washington, DC: WRI, 2001), 19.

6. Food and Agriculture Organization, *World Review of Fisheries and Aquaculture* (Rome: FAO, 2006), 29, http://www.fao.org/docrep/009/A0699e/A0699e00.htm; and Ransom A. Myers and Boris Worm, "Rapid World-wide Depletion of Predatory Fish Communities," *Nature* 423 (2003): 280. Some analysts put the proportion of ocean fisheries overexploited or collapsed significantly lower. See also Fred Pearce, "Oceans Raped of Their Former Riches," *New Scientist*, August 2, 2003, 4.

7. MEA, *Ecosystems and Human Well-Being: Synthesis*, 2.

8. MEA, *Ecosystems and Human Well-Being: Synthesis*, 5, 36.

9. Tim Radford, "Scientist Warns of Sixth Great Extinction of Wildlife," *The Guardian*, November 29, 2001. See also Nigel C. A. Pitman and Peter M. Jorgensen, "Estimating the Size of the World's Threatened Flora," *Science* 298 (2002): 989; and F. Stuart Chapin III et al., "Consequences of Changing Biodiversity," *Nature* 405 (2000): 234–242.

10. U.N. Environment Programme, *Global Environment Outlook 3* (London: Earthscan, 2002), 64–65. Drylands cover about 40 percent of the earth's land surface, and an estimated 10–20 percent suffer from "severe" degradation. James F. Reynolds et al., "Global Desertification: Building a Science for Dryland Development," *Science* 316 (2007): 847. See also "Key Facts About Desertification," Reuters/Planet Ark, June 6, 2006, summarizing United Nations estimates.

11. Fred Pearce, "Northern Exposure," *New Scientist*, May 31, 1997, 25; Martin Enserink, "For Precarious Populations, Pollutants Present New Perils," *Science* 299 (2003): 1642. See also the data reported in Joe Thornton, *Pandora's Poison* (Cambridge, MA: MIT Press, 2000), 1–55.

12. U.N. Environment Programme, *Global Outlook for Ice and Snow*, June 4, 2007, http://www.unep.org/geo/geo_ice. See also http://www.geo.unizh.ch/wgms and http://www.unep.org/geo/geo_ice/PDF/GEO_C6_A_LowRes.pdf. See generally William Collins et al., "The Physical Science Behind Climate Change," *Scientific American*, August 2007, 64. And see "Arctic Sea Ice Drops to Record Low," *Nature newsblog*, September 15, 2011, 254, http://blogs.nature.com/news/2011/09/arctic_sea_ice_drops_to_record.html.

13. See "UN Reports Increasing 'Dead Zones' in Oceans," Associated Press, October 20, 2006; Mark Shrope, "The Dead Zones," *New Scientist*, December 9, 2006, 38; and Laurence Mee, "Reviving Dead Zones," *Scientific American*, November 2006, 79. On nitrogen pollution, see Charles Driscoll et al., "Nitrogen Pollution," *Environment* 45, no. 7 (2003): 8; and Mark Sutton, "Too Much of a Good Thing," *Nature* 472 (2011): 159.

14. Peter M. Vitousek et al., "Human Appropriation of the Products of Photosynthesis," *Bioscience* 36, no. 6 (1986): 368; S. Rojstaczer et al., "Human Appropriation of Photosynthesis Products," *Science* 294 (2001): 2549. See also Helmut Haberl et al.,

"Quantifying and Mapping the Human Appropriation of Net Primary Production in Earth's Terrestrial Ecosystems," *Proceedings of the National Academy of Sciences* 104 (2007): 12942–12947.

15. U.N. Environment Programme, "At a Glance: The World's Water Crisis," http://www.ourplanet.com/imgversn/141/glance.html.

16. MEA, *Ecosystem and Human Well-Being: Synthesis*, 32.

17. Michael R. W. Rands et al., "Biodiversity Conservation: Challenge Beyond 2010," *Science* 329 (2010): 1299.

18. See Michael Hoffman et al., "The Impact of Conservation on the Status of the World's Vertebrates," *Science* 330 (December 10, 2010): 1503; "Plants Under Threat," *Nature* 467 (2010); and "Beastly Tales," *The Economist*, June 1, 2011, http://www.economist.com/blogs/dailychart/2011/06/endangered-species.

19. "Africa's National Parks Hit by Mammal Declines," *Science Daily*, July 13, 2010, http://www.sciencedaily.com/releases/2010/07/100712141851.htm.

20. Paul Rauber, "Race to Raze," *Sierra*, http://www.sierraclub.org/sierra/201011/grapple 3.aspx.

21. "World's Mangroves Retreating at Alarming Rate," Reuters Planet Ark, July 15, 2010.

22. Sebastian Smith, "Oceans' Fish Could Disappear in 40 Years: UN," AFP, May 17, 2010.

23. World Resources Institute (WRI) in collaboration with United Nations Development Programme, United Nations Environment Programme, and World Bank, *World Resources 2010–2011: Decision Making in a Changing Climate—Adaptation Challenges and Choices* (Washington, DC: WRI, 2011), 14.

24. See Intergovernmental Panel on Climate Change, "Contribution of Working Group II to the Fourth Assessment Report of the Intergovernmental Panel on Climate Change: Summary for Policymakers," April 2007, http://www.ipcc.ch/pdf/assessment-report/ar4/wg2/ar4-wg2-spm.pdf, 11. See also Elisabeth Rosenthal, "For Many Species, No Escape as Temperature Rises," *New York Times*, January 21, 2011; and Suzanne Goldenberg, "Canadian Seal Cull 'Unnecessary Due to Climate Change,'" *The Guardian*, January 5, 2012, http://www.guardian.co.uk/environment/2012/jan/05/canadian-seal-cull-unnecessary-climate-change.

25. Jim Robbins, "What's Killing the Great Forests of the American West?" *Yale Environment 360*, March 15, 2010; Dina Fine Maron, "How Pine Bark Beetles Created an Elaborate and Deadly Mess," *New York Times*, October 28, 2010; and Andrew Nikiforuk, "Beetlemania," *New Scientist*, November 15, 2011, 38.

26. On November 18, 2011, the Intergovernmental Panel on Climate Change released its *Special Report on Managing the Risks of Extreme Events and Disasters* (SREX), http://ipcc-wg2.gov/SREX, which concluded it likely that climate change already has or will contribute to high temperature extremes, sea level rise, heavy precipitation events, and droughts. See also Quirin Schiermeier, "Extreme Measures," *Nature* 477 (2011): 148–149; and Richard A. Kerr, "Humans Are Driving Extreme Weather," *Science* 334 (2011): 1040.

27. Deborah Zabarenko, "Drought Could Hit World's Most Populous Areas," Reuters, October 19, 2010, http://www.mnn.com/earth-matters/wilderness-resources/stories/drought-could-hit-worlds-populous-areas; "Droughts to Be More Common by 2030, Extreme by 2100," ClimateWire (www.eenews.net/cw), October 21, 2010.

28. Lauren Morello, "Scientists See the Southwest as First Major U.S. Climate Change Victim," ClimateWire (www.eenews.net/cw), December 14, 2010; "The Drying of the

West," *The Economist*, January 29, 2011, 32; Jon Gertner, "The Future Is Drying Up," *New York Times Magazine*, October 21, 2007. See generally Joseph Romm, "The Next Dust Bowl," *Nature* 478 (2011): 450–451; and William deBuys, *The Great Aridness* (Oxford: Oxford University Press, 2011).

29. World Resources Institute et al., *World Resources 2010–2011*, 14.

30. Thomas Jacob et al., "Recent Contributions of Glaciers and Ice Caps to Sea Level Rise," *Nature*, published online February 8, 2012, http://www.nature.com/nature/journal/vaop/ncurrent/full/nature10847.html.

31. Mari N. Jensen, "Rising Seas Will Affect Major U.S. Coastal Cities by 2100," University of Arizona, February 14, 2011; Shanta Barley, "A World 4°C Warmer," *New Scientist*, October 3, 2009, 14; Jeremy Hance, "Sea Levels to Rise More Than Expected Due to 'Deeply Surprising' Greenland Melt," Environmental News Network, December 15, 2009, reproduced from http://news.mongabay.com/2009/1214-hance_greenmelt.html; Catherine Brahic, "If Sea Levels Rise a Meter, Watch Out," *New Scientist*, September 6, 2008, 12; Rob Young and Orrin Pilkey, "How High Will Seas Rise? Get Ready for Seven Feet," *Yale Environment 360*, January 14, 2010; Fen Montaigne, "A World Centered on Sea Ice Is Changing Swiftly at the Poles," *Yale Environment 360*, June 28, 2011; "Greenland's Going Rate," *Science*, April 29, 2011, 515; and "More and More Melting," *Science*, March 28, 2011, 1367.

32. Anil Ananthaswamy, "Greenland Poised on a Knife Edge," *New Scientist*, January 8, 2011, 8.

33. Barley, "A World 4°C Warmer," 14.

34. Hannah Hoag, "Report Maps Perils of Warming," *Nature* 466 (2010), 425.

35. "Heat Waves Could Be Commonplace in the U.S. by 2039," *Science Daily*, July 9, 2010, http://www.sciencedaily.com/releases/2010/07/100708122617.htm.

36. Heidi Cullen, "Sizzle Factor for a Restless Climate," *New York Times*, July 19, 2011.

37. Barley, "A World 4°C Warmer," 15. See also A. de Sherbinin et al., "Preparing for Resettlement Associated with Climate Change," *Science*, October 28, 2011, 456.

38. Geoffrey York, "On the Move in a Warming World: The Rise of Climate Refugees," *Toronto Globe and Mail*, December 17, 2010.

39. Morris A. Bender et al., "Modeled Impact of Anthropogenic Warming on the Frequency of Intense Atlantic Hurricanes," *Science* 327 (2010): 454.

40. Justin Gillis, "Heavy Rains Linked to Humans," *New York Times*, February 16, 2011. See http://www.nature.com/news/2011/110216/full/470316a.html. See also Jenny Mandel, "Natural Disasters: 2011 Already the Costliest Year on Record," *Environment and Energy Daily*, http://www.eenews.net, July 12, 2011. And see generally National Academy of Sciences et al., *Expert Consensus Report: America's Climate Choices* (Washington, DC: National Academies Press, 2011), at www.americasclimatechoices.org.

41. National Research Council, *Abrupt Climate Change: Inevitable Surprises* (Washington, DC: National Academy Press, 2002). See also Paul Valdes, "Built for Stability," *Nature Geoscience* 4 (2011): 414–416. And see Edward A. G. Schuur and Benjamin Abbott, "High Risk of Permafrost Thaw," *Nature* 480 (2011): 32–33.

42. See Steve Connor, "Vast Methane 'Plumes' Seen in Arctic Ocean as Sea Ice Retreats," *The Independent (UK)*, December 13, 2011. And see Matthew Reagan et al., "Marine Methane Cycle Simulations for the Period of Early Global Warming," *Journal of Geophysical Research*, January 28, 2011.

43. Richard Kerr, "Ocean Acidification Unprecedented, Unsettling," *Science* 328 (2010): 1501. Warmer seas also mean less dissolved oxygen, compounding the threat to ocean life. See Carl Zimmer, "A Looming Oxygen Crisis and Its Impact on World's Oceans," *Yale Environment 360*, August 5, 2010. And see also Daniel G. Boyce et al., "Global Phytoplankton Decline over the Past Century," *Nature* 466 (2010): 591.

44. Kerr, "Ocean Acidification Unprecedented, Unsettling," 1501.

45. Juliet Eilperin, "UN Report Stresses Value of Nature to World's Economies," *Washington Post*, October 20, 2010; J. E. N. Veron, "Is the End in Sight for the World's Coral Reefs?," *Yale Environment 360*, December 6 2010.

46. H. Charles J. Godfray et al., "Food Security: The Challenge of Feeding Nine Billion People," *Science* 327 (2010): 812.

47. N. V. Fedoroff et al., "Radically Rethinking Agriculture for the Twenty-first Century," *Science* 327 (2010): 833. See also Justin Gillis, "A Warming Planet Struggles to Feed Itself," *New York Times*, June 5, 2011, 1.

48. C. J. Vorosmarty et al., "Global Threats to Human Water Security and River Biodiversity," *Nature* 467 (2010): 555.

49. American Geophysical Union, "Groundwater Depletion Rate Accelerating Worldwide," AGU Release No. 10–30, September 23, 2010. See also "Deep Waters, Slowly Drying Up," *The Economist*, October 9, 2010, 86; Li Jiao, "Water Shortages Loom as Northern China's Aquifers Are Sucked Dry," *Science* 328 (2010): 1462.

50. Pacific Institute, "Climate Change and Transboundary Waters," http://www.pacinst.org/reports/transboundary_waters/index.htm.

51. Lester Brown, "Could Food Shortages Bring Down Civilization?" *Scientific American*, May 2009, 52, 55. See also the articles collected in "The Food Issue," *Foreign Policy*, May/June 2011, 53.

52. United Nations Environment Programme, *From Conflict to Peacebuilding* (Nairobi: UNEP, 2009), 6–8.

53. Michael T. Klare, "The Permanent Energy Crisis," TomPaine.com, February 13, 2006, http://www.tompaine.com/print/the_permanent_energy_crisis.php. See also Michael T. Klare, "The New Thirty Years War," TomDispatch.com, June 26, 2011, http://www.tomdispatch.com/blog/175409; "Canadian Report Says Climate Change Could Lead to War," *ClimateWire*, www.eenews.net, June 30, 2011; and Christian Parenti, *Tropic of Chaos* (New York: Nation Books, 2011).

54. John M. Broder, "Climate Change Seen as Threat to U.S. Security," *New York Times*, August 9, 2009.

55. Ian Morris, *Why the West Rules—for Now* (New York: Farrar, Straus and Giroux, 2010), 598–613.

56. See, e.g., Kevin Anderson and Alice Bows, "Reframing the Climate Change Challenge in Light of Post-2000 Emission Trends," *Philosophical Transactions of the Royal Society* 366 (2008): 3863–3882; Clive Hamilton, *Requiem for a Species* (London: Earthscan, 2010); and Michael Marshall, "Climate's Dark Dawn," *New Scientist*, December 3, 2011, 6. See also the online presentation of Kevin Anderson, deputy director of the Tyndall Centre, the United Kingdom's leading academic climate change research organization, www.dfid.gov.uk/Stories/Podcasts/Professor-Kevin-Anderson/.

57. United Nations Environment Programme, *The Emissions Gap Report—Technical Summary*, November 2010, 6. See also Joeri Rogelj et al., "Emission Pathways Consistent

with a 2°C Global Temperature Limit," *Nature Climate Change* 1 (2011): 413–418. And see Gerard Wynn, "Extreme Steps Needed to Meet Climate Target," *Reuters/Planet Ark*, September 21, 2011.

58. In November 2011, the International Energy Agency released its 2011 *World Energy Outlook*, which warned that nations have only a few years to avoid locking into an unsustainable energy future. It pointed out that four-fifths of the total energy-related carbon dioxide emissions permitted to 2035 in its +2°C scenario are already locked in by existing power plants, buildings, and factories. New energy construction planned between now and 2017 will generate all the carbon dioxide emissions allowed in its +2°C scenario up to 2035. "The World Is Locking Itself into an Unsustainable Energy Future Which Would Have Far-Reaching Consequences, IEA Warns," press release, International Energy Agency, London, November 9, 2011.

59. See generally Anderson and Bows, "Reframing the Climate Change Challenge"; German Advisory Council on Global Change (WGBU), *Solving the Climate Dilemma: The Budget Approach* (Berlin: WGBU, 2009); and Malte Meinshausen et al., "Greenhouse-Gas Emission Targets for Limiting Global Warming to 2°C," *Nature* 458 (2009): 1158–1163. See also Clive Hamilton, *Requiem for a Species* (London: Earthscan, 2010); and Paul Gilding, *The Great Disruption* (New York: Bloomsbury, 2011).

60. Tim Jackson, *Prosperity Without Growth: Economics of a Finite Planet* (London: Earthscan, 2009), 80–81.

61. David Biello, "Green Energy's Big Challenge: The Daunting Task of Scaling Up," *Yale Environment 360*, January 20, 2011.

62. Michael Klare, "Clean, Green, Safe and Smart," *The Nation*, August 2–9, 2010, 14.

63. 2010 Annual Report, Global CCS Institute. See Alister Doyle, "Carbon Projects Up in 2010, Despite Costs," Reuters, March 10, 2011, http://in.reuters.com/article/2011/03/09/us-climate-carbon-idINTRE72829Y20110309. See also Stuart Haszeldine and Vivian Scott, "Carbon Capture and Storage," *New Scientist*, April 2, 2011.

64. Carbon capture and storage may prove highly valuable in realizing "negative emissions"—taking carbon dioxide out of the atmosphere—which many analysts now believe will be necessary. Producing wood and biomass absorbs carbon dioxide from the air. This biomass would then be burned to produce energy, and the resulting carbon dioxide releases would be captured and sequestered geologically.

65. See, e.g., Jeff Goodell, *Big Coal: The Dirty Secret Behind America's Energy Future* (New York: Houghton Mifflin, 2007).

66. "Energy Subsidies Black, Not Green," press release, Environmental Law Institute, September 18, 2009, http://www.eli.org/pdf/Energy_Subsidies_Black_Not_Green.pdf.

67. Philip Shabecoff, "U.S. Study Warns of Extensive Problems from Carbon Dioxide Pollution," *New York Times*, January 14, 1981, A13.

68. Johan Rockstrom et al., "Planetary Boundaries: Exploring a Safe Operating Space for Humanity," *Ecology and Society* 14 (2009): 32. See also Johan Rockstrom et al., "A Safe Operating Space for Humanity," *Nature* 461 (2009): 472.

Chapter 5. America the Possible

1. Preston Cloud, *Cosmos, Earth and Man* (New Haven: Yale University Press, 1978), 302–304.

2. Drew Dellinger, "Hieroglyphic Stairway," in *Love Letter to the Milky Way* (Mill Valley, CA: Planetize the Movement Press, 2010), 1.

3. Paul Raskin et al., *Great Transition* (Boston: Stockholm Environment Institute, 2002), 42–43.

4. Mary Evelyn Tucker and John Grim, "Daring to Dream: Religion and the Future of the Earth," *Reflections—The Journal of the Yale Divinity School*, Spring 2007, 4.

5. See www.journeyoftheuniverse.org. See also Brian Thomas Swimme and Mary Evelyn Tucker, *Journey of the Universe* (New Haven: Yale University Press, 2011). And see Thomas Berry, *The Great Work* (New York: Bell Tower, 1999), and *The Dream of the Earth* (San Francisco: Sierra Club Books, 1988).

6. See, e.g., Paul R. Ehrlich and Donald Kennedy, "Millennium Assessment of Human Behavior," *Science* 309 (2005): 562–563. See also Paul R. Ehrlich, *Human Natures: Genes, Cultures, and the Human Prospect* (Washington, DC: Island Press, 2000); and William Rees, "What's Blocking Sustainability? Human Nature, Cognition, and Denial," *Sustainability: Science, Practice, and Policy*, Fall 2010, http://sspp.proquest.com/archives/vol6iss2/1001-012.rees.html. And see Erich Fromm, *To Have or to Be* (London: Continuum, 1977); and Aldo Leopold, *A Sand County Almanac* (New York: Oxford University Press, 1949).

7. Quoted in Lawrence E. Harrison, *The Central Liberal Truth* (Oxford: Oxford University Press, 2006), xvi. For an excellent handbook on changing values, see Pubic Interest Research Center, *The Common Cause Handbook* (Machynlleth, Wales: Public Interest Research Center, 2011), at www.pirc.info and www.valuesandframes.org. See also Tom Crompton and Tim Kasser, *Meeting Environmental Challenges: The Role of Human Identity* (Surrey, UK: World Wildlife Fund–UK, 2009).

8. See Thomas Homer-Dixon, *The Upside of Down: Catastrophe, Creativity, and the Renewal of Civilization* (Washington, DC: Island Press, 2006), 6, 109, 254, 281.

9. Milton Friedman, *Capitalism and Freedom* (Chicago: University of Chicago Press, 2002), xiv.

10. Naomi Klein, *The Shock Doctrine: The Rise of Disaster Capitalism* (New York: Metropolitan Books, 2007).

11. Howard Gardner, *Changing Minds: The Art and Science of Changing Our Own and Other People's Minds* (Boston: Harvard Business School Press, 2006), 69, 82. See also James MacGregor Burns, *Transforming Leadership: A New Pursuit of Happiness* (New York: Grove Press, 2003).

12. Bill Moyers, "The Narrative Imperative," TomPaine.com, January 4, 2007, 2, 5, http://www.tompaine.com/print/the_narrative_imperative.php.

13. James Gustave Speth, *The Bridge at the Edge of the World: Capitalism, the Environment, and Crossing from Crisis to Sustainability* (New Haven: Yale University Press, 2008), 163.

14. Mary Evelyn Tucker, *Worldly Wonder: Religions Enter Their Ecological Phase* (Chicago: Open Court, 2003), 9, 43.

15. Bob Edgar, *Middle Church* (New York: Simon and Schuster, 2006); Jim Wallis, *The Soul of Politics* (New York: The New Press, 1994). See also Steven C. Rockefeller and John C. Elder, *Spirit and Nature* (Boston: Beacon Press, 1992).

16. Rachel Donadio and Laurie Goodstein, "Pope Urges Forming New World Economic Order to Work for the 'Common Good,'" *New York Times*, July 8, 2009, A6.

17. See Bruce Rich, *To Uphold the World* (Boston: Beacon, 2010); Albert Schweitzer, *Out of My Life and Thought* (New York: Henry Holt, 1933); Leopold, *A Sand County Almanac;* Thomas Berry (Mary Evelyn Tucker, ed.), *Evening Thoughts* (San Francisco: Sierra Club Books, 2006); E. O. Wilson, *The Creation* (New York: Norton, 2006); and Terry Tempest Williams, *Refuge* (New York: Vintage, 2001). See also Stephen R. Kellert and James Gustave Speth, eds., *The Coming Transformation* (New Haven: Yale School of Forestry and Environmental Studies, 2009).

  Numerous organizations are working to promote a new consciousness and deeper change including the Forum on Religion and Ecology, www.fore.research.yale.edu; the Center for Humans and Nature, www.humansandnature.org; Awakening the Dreamer, www.awakeningthedreamer.org; Four Years. Go, www.fouryearsgo.org; Quaker Earth care Witness, www.quakerearthcare.org; and the various state-level Interfaith Power and Light organizations.

18. Among the many books written about the possibility of large-scale economic, environmental, and social breakdown are Jared Diamond, *Collapse: How Societies Choose to Fail or Succeed* (New York: Viking, 2005); Fred Pearce, *The Last Generation* (London: Transworld, 2006); Martin Rees, *Our Final Hour* (New York: Basic Books, 2003); Richard A. Posner, *Catastrophe* (New York: Oxford University Press, 2004); James Lovelock, *The Revenge of Gaia* (London: Penguin, 2006); James Martin, *The Meaning of the 21st Century* (New York: Penguin, 2006); Homer-Dixon, *The Upside of Down;* Mayer Hillman, *The Suicidal Planet* (New York: St. Martin's Press, 2007); James Howard Kunstler, *The Long Emergency* (New York: Grove Press, 2005); Richard Heinberg, *Power Down* (Gabriola Island, BC: New Society Publishers, 2004); Ronald Wright, *A Short History of Progress* (New York: Carroll and Graf, 2004); John Leslie, *The End of the World* (London: Routledge, 1996); Colin Mason, *The 2030 Spike* (London: Earthscan, 2003); Michael T. Klare, *Resource Wars: The New Landscape of Global Conflict* (New York: Henry Holt, 2001); and Roy Woodbridge, *The Next World War* (Toronto: University of Toronto Press, 2004).

19. Jon Mooallem, "The End Is Near! (Yea!)," *New York Times*, April 19, 2009.

20. Millennium Ecosystem Assessment, Statement from the Board, *Living Beyond Our Means: Natural Assets and Human Well-Being*, March 2005, 5. See also Jonathan A. Foley et al., "Global Consequences of Land Use," *Science* 309 (2005): 570.

21. World Wildlife Fund—International, *Living Planet Report 2006* (Gland, Switzerland: WWF, 1006), 2–3.

22. David M. Potter, *People of Plenty* (Chicago: University of Chicago Press, 1958).

23. Tim Jackson, *Prosperity Without Growth: Economics of a Finite Planet* (London: Earthscan, 2009), 13–16.

24. Jeff Rubin, *Why Your World Is About to Get a Whole Lot Smaller* (New York: Random House, 2009), 22–24.

25. Christopher Steiner, *$20 Per Gallon: How the Inevitable Rise in the Price of Gasoline Will Change Our Lives for the Better* (New York: Grand Central Publishing, 2009).

26. David Holmgren, *Future Scenarios: How Communities Can Adapt to Peak Oil and Climate Change* (White River Junction, VT: Chelsea Green, 2009), 3–4.

27. Kunstler, *The Long Emergency*, 5, 239.

28. Ed Diener and Martin E. P. Seligman, "Beyond Money: Toward an Economy of Well-Being," *Psychological Science in the Public Interest* 5, no. 1 (2004): 3–5; Avner Offer, *The*

Challenge of Affluence (Oxford: Oxford University Press, 2006), 15–38. See also the diagrams reproduced in Speth, *The Bridge at the Edge of the World*, Chapter 6.

29. United States: Jonathon Porritt, *Capitalism as If the World Matters* (London: Earthscan, 2005), 54; United Kingdom: Nick Donovan and David Halpern, *Life Satisfaction: The State of Knowledge and the Implications for Government*, UK Cabinet Office Strategy Unit, December 2002, 17; Japan: Bruno S. Frey and Alois Stutzer, *Happiness and Economics: How the Economy and Institutions Affect Human Well-Being* (Princeton, NJ: Princeton University Press, 2002), 9.

30. Richard A. Easterlin and Laura Angelescu, "Happiness and Growth the World Over: Time Series Evidence on the Happiness-Income Paradox," Institute for the Study of Labor, Bonn, Germany, Discussion Paper No. 4060, March 2009.

31. Diener and Seligman, "Beyond Money," 3.

32. Peter C. Whybrow, *American Mania* (New York: Norton, 2005), 4. Bipolar disorder diagnoses account for most of the 50 percent growth between 1996 and 2004 in American children diagnosed with psychiatric illness. See Andy Coghlan, "Young and Moody or Mentally Ill?," *New Scientist*, May 19, 2007, 6.

33. Diener and Seligman, "Beyond Money," 10.

34. Martin E. P. Seligman, *Flourish* (New York: Free Press, 2011), 20.

35. David G. Myers, "What Is the Good Life?" *Yes! A Journal of Positive Futures*, Summer 2004, 15. See also David G. Myers, *The American Paradox: Spiritual Hunger in an Age of Plenty* (New Haven: Yale University Press, 2000).

36. See, e.g., Juliet Schor, *Plenitude: The New Economics of True Wealth* (New York: Penguin, 2010); David C. Korten, *The Great Turning* (San Francisco: Berrett-Koehler, 2006); Duane Elgin, *Voluntary Simplicity* (New York: Harper, 2010); David Wann, *The New Normal* (New York: St. Martin's, 2010); Thomas Princen, *Treading Softly* (Cambridge, MA: MIT Press, 2010); Bill McKibben, *Deep Economy* (New York: Times Books, 2007); Jay Walljasper, *All That We Share* (New York: The New Press, 2010); Janelle Orsi and Emily Doskow, *The Sharing Solution* (Berkeley, CA: NOLO, 2009); and Fritjof Capra and Hazel Henderson, *Qualitative Growth* (Institute of Chartered Accountants in England and Wales, jointly published with Tomorrow's Company, 2009), available at http://www.icaew.com/search?q=capra+and+henderson.

37. See www.biophilicdesign.net. See also Stephen R. Kellert et al., *Biophilic Design* (New York: Wiley, 2008); David W. Orr, *The Nature of Design* (Oxford: Oxford University Press, 2004); and William McDonough and Michael Braungart, *Cradle to Cradle* (San Francisco: North Point Press, 2002).

38. John Maynard Keynes, "Economic Possibilities for Our Grandchildren," in Keynes, *Essays in Persuasion* (New York: Norton, 1963 [originally published 1933]), 365–373.

Chapter 6. A Sustaining Post-Growth Economy

1. Herman E. Daly and Joshua Farley, *Ecological Economics* (Washington, DC: Island Press, 2004), 231. And see Herman E. Daly, "Uneconomic Growth in Theory and in Fact," Feasta Lecture, Trinity College, Dublin, April 26, 1999.

2. 2008 GDP per capita at purchasing power parity. Norway's is higher than the United State's. OECD, *OECD in Figures 2009* (Paris: OECD, 2009), 12–13.

3. See generally Herman E. Daly, *Beyond Growth* (Boston: Beacon Press, 1996); Clive Hamilton, *Growth Fetish* (London: Pluto Press, 2004); Peter A. Victor, *Managing Without Growth* (Northampton, MA: Edward Elgar, 2008); James Gustave Speth, *The Bridge at the Edge of the World: Capitalism, the Environment, and Crossing from Crisis to Sustainability* (New Haven: Yale University Press, 2008); and Tim Jackson, *Prosperity Without Growth: Economics of a Finite Planet* (London: Earthscan, 2009). See also Charles A. S. Hall and John W. Day, Jr., "Revisiting the Limits to Growth After Peak Oil," *American Scientist*, May–June 2009, 230.

4. World Wildlife Fund—International, *Living Planet Report 2010* (Gland, Switzerland: WWF, 2010), 8.

5. Paul Krugman, "The Finite World," *New York Times*, December 26, 2010. See also Jeff Rubin, *Why Your World Is About to Get a Whole Lot Smaller* (New York: Random House, 2009).

6. See, e.g., Keith Bradsher, "Supplies Squeezed, Rare Earth Prices Surge," *New York Times*, May 2, 2011. See also Fred Pearce, "Phosphate: A Critical Resource Misused and Now Running Low," *Yale Environment 360*, July 7, 2011.

7. Jeremy Grantham, "Time to Wake Up: Days of Abundant Resources and Falling Prices Are Over Forever," *GMO Quarterly Letter*, April 2011.

8. Richard Heinberg, *The End of Growth* (Gabriola Island, BC: New Society Publishers, 2011), 2–3.

9. Richard A. Kerr, "Splitting the Difference Between Oil Pessimists and Optimists," *Science* 326 (2009): 1048; and Richard Kerr, "Peak Oil Production May Already Be Here," *Science*, March 25, 2011, 1510.

10. Daniel Yergin, *The Quest* (New York: Penguin, 2011), 228, 239, 262.

11. Robert L. Hirsch et al., *Peaking of World Oil Production*, report prepared for the U.S. Department of Energy, February 2005, http://www.netl.doe.gov/publications/others/pdf/Oil_Peaking_NETL.pdf.

12. See Eric Pooley, "A Rich History and a Strange Reticence," *The American Prospect*, October 2011, 59.

13. Bill McKibben, *Eaarth* (New York: Henry Holt, 2010), 28, 47–48, 97–99 (emphasis in original).

14. Stephen Marglin, "Premises for a New Economy," New York, May 10, 2010, http://www.un.org/esa/dsd/dsd_aofw_sdkp/sdkp_uncsd_workshop_0510.

15. Thomas Homer-Dixon, "Economies Can't Just Keep on Growing," *Foreign Policy*, January/February 2011, 56, www.foreignpolicy.com/articles/2011/01/02/unconventional_wisdom?page=0,1. See also Paul Gilding, *The Great Disruption* (New York: Bloomsbury, 2011).

16. See Juliet Schor, *Plenitude: The New Economics of True Wealth* (New York: Penguin, 2010); Juliet Schor, "Sustainable Consumption and Worktime Reduction," *Journal of Industrial Ecology* 9 (2005): 37–50.

17. Schor, *Plenitude*, 105.

18. See generally New Economy Working Group, *Jobs: A Main Street Fix for Wall Street's Failure*, http://neweconomyworkinggroup.org/new-economy-story/main-street-fix-wall-streets-failure.

19. William Greider, "The End of Free-Trade Globalization," *The Nation*, November 22, 2010, http://www.thenation.com/article/155848/end-free-trade-gobalization.

20. Center for the Advancement of the Steady State Economy and Economic Justice for All, *Enough Is Enough*, November 2010, http://www.steadystate.org/enough-is-enough. See also Herman E. Daly, "Economics in a Full World," *Scientific American*, September 2005, 100; Peter A. Victor, "Ecological Economics and Economic Growth," *Annals of the New York Academy of Sciences* 1185 (2010): 237–245; W. E. Rees, "Achieving Sustainability," *Journal of Planning Literature* 9, no. 4 (1995): 343–361; Stephen Spratt et al., *The Great Transition* (London: New Economics Foundation, 2009).

21. Herman E. Daly, "Toward Some Operational Principles of Sustainable Development," *Ecological Economics* 2, no. 1 (1990): 1–6.

22. Victor, *Managing Without Growth*, 192–193.

23. Peter Victor, "Questioning Economic Growth," *Nature* 468 (18 November 2010), 370–371. See also Joan Martinez Alier, "Socially Sustainable Economic Degrowth," *Development and Change* 40, no. 6 (2009): 1099–1119; Richard Smith, "Green Capitalism: The God That Failed," *Real-World Economics Review*, no. 56 (2011): 112; and Servaas Storm, "Capitalism and Climate Change," *Development and Change* 40, no. 6 (2009): 1.

24. Victor, "Questioning Economic Growth," 370–371. See also Richard Smith, "Beyond Growth or Beyond Capitalism," *Real-World Economics Review*, no. 53 (2010): 28; and Philip Lawn, "Is Steady-State Capitalism Viable?," *Annals of the New York Academy of Sciences* 1219 (2011): 1–25. See also Ted Trainer, "The Radical Implications of a Zero Growth Economy," *Real-World Economics Review*, no. 57 (2011): 71.

25. Jackson, *Prosperity Without Growth*, 177–178.

26. Gar Alperovitz, *America Beyond Capitalism* (Hoboken, NJ: John Wiley, 2005), 79.

27. See, e.g., Gar Alperovitz, "Worker-Owners of America, Unite!" *New York Times*, December 14, 2011.

28. William Greider, *The Soul of Capitalism: Opening Paths to a Moral Economy* (New York: Simon and Schuster, 2003), 65.

29. Jeff Gates, *The Ownership Solution* (Reading, MA: Addison-Wesley, 1998).

30. Alperovitz, *America Beyond Capitalism*, 88–89.

31. These ideas have been creatively developed by Peter Barnes in *Capitalism 3.0: A Guide to Reclaiming the Commons* (San Francisco: Berrett-Koehler, 2006).

32. Personal communication from Peter Barnes, September 20, 2011.

33. See Stephen Davis et al., *The New Capitalists* (Boston: Harvard Business School Press, 2006).

34. See, e.g., Stephanie Strom, "Make Money, Save the World," *New York Times*, May 6, 2007, Sunday Business, 1; Mary Anne Ostrom, "Global Philanthropy Forum Explores New Way of Giving," *San José (CA) Mercury News*, April 12, 2007; Andrew Jack, "Beyond Charity? A New Generation Enters the Business of Doing Good," *Financial Times*, April 5, 2007, 11.

35. A still valuable trove of ideas is Martin Carnoy and Derek Shearer, *Economic Democracy* (White Plains, NY: M. E. Sharpe, 1980).

36. Richard A. Rosen and David Schweickart, "Visions of Regional Economies in a Great Transition World," Great Transition Initiative Paper 4, Tellus Institute, Boston, 2006, http://www.gtinitiative.org/documents/pdffinals/4economy.pdf. See also David Schweickart, *After Capitalism* (Lanham, MD: Rowman and Littlefield, 2011); and Richard A. Rosen, "How Should the Economy Be Regulated?," 2009 Summit on the Future of the Corporation, Paper No. 7, Corporation 20/20, Tellus Institute, 2009.

Chapter 7. System Changes

1. Peter S. Goodman, "The Free Market: A False Idol After All?," *New York Times*, December 30, 2007, 4.

2. James K. Galbraith, *The Predator State* (New York: Free Press, 2008), 165.

3. Galbraith, *The Predator State*, 195.

4. For a skillful application of this approach to the climate issue, see Robert Repetto, *America's Climate Problem: The Way Forward* (Washington, DC: Earthscan, 2011).

5. See, for example, Barbara Ehrenreich, *Nickel and Dimed: On (Not) Getting By in America* (New York: Henry Holt, 2001).

6. Robert Kuttner, *Everything for Sale* (Chicago: University of Chicago Press, 1999), 49.

7. For extensive data on multinationals, see Medard Gabel and Henry Bruner, *Global Inc.: An Atlas of the Multinational Corporation* (New York: New Press, 2003).

8. Robert Repetto, "Best Practice in Internal Oversight of Lobbying Practice," http://www.yale.edu/envirocenter/WP200601-Repetto.pdf.

9. Lee Drutman, "Perennial Lobbying Scandal," TomPaine.com, February 28, 2007, http://www.tompaine.com/articles/2007/02/28/perennial_lobbying_scandal.php.

10. G. William Domhoff, *Who Rules America?* (Boston: McGraw-Hill, 2006), xi, xiii–xiv. See also Jeff Faux, *The Global Class War* (Hoboken, NJ: John Wiley and Sons, 2006).

11. Marjorie Kelly and Allen White, "Corporate Design: The Missing Business and Public Policy Issue of Our Time," Corporation 20/20, Tellus Institute, November 2007. See also Allen White, "Transforming the Corporation," Great Transition Initiative Paper No. 5, Tellus Institute, 2006, http://gtinitiative.org/documents/PDF FINALS/5Corporations.pdf; and Steven Hill, "Europe's Answer to Wall Street," *The Nation*, May 10, 2010, 23.

12. Michael Marx et al., "Strategic Corporate Initiative: Toward a Global Citizens' Movement to Bring Corporations Back Under Control," Corporate Ethics International, September 2007, http://www.corpethics.org/downloads/SCI_Report_September_2007.pdf. See also Allen D. Kanner, "Shasta and Goliath: Bringing Down Corporate Rule," *Tikkun*, Winter 2011, 15.

    On the commons, see Peter Barnes, *Capitalism 3.0: A Guide to Reclaiming the Commons* (San Francisco: Berrett-Koehler, 2006); Michael Hardt and Antonio Negri, *Commonwealth* (Cambridge, MA: Harvard University Press, 2009); Peter Linebaugh, *The Magna Carta Manifesto* (Berkeley: University of California Press, 2008); and Jay Walljasper, *All That We Share* (New York: The New Press, 2010).

13. See Neva Goodwin, "What Can We Hope for the World in 2075?" E. F. Schumacher Lecture, New Economics Institute, November 2010, 13.

14. Charles Cray, "Revisiting Corporate Charters," 2007 Summit on the Future of the Corporation, Paper No. 7, in Allen White and Marjorie Kelly, eds., *Paper Series on Corporate Design*, Corporation 20/20, Tellus Institute, November 2007, 67.

15. Cray, "Revisiting Corporate Charters," 67–68.

16. Allen White, "When the World Rules Corporations: Pathway to a Global Corporate Charter," Great Transition Initiative Perspectives on Critical Issues, Tellus Institute, August 2010, http://gtinitiative.org/documents/IssuePerspectives/GTI-Perspectives-Global_Corporate_Charters.pdf. The title plays off David Korten's book, *When Corporations Rule the World* (San Francisco: Berrett-Koehler, 2001).

17. Richard A. Rosen, "How Should the Economy Be Regulated?," 2009 Summit on the Future of the Corporation, Paper No. 7, Corporation 20/20, Tellus Institute, 2009, 55–56. For an excellent discussion of the corporate future, see Neva Goodwin, "What Can We Hope for the World in 2075?" See www.neweconomicsinstitute.org.

18. See www.asbcouncil.org.

19. See www.livingeconomies.org.

20. See www.bcorporation.net.

21. See www.fourthsector.net.

22. Gar Alperovitz, "The New Economy Movement," *The Nation*, June 13, 2011, 21. See also Gar Alperovitz, Ted Howard, and Thad Williamson, "The Cleveland Model," *The Nation*, February 11, 2010.

23. See generally Deborah B. Warren and Steve Dubb, *Growing a Green Economy for All: From Green Jobs to Green Ownership*, The Democracy Collaborative at the University of Maryland, July 2010.

24. Marjorie Kelly, *The Divine Right of Capital* (San Francisco: Berrett-Koehler, 2003).

25. Marjorie Kelly, "Not Just for Profit," 2009 Summit on the Future of the Corporation Paper No. 5, Corporation 20/20, Tellus Institute, 2009, 34–36.

26. See also Joel Bakan, *The Corporation* (London: Constable, 2005); John Cavanagh et al., *Alternatives to Economic Globalization: A Better World Is Possible* (San Francisco: Berrett-Koehler, 2002); Korten, *When Corporations Rule the World* and *The Post-Corporate World* (San Francisco: Berrett-Koehler, 1999); and Sharon Beder, *Suiting Themselves: How Corporations Drive the Global Agenda* (London: Earthscan, 2006). See also the "Stand Up to Corporate Power" issue of *Yes! Magazine*, Fall 2007.

27. David Korten, *How to Liberate America from Wall Street Rule*, A Report of the New Economy Working Group, July 2011. See www.neweconomyworkinggroup.org.

28. Thomas H. Greco, Jr., *The End of Money and the Future of Civilization* (White River Junction, VT: Chelsea Green, 2009), 35.

29. Quoted in Greco, *The End of Money and the Future of Civilization*, 38.

30. John Kenneth Galbraith, *Money: Whence It Came and Where It Went* (London: Penguin, 1975), 18–19.

31. Mary Mellor, "Could the Money System Be the Basis of a Sufficiency Economy?" *Real World Economics Review*, no. 54 (2010): 79.

32. Otto Scharmer, "Seven Acupuncture Points for Shifting Capitalism to Create a Regenerative Ecosystem Economy," Roundtable on Transforming Capitalism to Create a Regenerative Economy, MIT, Cambridge, Massachusetts, June 8–9, September 21, 2009, 19.

33. Korten, *How to Liberate America from Wall Street Rule*.

34. Korten, *How to Liberate America from Wall Street Rule*, 6–7. See also William Greider, "Fixing the Fed," *The Nation*, March 30, 2009, and "Dismantling the Temple," *The Nation*, August 3, 2009.

35. On complementary currencies generally, see Gwendolyn Hallsmith and Bernard Lietaer, *Creating Wealth: Growing Local Economies with Local Currencies* (Gabriola Island, BC: New Society Publishers, 2011). One notable example of a local currency is the BerkShares developed with support from the E. F. Schumacher Society (now New Economics Institute) for the southern Berkshires region of Massachusetts. See www

.berkshares.org and www.neweconomicsinstitute.org. See also Bill McKibben, "A Bang for Your Buck in the Berkshires," *Yankee*, September/October 2010, 93.

36. See generally Greco, *The End of Money and the Future of Civilization*.

37. Herman E. Daly, "Moving from a Failed Growth Economy to a Steady State Economy," April 21, 2011, unpublished manuscript, forthcoming in volume from Palgrave Publishers. See also Herman E. Daly, "Moving from a Failed Growth Economy to a Steady State Economy," *Solutions*, March/April 2010, 37.

38. Quoted in Mike Nickerson, *Life, Money and Illusion* (Lanark, ON: Seven Generations, 2006), 188.

39. James Truslow Adams, *The Epic of America* (New York: Little, Brown, 1934).

40. Sarah Treuhaft and David Madland, "Prosperity 2050: Is Equity the Superior Growth Model?," Center for American Progress, April 2011, http://www.americanprogress.org/issues/2011/04/prosperity_2050.html.

41. Robert Reich, *Aftershock* (New York: Alfred A. Knopf, 2010), 127.

42. Robert H. Frank, "Post-Consumer Prosperity," *The American Prospect*, March 24, 2009. See also Robert Frank et al., "Expenditure Cascades," http://papers.ssrn.com/sol3/papers.cfm?abstract_id=1690612.

43. Gar Alperovitz and Lew Daly, *Unjust Deserts* (New York: The New Press, 2008), 5.

44. Quoted in Alperovitz and Daly, *Unjust Deserts*, 14.

45. Alperovitz and Daly, *Unjust Deserts*, 16.

46. Peter Corning, *The Fair Society* (Chicago: University of Chicago Press, 2011).

47. The books and articles here are voluminous. Still useful is Mark Robert Rank, *One Nation, Underprivileged* (Oxford: Oxford University Press, 2004).

48. Herman E. Daly, "From a Failed-Growth Economy to a Steady State Economy," *Solutions*, March–April 2010, 41.

49. Howard Gardner, "An Embarrassment of Riches," *Foreign Policy*, May/June 2007, 39.

50. Reich, *Aftershock*, 129–130.

51. Reich, *Aftershock*, 131.

52. Bruce Ackerman and Anne Alstott, *The Stakeholder Society* (New Haven: Yale University Press, 1999), 4–5.

53. John Cavanagh et al., "Reversing the Great Tax Shift," Institute for Policy Studies, April 8, 2009. And see Sarah Anderson and John Cavanagh, eds., "America Is Not Broke," Institute for Policy Studies, November 21, 2011, http://www.fpif.org/reports/america_is_not_broke. See also William H. Gates, Sr., and Chuck Collins, *Wealth and Our Commonwealth* (Boston: Beacon Press, 2003); and Bernie Becker, "Study Finds Many Corporations Pay Effective Tax Rate of Zero," *The Hill*, June 1, 2011.

54. Quoted in Clifford Cobb et al., "If the GDP Is Up Why Is America Down?" *The Atlantic Monthly*, October 1995, 59.

55. Quoted in Robert Costanza et al., *Beyond GDP: The Need for New Measures of Progress*, The Pardee Papers No. 4, Pardee Center, Boston University, January 2009, 7.

56. See generally the excellent Demos report by Lew Daly and Stephen Posner, *Beyond GDP: New Measures for a New Economy* (New York: Demos, 2011), www.demos.org/publication/beyond-gdp-new-measures-new-economy. See also Joseph Stiglitz et al., *Mismeasuring Our Lives: Why GDP Doesn't Add Up* (New York: The New Press, 2010); and Jon Gertner, "The Rise and Fall of the GDP," *New York Times Magazine*, May 16,

2010, 60. On June 8, 2011, the European Parliament passed a far-reaching resolution, "GDP and Beyond: Measuring Progress in a Changing World," which *inter alia* noted that "the need to improve data and indicators to complement GDP for overall societal development is increasingly recognized by all international institutions."

57. See the discussion in James Gustave Speth, *The Bridge at the Edge of the World: Capitalism, the Environment, and Crossing from Crisis to Sustainability* (New Haven: Yale University Press, 2008), Chapter 6. See also the Happiness Initiative, Sustainable Seattle, www.sustainableseattle.org.

58. See Tim Jackson and Susanna Stymne, *Sustainable Economic Welfare in Sweden* (Stockholm: Stockholm Environment Institute, 1996), http://www.sei.se/dload/1996/SEWISAPI.pdf. On the ISEW generally, see Philip A. Lawn, "An Assessment of the Valuation Methods Used to Calculate the Index of Sustainable Economic Welfare (ISEW), Genuine Progress Indicator (GPI), and Sustainable Net Benefit Index (SNBI)," *Environment, Development and Sustainability* 7 (2005): 185. On indicators, see also John Talberth et al., *The Genuine Progress Indicator 2006* (Oakland, CA: Redefining Progress, 2006), http://www.environmental-expert.com/Files%5C24200%5Carticles%5C12128%5CGPI202006.pdf; Marque-Luisa Miringoff and Sandra Opdycke, *America's Social Health* (Armonk, NY: M. E. Sharpe, 2007); *Environmental Performance Index 2010*, at www.epi.yale.edu; *The Ecological Wealth of Nations 2010, Global Footprint Network*, www.footprintnetwork.org; Economist Intelligence Unit, *Democracy Index 2010: Democracy in Retreat*, at www.eiu.com; and New Economics Foundation, *Measuring Our Progress* (London: New Economics Foundation, 2011), 59. See, e.g., Philip A. Lawn, *Toward Sustainable Development* (Boca Raton: Lewis Publishers, 2001), 240–242.

60. See Jason Venetoulis and Cliff Cobb and the Redefining Progress Sustainability Indicators Program, *The Genuine Progress Indicator, 1950–2002 (2004 Update)*, March 2004, http://www.rprogress.org/publications/2004/gpi_march2004update.pdf.

61. William D. Nordhaus and James Tobin, "Is Growth Obsolete?," in Milton Moss, ed., *The Measurement of Economic and Social Performance* (New York: Columbia University Press, 1973).

62. See the Canadian Index of Well-Being site at www.ciw.ca.

63. Lizabeth Cohen, *A Consumers' Republic: The Politics of Mass Consumption in Postwar America* (New York: Alfred A. Knopf, 2003), 403.

64. Important recent works on consumerism include Juliet B. Schor, *The Overspent American* (New York: Harper, 1998) and *Plenitude: The New Economics of True Wealth* (New York: Penguin, 2010); Gary Cross, *An All-Consuming Century* (New York: Columbia University Press, 2000); Thomas Princen, *Treading Softly* (Cambridge, MA: MIT Press, 2010) and *The Logic of Sufficiency* (Cambridge, MA: MIT Press, 2005); John R. Ehrenfeld, *Sustainability by Design* (New Haven: Yale University Press, 2008); Andres R. Edwards, *Thriving Beyond Sustainability* (Gabriola Island, BC: New Society Publishers, 2010); Benjamin R. Barber, *Consumed* (New York: Norton, 2007); Annie Leonard, *The Story of Stuff* (New York: Free Press, 2010); John de Graaf, *Affluenza* (San Francisco: Berrett-Koehler, 2005); David Wann, *The New Normal* (New York: St. Martin's Press, 2010); Worldwatch Institute, *State of the World 2010* (New York: Norton, 2010); Robert H. Frank, *Luxury Fever* (Princeton, NJ: Princeton University Press, 1999); Peter Dauvergne, *The Shadows of Consumption* (Cambridge, MA: MIT Press, 2008); Thomas

Princen, Michael Maniates, and Ken Conca, eds., *Confronting Consumption* (Cambridge, MA: MIT Press, 2001); Duane Elgin, *Voluntary Simplicity* (New York: Harper, 2010); Clive Hamilton, *Affluenza* (Crows Nest, Australia: Allen and Unwin, 2005); Tim Kasser, *The High Price of Materialism* (Cambridge, MA: MIT Press, 2002); and Maurie J. Cohen et al., "The New Politics of Consumption," *Sustainability: Science, Practice, and Policy* 1, no. 1 (2005).

65. Richard Layard, *Happiness* (New York: Penguin, 2005), 48–49.

66. See Layard, *Happiness*, 43–48; Ed Diener and Martin E. P. Seligman, "Beyond Money," *Psychological Science in the Public Interest* 5, no. 1 (2004), 10; Andrew Oswald, "The Hippies Were Right All Along About Happiness," *Financial Times*, January 19, 2006, 17. See also Gary Rivlin, "The Millionaires Who Don't Feel Rich," *New York Times*, August 5, 2007, 1A.

67. Christopher Swann, "Consuming Concern," *Financial Times*, January 20, 2006, 11.

68. Diener and Seligman, "Beyond Money," 18–19.

69. Robert E. Lane, *The Loss of Happiness in Market Democracies* (New Haven: Yale University Press, 2001), 6, 9, 319–324. In 2006, sociologists reported that a quarter of Americans said they had no one with whom to discuss important matters, almost triple the number similarly isolated in 1985. Miller McPherson et al., "Social Isolation in America," *American Sociological Review* 71 (2006): 353. See generally Robert D. Putnam, *Bowling Alone* (New York: Simon and Schuster, 2000).

70. Amitai Etzioni, "Spent: America After Consumerism," *The New Republic*, June 17, 2009.

71. Cohen, *A Consumers' Republic*, 403–405. See also Jeffrey Kaplan, "The Gospel of Consumption and the Better Future We Left Behind," *Orion*, May/June 2008, 39.

72. Cohen, *A Consumers' Republic*, 403–405.

73. David E. Shi, *The Simple Life: Plain Living and High Thinking in American Culture* (Athens: University of Georgia Press, 2007), 3, 277. The leading work on the modern simplicity movement is Elgin, *Voluntary Simplicity*.

74. Etizioni, "Spent: America After Consumerism."

75. Schor, *Plenitude*, 4–7.

76. See Frank, "Post-Consumer Prosperity"; Laurence S. Seidman and Kenneth A. Lewis, "Two Ways to Tax Very-High-Income Households," *Tax Notes*, June 22, 2009, 1466; and Frank, *Luxury Fever*.

77. See Derek Thompson, "America's Post-Ownership Future," *The Atlantic*, http://www.theatlantic.com/business/archive/2011/04/americas-post-ownership-future/237825; Danielle Sacks, "The Sharing Economy," FastCompany.com, April 18, 2011, http://www.fastcompany.com/magazine/155/the-sharing-economy.html; and "Schumpeter: The Business of Sharing," *The Economist*, October 16, 2010, 82.

78. See Reid Lifset and Thomas Lindquist, "Producer Responsibility at a Turning Point?" *Journal of Industrial Ecology* 12, no. 2 (April 2008): 144; Ehrenfeld, *Sustainability by Design*; Ellen Ruppel Shell, *Cheap: The High Cost of Discount Culture* (New York: Penguin, 2009); and Giles Slade, *Made to Break: Technology and Obsolescence in America* (Cambridge, MA: Harvard University Press, 2006).

79. See generally Erik Assadourian, "Cultural Change for a Bearable Climate," *Sustainability: Science, Practice, and Policy* 6, no. 2 (2010), 1.

Two groups working effectively to try to move America beyond consumerism are the Center for a New American Dream, www.newdream.org; and Green America, www.greenamerica.org.

80. See Juliet B. Schor, "Sustainable Consumption and Worktime Reduction," *Journal of Industrial Ecology* 9, no. 1–2 (2005): 37; John de Graaf, "Reducing Work Time as a Path to Sustainability," in Worldwatch Institute, *State of the World 2010* (New York: Norton, 2010), 173; James K. Galbraith, "Early Retirement as a Fix for Unemployment," *The American Prospect*, March 2011; and Charles Siegel, *The Politics of Simple Living*, http://www.uiowa.edu/~lsahunni/200/siegel%20PoliticsOfSimpleLiving.pdf. See also "Take Back Your Time," www.timeday.org.

81. See Tim Kasser, Tom Crompton, and Susan Linn, "Children, Commercialism, and Environmental Sustainability," *Solutions*, March/April 2010, 14; David Sirota, "Time to Crack Down on Child-Focused Ads," Truthout, May 27, 2011, http://truth-out.org/time-crackdown-child-focused-ads/1306503495.

82. Elizabeth Gettelman and Dave Gilson, "Ad Nauseam," *Mother Jones*, January/February 2007, 23.

83. "Billboard Boom," *The Economist*, April 23, 2011, 71.

84. See Kasser et al., "Children, Commercialism, and Environmental Sustainability"; and Allen Kanner, "Protecting Your Child from Capitalism," *Tikkun*, November/December 2008, 30, and "Corporate Free Speech: A Progressive Trap," *Tikkun*, March/April 2008, 42.

85. E. F. Schumacher, *Small Is Beautiful: Economics as If People Mattered* (New York: Harper, 1973), 70.

86. Thad Williamson et al., *Making a Place for Community: Local Democracy in a Global Era* (New York: Routledge, 2003), xiii–xiv.

87. Commission on a National Agenda for the Eighties, *A National Agenda for the Eighties* (Washington, DC: U.S. Government Printing Office, 1980), 166–167.

88. Williamson et al., *Making a Place for Community*, 5, 7, 9.

89. Williamson et al., *Making a Place for Community*, 5.

90. See Ed Douglas, "Better by Design," *New Scientist*, January 6, 2007, 31, 34.

91. Schumacher, *Small Is Beautiful*, 61.

92. See, e.g., Joan Fitzgerald, *Emerald Cities: Urban Sustainability and Economic Development* (Oxford: Oxford University Press, 2010).

93. Gar Alperovitz et al., "Rebuilding American Communities: A Comprehensive Community Wealth Building Federal Policy Proposal," The Democracy Collaborative at the University of Maryland, April 2010, http://www.community-wealth.org/_pdfs/news/recent-articles/04–10/report-alperovitz-et-al.pdf. See also Thad Williamson et al., *Climate Change, Community Stability, and the Next 150 Million Americans*, The Democracy Collaborative at the University of Maryland, 2010, http://www.community-wealth.org/_pdfs/news/recent-articles/10–10/report-williamson-dubb-alperovitz.pdf. See generally http://community-wealth.com and Steve Dubb et al., *Building Wealth*, The Aspen Institute, April 2005. On community development corporations, see http://naceda.org, and on community development finance institutions, see www.cdfi.org.

94. Michael H. Shuman, *Going Local: Creating Self-Reliant Communities in a Global Age* (New York: Free Press, 1998).

95. Michael H. Shuman, "20 Measures for a Successful Local Living Economy," *Business Alliance for Local Living Economies*, March 31, 2011. See www.livingeconomies.org. See also Stacy Mitchell, "Localism Index," *The Nation*, April 25, 2011, 23. See also Institute for Local Self-Reliance, www.ilsr.org, and the material posted there.

96. See, e.g., "Food for Everyone," *Yes! Magazine*, Spring 2009; "A Resilient Community," *Yes! Magazine*, Fall 2010; and "New Livelihoods," *Yes! Magazine*, Fall 2011.

97. See, e.g., Business Alliance for Local Living Economies, www.livingeconomies.org; Institute for Local Self-Reliance, www.ilsr.org; Green America, www.greenamerica .org; Center for a New American Dream, www.newdream.org; Institute for Sustainable Communities, www.iscvt.org; Center for Community Change, www.communitychange .org; Institute for Whole Communities, www.wholecommunities.org; TransitionUS, www.transitionus.org; Sustainable Communities Online, www.sustainable.org; and Sustainable Communities Coalition, http://smartstrategy.newamerica.net/nscc.

98. Robert Gates, "Remarks at the 2008 U.S. Global Leadership Campaign Tribute Dinner," Washington, DC, July 15, 2008.

99. Quoted in Gordon Lubold, "Admiral Mullen: Foreign Policy Is Too Dominated by the Military," *Christian Science Monitor*, March 3, 2010.

100. Center for a New American Security, "The Sacrifice Ahead: The 2012 Defense Budget," Policy Brief, February 2011, 1 (emphasis added).

101. Institute for Policy Studies, "Report of the Task Force on a Unified Security Budget for the United States," August 2010, 2–3.

102. See Robert Dreyfuss, "Taking Aim at the Pentagon Budget," *The Nation*, April 11, 2011, 22; "Threatening a Sacred Cow," *The Economist*, February 12, 2011, 33; William Pfaff, "Budget Problems, America? Try Ending Your Many Wars," Truthdig, June 1, 2011, http://www.truthdig.com/report/item/budget_problems_america_try_ending_your_many_wars_20110601/.

103. Wayne Porter and Mark Mykleby, "A National Strategic Narrative," Woodrow Wilson Center, 2011, 6–7. See also David W. Orr, "National Security and Sustainability," *Journal of Environmental Studies and Sciences* 1 (2011): 36.

104. Porter and Mykleby, "A National Strategic Narrative," 7–8.

105. Andrew J. Bacevich, *Washington Rules: America's Path to Permanent War* (New York: Metropolitan Books, 2010), 14, 238–239 (emphasis in original).

106. William Pfaff, *The Irony of Manifest Destiny: The Tragedy of America's Foreign Policy* (New York: Walker & Company, 2010), 178. See also Karen J. Greenberg, "How to End the War on Terror," TomDispatch.com, June 19, 2011, http://www.tomdispatch .com/blog/175406.

107. See William J. Astore, "American Militarism Is Not a Fairy Tale: How the Military and the Civilian Are Blurring in Washington," TomDispatch.com, June 14, 2011, http:// www.tomdisptach.com/blog/175404; and Tom Englehardt, "Post-Legal America and the National Security Complex," TomDispatch.com, May 30, 2011, http://www.tom dispatch.com/blog/175398.

108. Frederick A. O. Schwarz and Aziz Z. Huq, *Unchecked and Unbalanced: Presidential Power in a Time of Terror* (New York: The New Press, 2007), 201, 203. See also Jane Mayer, *The Dark Side: The Inside Story of How the War on Terror Turned into a War on American Ideals* (New York: Doubleday, 2008).

109. Schwarz and Huq, *Unchecked and Unbalanced*, 203–205.

110. Schwarz and Huq, *Unchecked and Unbalanced*, 205–206.

111. Schwarz and Huq, *Unchecked and Unbalanced*, 207.

112. Once the top focus of U.S. foreign policy has shifted to addressing a broader set of security concerns and related international threats, such as those reviewed in Chapters 2 and 3, the question becomes one of the policies and institutions needed to address these "unconventional" threats. Here, of course, there is a vast literature, including the author's contribution on meeting global-scale environmental challenges. See James Gustave Speth, *Red Sky at Morning: America and the Crisis of the Global Environment* (New Haven: Yale University Press, 2005). And see, e.g., Jim Garrison, *America as Empire: Global Leader or Rogue Power* (San Francisco: Berrett-Koehler, 2004); Anne-Marie Slaughter, *A New World Order* (Princeton, NJ: Princeton University Press, 2004); Robin Broad and John Cavanagh, *Development Redefined* (Boulder, CO: Paradigm, 2009); Amartya Sen, *Development as Freedom* (New York: Anchor, 2000); David C. Korten, *Agenda for a New Economy* (San Francisco: Berrett-Koehler, 2010); Peter G. Brown and Geoffrey Garver, *Right Relationship: Building a Whole Earth Economy* (San Francisco: Berrett-Koehler, 2009); Amitai Etzioni, *From Empire to Community* (New York: Palgrave Macmillan, 2004); Dani Rodrik, *The Globalization Paradox* (New York: Norton, 2011); Jeffrey D. Sachs, *The End of Poverty* (New York: Penguin, 2006); Al Gore, *Our Choice: A Plan to Solve the Climate Crisis* (Emmaus, PA: Rodale, 2009); Robert Repetto, *America's Climate Problem: The Way Forward* (Washington, DC: Earthscan, 2011); David Sandalow, *Freedom from Oil* (New York: McGraw-Hill, 2008); Julian Cribb, *The Coming Famine: The Global Food Crisis and What We Can Do to Avoid It* (Berkeley: University of California Press, 2010); Fred Pearce, *The Coming Population Crash* (Boston: Beacon Press, 2010); Sudhir Chella Rajan, "Global Politics and Institutions," Tellus Institute, Great Transition Paper Series, No. 3 (2006), http://gtinitiative .org/documents/PDFFINALS/3Politics.pdf; Charles Knight, "Security in the Great Transition," Tellus Institute, Great Transition Paper Series, No. 7 (2006), http://www .comw.org/pda/fulltext/06GTISecurity.pdf; Paul Raskin, "World Lines: Pathways, Pivots, and the Global Future," Tellus Institute, Great Transition Paper Series, No. 16 (2006), http://www.gtinitiative.org/documents/PDFFINALS/16WorldLines.pdf; Nayan Chanda "Runaway Globalization Without Governance," *Global Governance* 14 (2008): 119; William Greider, "The End of Free Trade Globalization," *The Nation*, November 22, 2010, 20; Nancy Birdsall and Francis Fukuyama, "The Post-Washington Consensus: Development After the Crisis," *Foreign Affairs*, March/April 2011, 45; Harold Meyerson, "A Global New Deal," *The American Prospect*, January/February 2009, 10; Uchita de Zoysa, "Millennium Consumption Goals: A Fair Proposal from the Poor to the Rich," *Sustainability Science, Practice, and Policy* 7, no. 1 (2011): 1; Robert Costanza, "Stewardship in a 'Full' World," *Current History*, January 2008, 30; Brian Walker et al., "Looming Global-Scale Failures and Missing Institutions," *Science* 325 (2009): 1345; and Maja Gopel, "Guarding Our Future: How to Protect Future Generations," *Solutions*, November/December 2010, 62.

Chapter 8. Realizing Democracy

1. Jacob S. Hacker and Paul Pierson, *Off Center* (New Haven: Yale University Press, 2005), 43–44.

2. Allan J. Lichtman, *White Protestant Nation* (New York: Grove Press, 2008), 6. See also Marc J. Hetherington and Jonathan D. Weiler, *Authoritarianism and Polarization in American Politics* (Cambridge: Cambridge University Press, 2009); and Kevin Phillips, *American Theocracy* (New York: Viking, 2006).

3. Lichtman, *White Protestant Nation*, 6. And see John J. Miller, *A Gift of Freedom* (San Francisco: Encounter Books, 2006); and Steven M. Teles, *The Rise of the Conservative Legal Movement* (Princeton, NJ: Princeton University Press, 2008).

4. Hacker and Pierson, *Off Center*, 5.

5. Jacob S. Hacker and Paul Pierson, "The Stalemate State," *The American Prospect*, October 18, 2010. The most disturbing critique of modern American politics may be that of Sheldon W. Wolin in *Democracy Inc.* (Princeton, NJ: Princeton University Press, 2008).

6. Jacob S. Hacker and Paul Pierson, *Winner-Take-All Politics* (New York: Simon and Schuster, 2010), 99.

7. See, e.g., Alan Wolfe, *Does American Democracy Still Work?* (New Haven: Yale University Press, 2006); Thomas E. Mann and Normal J. Ornstein, *The Broken Branch* (Oxford: Oxford University Press, 2008); Eric Alterman, *Kabuki Democracy* (New York: Nation Books, 2011); Hacker and Pierson, *Off Center* and *Winner-Take-All Politics;* Robert G. Kaiser, *So Damn Much Money* (New York: Vintage Books, 2010); Marc J. Hetherington and Jonathan D. Weiler, *Authoritarianism and Polarization in American Politics* (Cambridge: Cambridge University Press, 2009); Kevin Phillips, *American Theocracy* (New York: Viking, 2006); Robert F. Kennedy, Jr., *Crimes Against Nature* (New York: Harper Collins, 2004); and David W. Orr, *The Last Refuge* (Washington, DC: Island Press, 2004).

8. Lawrence R. Jacobs and Theda Skocpol, eds., *Inequality and American Democracy* (New York: Russell Sage Foundation, 2005). See also Larry M. Bartels, *Unequal Democracy* (Princeton, NJ: Princeton University Press, 2008).

9. See Bill Moyers, "Welcome to the Plutocracy!," address at Boston University, October 29, 2010, http://archive.truthout.org/bill-moyers-money-fights-hard-and-it-fights-dirty64766.

10. Hacker and Pierson, *Winner-Take-All Politics*, 291.

11. Kaiser, *So Damn Much Money*, 343–345.

12. James K. Galbraith, *The Predator State* (New York: Free Press, 2008), xviii–xix.

13. William Greider, *The Soul of Capitalism: Opening Paths to a Moral Economy* (New York: Simon and Schuster, 2003), 29.

14. Robert Kuttner, *A Presidency in Peril* (White River Junction, VT: Chelsea Green, 2010).

15. Quoted in Ari Berman, "Citizens Unite Against *Citizens United*," *The Nation*, August 16–23, 2010, 30.

16. Robert A. Dahl, *How Democratic Is the American Constitution?* (New Haven: Yale University Press, 2003), 163.

17. Katrina vanden Heuvel, "Just Democracy," *The Nation*, July 21–28, 2008, 31.

18. Bob Edgar, "A 21st-Century Agenda for Democratic Renewal," *The American Prospect*, January/February 2009, A2.

19. Mickey Edwards, "How to Turn Republicans and Democrats into Americans," *The Atlantic*, July/August 2011, 102.

20. See generally "Revitalizing Democracy: Special Report," *The American Prospect*, January/February 2009, A1.

The following are among the leading groups that work on prodemocracy political reforms, often against the odds when media and public attention are more focused on substantive, not procedural issues: Americans for Campaign Reform, www.acrreform .org; FairVote, www.fairvote.org; Demos, www.demos.org; Public Campaign, www .publicampaign.org; Common Cause, www.commoncause.org; America Votes, www .americavotes.org; Democracy 21, www.democracy21.org; Brennan Center for Justice, www.brennancenter.org; Center for Responsive Politics, www.opensecrets.org; Campaign Finance Institute, www.cfinst.org; Public Citizen, www.citizen.org; New America Foundation, www.newamerica.net; Campaign Legal Center, www.campaign legalcenter.org; and Democracy Matters, www.democracymatters.org. The author is associated with Demos as a fellow and with Americans for Campaign Reform as an adviser.

A promising new initiative dedicated to "fighting the corrupting influence of well-financed special interests" is United Republic: Democracy Is Not for Sale. See http:// unitedrepublic.org.

21. Larry Marx, "A Broader Definition of Democracy," *The American Prospect*, January/ February 2009, A3.

22. Stuart Comstock-Gay and Joe Goldman, "More Than the Vote," *The American Prospect*, January/February 2009, A8–A9. See also Benjamin R. Barker, *Strong Democracy* (Berkeley: University of California Press, 2003); Frances Moore Lappé, *Democracy's Edge* (San Francisco: Jossey-Bass, 2006); and Jared Duval, *Next Generation Democracy* (New York: Bloomsbury, 2010).

23. Bruce Ackerman and James S. Fishkin, *Deliberation Day* (New Haven: Yale University Press, 2004), 3.

24. Ackerman and Fishkin, *Deliberation Day*, 5.

25. F. A. O. Schwarz, "The National Security State and Other Dangers to Democracy in America," Lecture at the Free University of Berlin, November 11, 2010 (emphasis in original).

26. States already have responsibility for maintaining a database of registered voters. Steve Hill explains how this could be expanded: "This database, if merged with each state's census database, Social Security database, driver's license database, and others, would enable universal registration. The creation of the database can be done on a state-by-state or a national basis. Both options have their pluses and minuses, but the basic goal does not change: automatic and universal voter registration of all eligible adults 18 years or older." Steven Hill, *Ten Steps to Repair American Democracy* (Sausalito, CA: PoliPoint Press, 2006), 38.

Efforts have been made to restrict voter access, moving in exactly the wrong direction. See Katrina vanden Heuvel, "The Voter ID Laws Threaten Democracy," *Washington Post*, reprinted in *Valley News*, July 28, 2011, A8; Editorial, "The Republican Threat to Voting," *New York Times*, April 26, 2011.

27. Hill, *Ten Steps to Repair American Democracy*, 27–33.

28. Hill, *Ten Steps to Repair American Democracy*, 90.

29. This initiative is referred to as the National Popular Vote initiative. See www.national popularvote.com. See also Robert Richie, "Failing Electoral College," *The Nation*, October 1, 2007. See generally www.fairvote.org.

30. Hill, *Ten Steps to Repair American Democracy*, 102–103.

31. Joel Lefkowitz, "The Electoral College," in Ronald Hayduk and Kevin Mattson eds., *Democracy's Moment* (New York: Rowman and Littlefield, 2002), 195; Michael Lind, "Why Republicans Want Gridlock," Salon.com, March 2, 2010, http://www.salon.com/opinion/feature/2010/03/01/gridlock/print.html.

32. See generally www.fixtheprimaries.com. See also John Nichols, "The Money-Mad Primary Race," *The Nation*, January 21, 2008; and Kenneth Baer, "A Democratic Primary," *Democracy*, Spring 2008, 122.

33. Edwards, "How to Turn Republicans and Democrats into Americans," 103–104.

34. Hacker and Pierson, *Off Center*, 213. See also Edwards, "How to Turn Republicans and Democrats into Americans," 104.

35. Hill, *Ten Steps to Repair American Democracy*, 64–65, 70. See also Krist Novoselic and Rob Richie, "Eliminate Winner-Take-All to Broaden Representation," *Valley News*, July 25, 2011, A6.

36. Vanden Heuvel, "Just Democracy," 38. See also Alyssa Katz, "The Power of Fusion Politics," *The Nation*, September 12, 2005.

37. Lind, "Why Republicans Want Gridlock"; Hill, *Ten Steps to Repair American Democracy*, 114–115.

38. Mann and Ornstein, *The Broken Branch*, 87.

39. Lake Research Partners and Tarrance Group, "Congressional Fair Elections Coalition: Findings from a Nationwide Survey," February 2–6, 2009.

40. Fair Elections Now Coalition, "Clean Elections in Practice: Results from States and Municipalities," http://fairelectionsnow.org, April 14, 2009. The approach has worked well in New York City. See Angela Migally and Susan Liss, *Small Donor Matching Funds: The NYC Election Experience* (New York: Brennan Center for Justice, New York University School of Law, 2010).

41. See Americans for Campaign Reform, www.acrreform.org.

42. Mark Schmitt, "Can Money Be a Force for Good?" *The American Prospect*, January/February 2009, A14.

43. Linda Greenhouse, "Hurry Up and Wait," *Opinionator*, December 27, 2009.

44. Michael Waldman, *A Return to Common Sense* (Naperville, IL: Sourcebooks, 2008), 59.

45. Americans for Campaign Reform, "Fact Sheet: Money in Politics: Who Gives," December 7, 2010, http://www.acrreform.org/research/money-in-politics-who-gives/.

46. Americans for Campaign Reform, "Election Analysis: 2010 Midterm Bankrolled by Less than 1% of Americans," press release, December 9, 2010. On the corrupting influence of money in elections of state judges, see the articles collected at "For Sale," *The American Prospect*, October 2011, 33.

47. Americans for Campaign Reform, "Fact Sheet: Money in Politics: Who Gets," December 7, 2010, http://www.acrreform.org/research/money-in-politics-who-gets/.

48. Americans for Campaign Reform, "Fact Sheet: Wall Street Money in Politics," December 7, 2010, http://www.acrreform.org/research/wall-street-money-in-politics/.

49. Quoted in Waldman, *A Return to Common Sense*, 63. See also Merrill Goozner, "Financial PACs 'Invest' in Influential Freshmen," OpenSecrets blog, April 13, 2011, http://www.opensecrets.org/news/2011/04/financial-pacs-invest-in-influentia.html. This article is one of a three-part series jointly sponsored by OpenSecrets.org and *The Fiscal Times*. See Michael Bickel, "Business Targets Campaigns of Key Committee Members," OpenSecrets blog, April 13, 2011, http://www.opensecrets.org/news/2011/04/

business-targets-campaigns-of-key.html; and Eric Pianin et al., "Congressional Freshmen Saddled with Debt Turn to PACs," OpenSecrets blog, April 14, 2011, http://www.opensecrets.org/news/2011/04/congressional-freshmen-saddled-with.html.

50. Alan Simpson, "Special Interests Distort Elections," *Politico*, April 25, 2011. See also Editorial, "What the Secret Donors Want," *New York Times*, November 22, 2010. And see Hacker and Pierson, *Off Center*, 215.

51. See, e.g., Jonathan Crewdson et al., "Secret Donors, Toothless FEC," *Bloomberg News*, reprinted in *Valley News*, May 23, 2011, 1.

52. Ronald Dworkin, "The Decision That Threatens Democracy," *New York Review of Books*, May 13, 2010, 63. On Super PACs, see John Nichols and Robert McChesney, "The Assault of the Super PACs," *The Nation*, February 6, 2012, 11. And see Trevor Potter, "Was the Supreme Court Conned?" *Bloomberg News*, May 23, 2011; and Nicholas Confessore, "Lines Blur Between Candidates and PACs with Unlimited Cash," *New York Times*, August 27, 2011.

53. See Move To Amend, http://movetoamend.org. See also Ari Berman, "Citizens Unite Against *Citizens United*," *The Nation*, August 16–23, 2010, 29; Robert Weissman, "Citizens United: Bad Law, Worse Effects," *Valley News*, January 26, 2011; and David Sirota, "The Biggest Threat to Citizens United," Salon.com, http://www.salon.com/2012/01/06/the_biggest_threat_to_citizens_united/singleton.

54. David M. Herszenhorn, "Campaign Finance Bill Is Set Aside," *New York Times*, July 27, 2010.

55. The Supreme Court's attack on campaign finance laws continues. See Adam Liptak, "Justices Strike Down Arizona Campaign Finance Law," *New York Times*, June 27, 2011; Editorial, "The First Amendment, Upside Down," *New York Times*, June 27, 2011.

56. See, e.g., Bruce Ackerman and David Wu, "How to Counter Corporate Speech," *Wall Street Journal*, January 27, 2010. See also Lawrence Lessig, *Republic, Lost* (New York: Twelve, 2011).

57. This action and the preceding one are urged by Common Cause and others.

58. Hill, *Ten Steps to Repair American Democracy*, 150.

59. The Center for Responsive Politics maintains a database on lobbying spending at www.opensecrets.org.

60. "The Artful Dodgers: How a Dozen Multinational Corporations Spent a Billion Dollars on Lobbying and Campaign Contributions and Avoided Paying Taxes," Public Campaign, http://www.publicampaign.org/reports/artfuldodgers.

61. Alterman, *Kabuki Democracy*, 7.

62. Hacker and Pierson, *Winner-Take-All Politics*, 303.

63. Anne C. Mulkern, "Lobbying: Tiny Group of Deep-Pocketed Contributors Fueling U.S. Chamber's Advocacy," *New York Times*, November 23, 2009. See also Jeff Goodell, *Big Coal* (Boston: Houghton Mifflin, 2006).

64. Darren Samuelsohn, "Climate: Ad Buys Precede Senate Debate on Emissions Bill," *Greenwire*, May 27, 2008.

65. Anne C. Mulkern, "Lobbying: IRS Disclosures Show Extent of Oil and Coal Groups' Outreach," *Greenwire*, November 18, 2009, http://www.eenews.net/public/Greenwire/2009/11/18/1.

66. "Fact Sheet: Money in Politics and the Environment," Americans for Campaign Reform, December 7, 2010, http://www.acrreform.org/wp-content/uploads/2010/12/Fact-Sheet-Money-in-Politics-and-the-Environment.pdf.

67. Marianne Lavelle, "Tally of Interests on Climate Bill Tops a Thousand," Center for Public Integrity, August 10, 2009, http://www.publicintegrity.org/investigations/climate_change/articles/entry/1608/. See also Christa Marshall, "Lobbying: K Street Getting Hot for Climate Change," ClimateWire, May 27, 2008, http://www.opensecrets.org/news/2008/05/climate-change-a-hot-issue-on.html. See generally Jeff Goodell, "As the World Burns," *Rolling Stone*, January 6, 2010.

68. Jane Mayer, "Covert Operations: The Billionaire Brothers Who Are Waging a War Against Obama," *The New Yorker*, August 30, 2010. See also Jane Mayer, "State for Sale," *The New Yorker*, October 10, 2011.

69. Mayer, "Covert Operations," 2–3.

70. See the Koch Industries webpage http://www.greenpeace.org/usa/en/media-center/reports/Koch-Industries-Still-Fueling-Climate-Denial-2011-Update/ for "Koch Industries: Still Fueling Climate Denial 2011 Update," Executive Summary, May 6, 2011.

71. See Lee Drutman, "Three Fixes for Our Lobbyist Problem," *The American Prospect*, June 5, 2008. See also "Campaign Finance Reform: A New Era," Common Cause, http://www.commoncause.org/atf/cf/%7Bfb3c17e2-cdd1–4df6–92be-bd4429893665%7d/commoncausecampaignfinancereformagenda2009.pdf; and Anne C. Mulkern, "Lobbying: Bill Would Force More to Report Influence Efforts," *Greenwire*, June 24, 2011. On the revolving door, see Caitlin Ginley and M. B. Pell, "On Financial Reform Bill, 52 Percent of Lobbyists Worked in Government," June 20, 2010, http://www.iwatchnews.org/2010/06/10/2656/financial-reform-bill-52-percent-lobbyists-worked-government. And see Robert Repetto, "Best Practice in Internal Oversight of Lobbying Practice," Yale Center for Environmental Law and Policy, September 1, 2006.

72. See Press Release, "Federal Court Upholds CT Pay-to-Play Ban," Brennan Center for Justice, New York University, December 19, 2008.

73. Mann and Ornstein, *The Broken Branch*.

74. See Emmet Bondurant, "The Senate Filibuster Rule," http://www.commoncause.org (arguing that Senate Rule XXII is unconstitutional).

75. Sheldon Whitehouse and Sherrod Brown, "Protecting Our Government from Corporate Influence," *Huffington Post*, June 23, 2010.

76. Hacker and Pierson, *Off Center*, 193–206, and *Winner-Take-All Politics*, 302–306.

77. Wolfe, *Does American Democracy Still Work?*, 106–107, 135.

78. A number of impressive organizations have worked regularly to keep journalism strong, independent, and credible. See Media Matters, www.mediamatters.org; Fairness and Accuracy in Reporting (FAIR), www.fair.org; FreePress, www.freepress.net; Media Access Project, www.mediaaccess.org; Media and Democracy Coalition, www.media-democracy.net; Reclaim the Media, www.reclaimthemedia.org; Alliance for Community Media, www.allcommunitymedia.org; Center for Media and Democracy, www.prwatch.org; Center for Digital Democracy, www.democraticmedia.org; Save the News, www.savethenews.org; among others.

79. John Nichols and Robert W. McChesney, *The Death and Life of American Journalism* (New York: Nation Books, 2010).

80. John Nichols and Robert W. McChesney, "How to Save Journalism: The Patriotic Case for Government Action," *The Nation*, January 25, 2010, 13.

81. Nichols and McChesney, "How to Save Journalism," 13.

82. Nichols and McChesney, "How to Save Journalism," 16.

83. See "National Poll Ranks PBS #1 in Public Trust for Fourth Consecutive Year," PBS press release, March 22, 2007.

84. See generally *Media and Democracy in America Today: A Reform Plan for a New Administration*, Common Cause, August 2008, http://www.commoncause.org/atf/cf/%7Bfb3c17e2-cdd1–4df6–92be-bd4429893665%7D/MEDIAPLAN082108.PDF; and James Fallows, "How to Save the News," *The Atlantic*, June 2010, 44.

Chapter 9. The Movement

1. Harold Meyerson, "Without a Movement, Progressives Can't Aid Obama's Agenda," *Washington Post*, January 6, 2010, A15.

2. Deepak Bhargava, "Change We Can Believe In," *The American Prospect*, May 2010, 37, 39.

   In addition to the works cited elsewhere in this chapter, there are many good and thoughtful books that bear on organizing and building a progressive movement. See, e.g., Naomi Wolf, *Give Me Liberty* (New York: Simon and Schuster, 2008); David Gershon, *Social Change 2.0* (West Hurley, NY: High Point/Chelsea Green, 2009); Markos Moulitsas Zúniga, *Taking on the System* (New York: Penguin, 2008); Frances Moore Lappé, *Getting a Grip* (Cambridge, MA: Small Planet Media, 2010); Jonathan Isham and Sissel Waage, eds., *Ignition* (Washington, DC: Island Press, 2007); Todd Gitlin, *Letters to a Young Activist* (New York: Basic Books, 2003); and Bruce E. Levine, *Get Up, Stand Up* (White River Junction, VT: Chelsea Green, 2011). On international movements, see Paul Hawken, *Blessed Unrest* (New York: Viking, 2007); Tom Mertes, ed., *A Movement of Movements* (London: Verso, 2007); and Robin Broad, ed., *Global Backlash* (Lanham, MD: Rowman and Littlefield, 2002). And see the *Bill Moyers Journal* segment at http://www.pbs.org/moyers/journal/04302010/watch.html.

3. Frederick Douglass, "West India Emancipation," speech at Canandaigua, New York, August 3, 1857.

4. Dahvi Wilson and Jeni Krencicki, "The Progressive Movement's Strategic Deficit Disorder: Symptoms, Pathogenesis, Prognosis," Yale University School of Forestry and Environmental Studies, Spring 2006.

5. Jerome Armstrong and Markos Moulitsas Zúniga, *Crashing the Gate* (White River Junction, VT: Chelsea Green, 2006), 37.

6. David Roberts, "What Is the Dream Behind the American Dream Movement?" *Grist*, June 21, 2011.

7. See Democracy Alliance, www.democracyalliance.org; America Votes, www.americavotes.org; Center for Progressive Leadership, www.progressiveleaders.org; Campaign for Stronger Democracy, http://strongerdemocracy.org; and Netroots Nation, www.netrootsnation.org.

8. Personal communication from Betsy Taylor, Breakthrough Strategies and Solutions, August 24, 2011.

9. See the Institute for Policy Studies, www.ips-dc.org; Demos, www.demos.org; the Center for American Progress, www.americanprogress.org; the Campaign for America's

Future, www.ourfuture.org; the Tellus Institute, www.tellus.org; and the Progressive Ideas Network, www.progressiveideasnetwork.org.

10. See the Blue-Green Alliance, www.bluegreenalliance.org; and the Apollo Alliance, www.apolloalliance.org.

11. See the New Economics Institute,www.neweconomicsinstitute.org; the New Economy Working Group, www.neweconomyworkinggroup.org; and the New Economy Network, www.neweconomynetwork.org.

12. See MoveOn, www.moveon.org.

13. See the American Dream Movement, www.americandreammovement.net; and Rebuild the Dream, www.rebuildthedream.com.

14. See Bill McKibben, "Policy Reform to 350," *Solutions*, September/October 2010, 11; and www.350.org. And see Jonathan Isham, Jr., "How 350 Has Sparked Hope," *Solutions*, September/October 2010, 1; and Alec Loorz, "The Next Generation Takes on Climate Change," *Solutions*, September/October 2010, 38.

15. "The Widening Circle: Campaign for Advancing a Global Citizens Movement," http://wideningcircle.org.

16. See America Votes, www.americavotes.org; and State Voices, www.statevoices.org.

17. Personal communication from Betsy Taylor, Breakthrough Strategies and Solutions, August 24, 2011.

18. Alex Steffen, ed., *Worldchanging: A User's Guide to the Twenty-first Century* (New York: Abrams, 2006), 412.

19. Two effective groups in this regard are National People's Action, www.npa-us.org; and Center for Community Change, www.communitychange.org.

20. See "Imagine All the People: Advancing a Global Citizens Movement," Tellus Institute, Great Transition Initiative, December 2010, http://gtinitiative.org/documents/IssuePerspectives/GTI-Perspectives-Imagine_All_the_People.pdf. See also Paul Raskin, "Making the Great Transition," *Solutions*, May/June 2010, 12.

21. Steven Hill, *Europe's Promise* (Berkeley: University of California Press, 2010). But Europe has its difficulties. See Robert Kuttner, "History's Missed Moment," *The American Prospect*, October 2011, 18.

22. Quoted in Ben Stein, "In Class Warfare, Guess Which Class Is Winning," *New York Times*, November 26, 2006. See also Warren E. Buffett, "Stop Coddling the Super-Rich," *New York Times*, August 14, 2011.

23. Harold Laswell, *Politics: Who Gets What, When, and How* (New York: McGraw-Hill, 1936; Cleveland: Meridian, 1958), 13.

24. For another sign that the progressive movement is growing in America, see www.the99spring.com. And see generally the Occupy website, www.occupytogether.org.

25. Bill Moyer et al., *Doing Democracy* (Gabriola Island, Canada: New Society Publishers, 2001), excerpted in *Watershed Sentinel*, March/April 2008, 15–16.

26. Chris Hedges, "We Must Defy the Corporate Monsters Laying Waste to Our World," AlterNet, April 18, 2011, http://www.alternet.org/story/150652/hedges%3A_we_must_defy_the_corporate_monsters_laying_waste_to_our_world.

27. Seamus Heaney, *The Cure at Troy: A Version of Sophocles's Philocetes* (New York: Noonday Press, 1991).

Index

cummings, e. e., 87
customer stock ownership plans (CSOPs), 100

Dahl, Robert, 161
Daly, Herman, xiv, 92, 123–124, 128
Daly, Lew, xiv, 127, 128
Davis, Paige, xv
Dead Creek Wildlife Management Area, xiii–xiv
The Death and Life of American Journalism (Nichols and McChesney), 184
debt (national): increase in, 27, 38–39; reducing, 125, 130–131, 154; vision for the future, 71. *See also* budget deficit
debt (personal), 7. *See also* consumerism; home mortgages
Deepwater Horizon disaster, 181
deforestation, 53, 55, 56, 210–211n4
de Graaf, John, xiv
degrowth economies, 99. *See also* sustaining economy
Dellinger, Drew, 70
democracy: American empire a threat to, 46; breadth, 163; climate change a threat to, 190; deliberative democracy, 163–164; digital democracy, 182; local communities and, 143; principles of, 161–162; voter participation, 137, 165. *See also* political system and political economy (U.S.); prodemocracy reforms
Democracy Alliance, 188
Democracy Collaborative at the University of Maryland, xiii, 117–118, 144–145. *See also* Alperovitz, Gar
Democratic Party, 158–159, 173, 174
Demos, xiii, 24. *See also* Callahan, David
denial, 36–37
Department of Energy (U.S.), 43, 63, 94
Department of Homeland Security, 46
depression, 2, 5, 82
desertification and arable land loss, 54, 56–57, 58, 211n10
Diener, Ed, 82, 83, 136
digital democracy, 182
DISCLOSE Act, 174
Disney, 183–184
The Divine Right of Capital (Kelly), 118

Does American Democracy Still Work? (Wolfe), 182–183
Domhoff, William, 108–109
Donalbedian, Josh, xv
Douglas, Frederick, 187
drinking water. *See* freshwater
drought, 55–56
drug trafficking, 49–50
drug use, 30, 71, 154
Dubb, Steve, xiv
Dworkin, Ronald, 174
Dycus, Steven, xiv

Eaarth (McKibben), 94–95
Easterlin, Richard, 82
Ecological Footprint, 2, 80, 92–93
economic democracy, 99–102. *See also* income inequality
economic growth: and climate change containment goals, 61–62; consumer spending as driver, 136; costs, 92; environmental deterioration a threat to, 53; failure of, 128, 191; government interests served, 7; growth imperative, 4–5, 8, 128; growth rate, 53; income inequality and, 126–127; jobs not linked to, 35; limits *of*, 91–92; limits *to*, 92–95; measures of, 4, 131–132, 224n56 (*see also* GDP); negative consequences, 5, 80; transformation of, 10, 86, 94–95; and well-being, 82–83
economic insecurity, 23–28, 34–35, 71, 127–130. *See also* income inequality
"Economic Possibilities for Our Grand-children" (Keynes), 86–87
The Economist, 140
Edelman, Marian Wright, 103
Edgar, Bob, xv, 76
education: change needed, 96, 154; and cultural change, 77; decline (failure), 2, 27, 33–34; higher education, 30, 33–34, 200n1; high school completion, 2, 33, 200n1; measuring community progress, 146; as priority, 149; required for citizen/government competence, 105; vision for the future, 71, 86
Edwards, Mickey, 162, 167
Ehrenreich, Barbara, 23, 37–38
Eisenhower, Dwight D., 43, 44–45